The Savings and Loan Story, 1930-1960

A Business Reborn

JOSEPHINE HEDGES EWALT

Assistant Vice President and Washington Editor
United States League

American Savings and Loan Institute Press

Chicago, Illinois

Library of Congress Catalog Card Number 62-18605

Foreword

Nearly a full generation has come into being since the black day in 1929 when the stock market began its collapse and inaugurated what was to be the greatest depression the United States of America had ever known. Some of the changes in the life of the country during the years since then have been startlingly abrupt and others have been deceptively gradual. Some of them are traceable directly to the discouraging business conditions which lasted so long and penalized so many. Others have certain but limited lines of descent from the Great Depression.

The savings and loan system was nearly a century old when that depression began, but its ways and looks have changed so definitely since then that it is in many respects a new business. The associations do their traditional job of taking savings and making home loans; but the scope of their operations, the number of people who find their livelihood in them, the quarters they occupy and their sights on the future make it difficult for the casual observer to trace the resemblance to older building and loan institutions. This change belongs to the deceptively gradual category of post-depression developments; and certainly without the impetus of the business situation of the 1930s, it might never have happened.

The transformation makes an inspiring chapter in the story of

American finance. It is rife with the drama of legislation enacted by narrow margins; it witnesses to the ability of the leaders within a business to devise practical solutions and make them work; it benefits from the happy chance that an institution using its funds primarily for home financing should be in the forefront of the sources of credit needed by the nation after World War II.

In 1931 the United States Savings and Loan League published the *History of Building and Loan in the United States* by Morton Bodfish, telling the story of the first hundred years of the business and its development up to the time of the Great Depression. Time and the popularity of the volume have reduced it to the status of "out of print." In order to provide a hasty glimpse of this period for those who do not have the earlier volume on their shelves, this book carries Appendix two entitled "The First 100 Years: A Synopsis."

But as noted above, the savings and loan business today is in many respects a new business, one which began in the depression. The story of the business since then—which is the story of its remaking into the modern system we know today—deserves to be written while the memories of some of those who lived through this remarkable generation in the business are still intact.

As the trade association serving institutions of this type continuously since 1892, the United States League is the logical organization to sponsor this history.

Josephine Hedges Ewalt was commissioned to write the history. She is not only a trained journalist but also is uniquely qualified to author such a text, as she has occupied a key position on the staff of the United States League through almost this entire period. Few, if any, persons have had a better opportunity to know and to study the business since 1930 and to record its changes and development.

We undertook this task of telling the story of the business since 1930 with a mingling of humility and pride. The pride with which the League attempts this work is due to the fact that the officers and staff of the League itself were those largely responsible for harnessing the forces which turned a "movement" and a fringe-of-the-financial-world entity into the largest savings and home financing system the world has ever seen. This pride stems from the fact that the United States League, through the leadership it provided the business, contributed immeasurably to the dramatic changes that the business has undergone and to the record of the past 30 years.

The humility is due to the inevitable glossing over of events which the judgment of others might have given more prominence. It was a challenge to write the history of a period while so many who made the history and contributed to it are active in the business and in a position to disagree with one's interpretation of it.

Many people had much to do with the remaking of the business and its accomplishments in the years since the Great Depression. In fact, so many people have had so much to do with the accomplishments as a whole—accomplishments which in many respects were the results of united action of many people largely working through the United States League and their state leagues—that it was decided to omit references in the text to personalities. This decision is particularly unfair to a number of people who gave outstanding leadership and did notable work in the development of the modern savings and loan business and to whom the business owes a great debt of appreciation.

Notable among those to whom particular appreciation and recognition are due are: Morton Bodfish who, as the League's chief executive officer, more than any other person during the 1930s provided the vigorous and outstanding leadership that the times demanded; A. D. Theobald who worked very closely with Mr. Bodfish on the League staff during the critical years in the development of the modern savings and loan business; and Horace Russell who served for many years as general counsel for the Federal Home Loan Bank Board and later as general counsel for the United States League.

It would be completely unfair not to express here appreciation for the contribution made by Henry A. Bubb of Topeka, Kansas, during the latter years of the period covered by this history. He devoted probably more time, energy and leadership to the affairs of the business nationwide during this period than any other savings and loan executive, first as League president and then for many years as chairman of the League's Legislative Committee.

Many of the actions and much of the leadership attributed in this book to the League were actually the work of these individuals. Much of the responsibility was theirs. A great deal of the success of the business is the fruit of their ideas and their untiring work.

In addition to these men, significant contributions came from

League officers, chairmen and members of League committees, members of the Federal Home Loan Bank Board, presidents of the Federal Home Loan Banks and persons active in state organizations of savings and loan. The references to the League in the text refer also to the work done by several hundred persons who served in one or more of these capacities. So that there may be some record of those in positions of leadership and responsibility in the savings and loan business during the exciting and dramatic years 1930-1960, Appendix One lists the following: United States League presidents, directors and executive committeemen, the chairmen of its Legislative Committee and the key staff members; American Savings and Loan Institute presidents; executive officers of the state leagues; the members of the Federal Home Loan Bank Board; and the presidents of the Federal Home Loan Banks.

Yet, when one has listed these hundreds of savings and loan personalities as the source of the power and inspiration of the United States League, one is still conscious of another necessary omission. Many members of Congress over this 30-year period played an invaluable role in providing the opportunity for savings and loan institutions to mature and acquire stature. Their mention in the text is necessarily confined to those most conspicuous in their contributions. But the record is clear that their part was noteworthy.

The present generation of savings and loan men and women and future generations owe a debt of gratitude to the people who were responsible in these various ways for the large, successful and sound savings and loan business with which we entered the decade of the 1960s. Likewise, the nation can be thankful that we developed strong and useful thrift and home financing institutions, because the savings and loan business truly has helped make America a nation of home owners.

NORMAN STRUNK
Executive Vice President

October 1962

Acknowledgments

Periodicals and special publications of the United States Savings and Loan League form the basic record which substantiates my personal observations and experiences. I relied heavily on the League's *Savings and Loan Annals*, 1930-60; *Confidential Bulletins*, 1931-56; *Membership Bulletins*, 1957-61; *Savings and Loans*, 1942-44; *Savings and Loan News*, 1945-60; and *Fact Books*, 1954-61. *The Federal Home Loan Bank Review*, 1937-47, served as an additional source of detailed information. Frequently reference also was made to the official reports of the various government agencies, the *Congressional Record* and other documents of the Congress of the United States.

My special thanks go to those who helped in the preparation. Ray Stein collaborated on the research and first draft of the manuscript. A. D. Theobald, Horace Russell, A. R. Gardner and George L. Bliss made major suggestions for the rounding out of the record of this remarkable 30 years. Yoeman work was performed by Nancy Gilfillan and Cecelia Heenan to get the manuscript physically into shape. Helen E. Heggie was invaluable as editor. The Publications Department of The American Savings and Loan Institute, under the direction of Lawrence V. Conway, handled the publication of the book for the United States League.

I am grateful to Norman Strunk for the privilege of writing of a period and a business which have been a magnificent personal adventure to me.

Josephine Hedges Ewalt

Contents

contents, continued

Part one

The legacy
of the great depression

1931-1936

Chapter 1

The business
in perspective: late 1920s

The typical predepression association, known more often as a building and loan than as a savings and loan, was one of a national network of modest-sized community institutions. Though all were blood relatives, their family resemblance was not always easily seen. But the business which was then rounding out its first century of existence accounted for roughly 10% of the savings which the American people had accumulated by 1930, and it held mortgages on about 2,200,000 of their homes. In its first 100 years, it had financed a total of about 8 million home-owning families.

The people in savings and loan work thought of it as a social institution, a "movement," with overtones of something other than a "business." Julius Klein, Assistant Secretary of Commerce of the United States, in a radio address on January 3, 1931, said, "Let's extend congratulations on this occasion of its 100th birthday to our most signally successful *co-operative* business effort." (Italics are author's.) Earlier in this nationwide broadcast, the speaker had referred to what the then-President of the United States, the Honorable Herbert Hoover, had said of savings and loan associations when he was Secretary of Commerce, "They should be encouraged by the public-spirited citizens in every locality."

Prevalent and dominating the public impression of the associations at that time was the idea that they "helped people." It is not inappropriate to mention, as evidence of this consensus, the remark of a passerby at the Chicago Century of Progress Exposition in 1933. Picking up one of the pamphlets from the small but attractive savings and loan exhibit there he remarked, "No one can measure the good that has been done by these associations."

Between 1925 and 1930—a period of high activity in building and acquisition of homes—associations were lending about 35% of the money then being placed in mortgages on all nonfarm residences. Only to a very limited extent did they participate in construction lending. Most of their loans were on existing homes. Loans frequently amounted to a higher percentage of value than those made by other lenders. Consequently, savings and loan associations were coupled in the minds of some people with the poorer risks, i.e., borrowers with extremely limited incomes and to houses that never would have been shown on a "home of the week" page in any publication. Partly from this circumstance, of course, came the idea of "how they helped." Actually, there were exceptions—cities in which savings and loan institutions were already operating as the source of home financing for a full cross section of the income groups in the locality. But this situation was not widespread enough to give them the acknowledged status, nationwide, of the country's primary home lenders. They were, however, then as in mid-century, the only financial institutions created to specialize in lending on homes and very little else.

By the end of the prosperous decade of the 1920s, their assets approximated $9 billion. This figure was not negligible, in terms of 1929 thinking, but the associations were not known to the general public to anything like the extent their $9 billion warranted. The fact that at least 90% of them, as individual units, had less than $1 million in assets is an obvious reason for the limited public knowledge of them; fewer than 90 institutions throughout the country had resources of more than $10 million in 1930.

As an immediate consequence of the relative smallness of the individual unit, very few associations had business quarters large enough to attract the attention of the casual passerby; too often they operated from second floor locations; and very frequently they were housed with another business which got the name on the door in larger letters—a real estate or insurance company—or even a commercial bank. Under such circumstances, an association could be doing millions of dollars of lending a year and the people of the locality might not know of it unless a friend or business associate happened to mention that he obtained his loan there. The savings function was even less likely to be publicized by word of mouth.

The lack of uniformity in the name of the institutions played a significant part in preventing their identity from taking shape in the public mind of the 1920s. While the term "building and loan" association was most common, the now prevalent "savings and loan" had already become normal in New York state and many parts of Ohio and in Washington state. There was scattered use of "savings and loan" in other states whose laws permitted variety in designation of thrift and home financing institutions. In Massachusetts and some of the other New England states, "co-operative bank" was the only legal designation. Louisiana leaned heavily toward use of the word "homestead" somewhere in the title. The term "building association" had a substantial following, notably in the District of Columbia; and such combinations as "building and saving," "savings, building and loan" were not unusual.

State charters exclusively

All associations did business under state law—a situation that existed in the commercial banking field from the 1830s to 1863, when national banks were first chartered. State laws providing for the chartering and supervision of associations virtually ran the gamut in both important substance and details. They were adequate (according to the lights of the late 1920s) in a few states; inadequate, in retrospect at least, in most other states; in Maryland and South Carolina, nonexistent.

Variations in the laws from state to state caused the associations to operate differently in the various jurisdictions. Diversity in operations was, moreover, a tall stumbling block to those far-sighted leaders who tried to create a public consciousness of the institutions represented by $9 billion in total assets. One particular aspect on which state laws differed considerably should be mentioned here because the resolution of that difference figured largely in the plan for reconstructing savings and loan institutions in the 1930s. It was the provision for different types of accounts.

Types of accounts

Most state laws leaned heavily toward those types of accounts which brought into the association money fairly likely to stay with it for several years. These were the "installment shares" and the "prepaid shares." Under both concepts the saver had to carry through his savings program to a definite maturity date, if he was to get all the earnings possible on his savings. Through the device of forfeiture of a portion of earnings (it is still used in the U. S. Savings Bond Program) the association exercised control over withdrawals. In such a situation it was dealing essentially in long-term money.

Only two types of accounts permitted early withdrawals with no forfeiture of earnings: the full-paid, in multiples of $100, on which earnings were distributed in cash every six months, and the optional savings account closely resembling the savings bank account. While many state laws provided for full-paid "shares," only a few permitted optional savings. Money in such accounts came much nearer to accurate classification as "short-term" than did the funds in the other, much more frequently used, types of accounts. But such money represented in the 1920s only a small part of the funds with which savings and loan associations operated.

When the chips were down in the depression years, the savings and loan business abandoned its heavy reliance on the type of account that brought in essentially long-term money and overwhelmingly accepted the theory that it must make funds available, without forfeiture of earnings, when the savers wanted them. Chapters 7 and 11 will give more details of the events which caused this concept to prevail.

A phenomenal growth in the number of associations characterized the 1920s. There were 8,600 savings and loan units at the beginning of the decade; the number had mushroomed to more than 12,000 by the time of the 1929 crash. But this is not the whole story. Most spectacular was the growth in number of associations in such cities as Cincinnati, Philadelphia, Chicago, Milwaukee and

6

Baltimore. These were cities which already had a good complement of savings and loan institutions, but they saw hundreds of new ones spring up in the wake of the real estate boom. By 1931 it was apparent to some savings and loan leaders that during the recent prosperity too many small associations had been organized in fields inadequate to support them; supervision in the 1920s had failed signally to cope with this possibility.

The basic changes which took place in the savings and loan association structure and procedure during the years 1930 to 1960 will be mentioned in this volume as the chronology determines. These changes reach deeply into the basic relations that existed between the association and its savers and borrowers. Their principal direction was toward greater flexibility, greater capacity of the association to meet a wider variety of customer needs, and a basic adaptability to the inevitable march of time.

In looking at the business in perspective as of the beginning of the new generation, one would make a grave mistake, however, not to recognize that the changes in the 1930s were already foreshadowed by some of the advanced practices of the associations in the 1920s. The new ideas of the 1930s did not come out of thin air. A significant minority of associations were already providing a flexible service, permitting—as already indicated above—savers to make payments, if and when they wished, and offering a loan repayment arrangement almost equivalent to that which today's associations take for granted. Moreover a substantial number of associations even in the 1920s were operated on the principle that they were a financial business first and a social institution second. Few of the managers of those forward-looking associations would, however, have hazarded the prediction that their view of how the business should be conducted would become the norm before another generation had passed. They could not have predicted it because they could not foresee the open door to change which the experiences of the Great Depression would present to the business.

The challenge of the depression can be put very simply: The savings and loan institutions had to deal with conditions which were the reverse of those under which they had been built up. They owed three-fourths of their stature in 1930 to the growth of the previous 10 years—a period of uninterrupted prosperity.

Before the decade of the 1920s, the aggregate assets of the business were indeed modest—$2.5 billion. Then they entered a decade which is famous in the history of the United States for its headlong rush back to "normalcy," its deliberate disregard of lessons of the past, its emphasis on getting rich quickly and enjoying a high standard of living on credit, plus its naive faith that there would be no more major business setbacks. The period was characterized by an extraordinary expansion of the home building industry which brought savings and loan associations into a role they had not previously experienced; there was a constant demand over a period of years for an increasing volume of home mortgage money so that

Chart 1. Number of savings and loan associations and total assets, December 31, 1919-1929

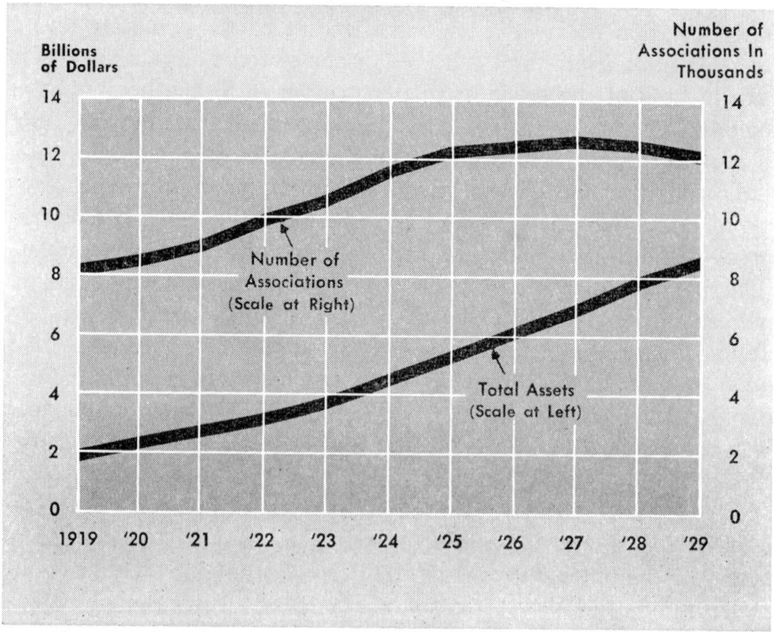

Source: *United States League, secretary-treasurer's annual reports*

the march forward of savings and loan was practically inevitable. Chart 1 reveals the trend in the number of associations and their total assets during the decade of the 1920s.

One look at the leaps ahead in some of the more populous states witnesses to unparalleled expansion as the order of the day. Between December 31, 1919, and December 31, 1929, the total assets

8

of California associations increased by 1,141% ($438 million), of New Jersey by 480% ($952 million), of New York by 320% ($321 million), of Illinois by 249% ($320 million), of Pennsylvania also by 249% ($999 million) and of Ohio by 236% ($902 million). Some other states, starting from a smaller base, approximated these rates of growth. Most of the men who were responsible for the operation of the associations thought with good reason the future held more of the same.

Full-time staffs for leagues

But there were many astute thinkers among them who foresaw that a business could not experience such growth without engendering some grave problems some day—even without considering the possibility of a depression (which few did). The wisest of their generation were already beginning to see that the day had passed when the individual savings and loan man could work out all of his problems alone. They saw that the only way to meet the possible problems of the future was through the city and state leagues and the United States Savings and Loan League; and accordingly they led the way toward full-time staffs for the leagues. They won support for the idea that more men should be employed by these leagues, which could then cease depending on certain savings and loan officials to devote the greater part of their time *gratis* for the benefit of the rest. In 1928 a strong movement started to supply the United States League with the "proper machinery" to carry out the plans which the conventions and governing councils made.

Let it be remembered that the savings and loan business from the time of its very beginning in the United States had had one piece of great good fortune: It had attracted to its leadership men and women of foresight and of mental ability far beyond that for which the associations could pay. Out of the minds of such people came the recognition in the late 1920s of the need for leagues to be adequately staffed. Some of the state leagues already had full-time executives before the same step was taken for the United States League. Notably those in Ohio, New York, Indiana, Illinois, California, Kansas, Washington and Pennsylvania were already demonstrating some of the advantages of this new approach.

Banding together of associations at the state level with a full-time executive to work for their common interests had been hastened by frequent brushes with the competitive-minded commercial bankers in the form of interpretations of Section 5219 of the U.S. Revised Statutes. This is the federal law which prohibits a state from taxing national banks more heavily than it taxes competing capital. Repeatedly, banks initiated court cases where they claimed that Section 5219 was being violated because a state was taxing national banks more heavily than it was taxing savings and loan associations. The bone of contention was that these institutions were competitors of the banks and that the banks, therefore, should not be paying taxes which the states failed to levy on the savings and loan associations. The courts continued to rule that these organizations were not competing financial institutions, but the litigation was frequent enough to create considerable work for a state savings and loan league executive. The legislative program of the United States League for many years included revision of Section 5219, with the objective of removing the cause of these frequently recurring court tests. The item was not removed from the League's legislative program until more pressing problems arose to be dealt with in Washington.

The 1920s were the great age of the formation of effective, powerful trade organizations in many businesses. The savings and loan leaders amended their United States League Constitution in 1929 to provide for the opening of a full-time office and appointment of an executive manager. The League president at the first annual convention held after this change predicted that the opening of the national office of the League in Chicago on June 1, 1930, would rank in importance in the history of the business with the founding of the first association in 1831 and the very organization of the League in 1892. Prophetically indeed, he added, "The problems of the future will demand the services of the most successful men connected with the building and loan movement."

And so it was that the savings and loan associations, $9 billion strong, collided with the Great Depression, armed with a trade association to conduct their warfare against economic misfortunes. Largely because of it they were able to cope with a serious loss of public confidence, with the business misjudgments of many association managements, and with the threat of a new and engulfing concept of the federal government, which could have swept the business into an economic role soon to be forgotten. In the

10

United States League they had a workable instrument for marshaling the thought within the business in order to arrive at solutions; and they had a staff in the League which took the responsibility of leading and implementing their thinking.

One other important fact of the preparation with which savings and loan associations faced the depression was that some of the possible remedies that later emerged had already been mellowing in the minds of a few leaders of the business. As early as the end of World War I federal charters and a system of home loan banks for the business had been discussed. When times had become easier and growth seemed inevitable, many of these earlier considerations had faded into the background. But the things that men think of ahead of their hour have a way of staying around in the shadows until their time is ripe; and these two ideas which savings and loan leaders of an older generation had discussed were the bases of two of the major lines of redevelopment which the business took in meeting its depression problems.

United States Savings and Loan League
and affiliated organizations

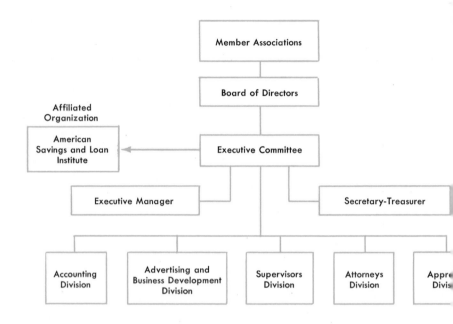

Committees

Federal Legislative Committee
Advisory Committee on State Legislation
Committee on Public Relations

Functions and Services

Convention Department

Handles arrangements for the League's Annual Convention.
Handles arrangements for conferences and other meetings of the League.

Advertising Service

Collects all forms of advertising materials and assembles them in special binders to be loaned out to League members for their examination.
Assists League members in the preparation of advertising pamphlets, statements and like materials.

Field Service

Acquaints nonmembers with the nature and extent of the League's service program and the benefits of belonging.
Serves the League's present members.
Cooperates with state and local leagues to provide greater service to the savings and loan business.

Secretarial Staff

Responsible for the routine functioning of th
Handles the clerical and stenographic wor

Publicity Bureau

Provides newspapers, periodicals, etc. with
publicity for the benefit of the League,
members and the American public.
Prepares exhibits for display at various tr
shows.

Publications

Publishes *Savings and Loan Annals*.
Publishes other printed materials for the L

Research Library

Provides reference resources on savings a
associations.
Develops course materials for the Institute.
Answers special inquiries from member associations.
Prepares the *History* volume.

Education and Research
(American Savings and Loan Institute)

Publishes the *Savings and Loans Journal*,
forerunner to *Savings and Loan News*.
Develops new chapters and cooperates wi
already existing chapters in increasing
membership and effectiveness of the Ins
Organizes the curricula, preparing whatev
materials are needed for new and revis
courses.

American Savings and Loan Institute

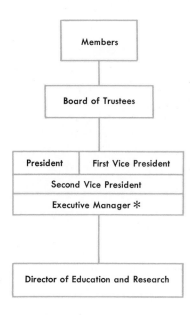

```
┌─────────────────┐
│     Members     │
└─────────────────┘
         │
┌─────────────────┐
│ Board of Trustees │
└─────────────────┘
         │
┌─────────────┬───────────────────┐
│  President  │ First Vice President │
├─────────────┴───────────────────┤
│      Second Vice President       │
├──────────────────────────────────┤
│       Executive Manager ✳        │
└──────────────────────────────────┘
         │
┌──────────────────────────────────┐
│ Director of Education and Research │
└──────────────────────────────────┘
```

✳ Also Executive Manager of the
United States Savings and Loan League

ffice.

le

gue.

loan

Functions and Services

Development of an educational program.
Organization of chapters.
Preparation of several texts.

te.

Chapter 2

Colliding
with depression

Economic catastrophe befell the United States in late 1929 and afflicted the people with increasing intensity in the first years of the 1930s. This prolonged and mammoth event is too well known for elaboration here, and a generation later it still substantially affects the thinking of many leaders in public life. But it brought the savings and loan associations no appreciable trouble until the growing list of commercial bank failures concentrated the crisis in the financial sector of the economy. Indeed every local bank failure had repercussions in any number of businesses in the community so that it has never been possible since then to isolate for study the problems of any one business in the depression, so dominant in the initial misfortunes of so many was the banking situation.

Before "Black Thursday" on Wall Street in October 1929, there was a relatively slight disruption of the normal world of the savings and loan "secretary" (the usual term for the full-time man in the associations in those days). The growing absorption of the nation with speculative profits brought about successive waves of withdrawals from savings and loan institutions by savers who wanted to take their fling in the stock market. The inflow of savings also materially slackened and for the same reason. Accordingly there was a dearth of money for making mortgage loans. The United States League secretary-treasurer's report put it this way: "The usual business of the building and loan associations was seriously disturbed."

Gradually after the stock market crash more normal conditions returned to savings and loan associations. Steady improvement was envisioned by nearly all managers of such institutions by the first quarter of 1930, even though there were some areas in which the improvement was slight. By the summer of 1930 the business as a whole believed its main troubles were over. In fact, the leaders of almost all businesses at this time, as well as the political leaders of the nation, believed that recovery was around the corner: The never-to-be-forgotten phrase with which the Administration of President Herbert Hoover was tagged by its opponents in the next national election was—"prosperity just around the corner." It became a political shibboleth of devastating impact, because it proved to be a serious misjudgment.

Bank failures, 1930-1932

Such prognosticators were, amazingly, overlooking the menace of the continuing incidence of bank failures. In 1930 there were 1,352 such suspensions; in 1931 another 2,294 banks closed their doors; and in 1932 another 1,456 went out of business. All of this, let it be remembered, happened before the banking "holiday" at the beginning of the Roosevelt Administration. While the great majority of the failed banks were not members of the Federal Reserve System, the highly regarded national banking system was nonetheless responsible for 846 of the failures during those three years. Nearly 200 state-chartered members of the Federal Reserve System also failed. The banks which collapsed in 1930, '31 and '32 had deposits of $3,259,658,000. In that statistic was cradled much of the depression predicament of the savings and loan business.

In late 1930 and early 1931 associations in many parts of the country found withdrawals taking on somewhat serious proportions. These months ushered in a period of some three years which brought discouragement, perplexity, alarm and finally, in some instances, near panic to the officers and boards of directors of thousands of associations. Terminology, graphically descriptive of the times, which has no meaning at all in the 1960s, entered the savings and loan vocabulary with unhappy frequency. One such term was "on notice": It meant paying withdrawals only as the money came in and keeping many customers waiting indefinite periods of time for the payment of their savings. Many associations adopted this practice as early as the fall of 1931.

A major problem arose for a savings and loan association when the bank in which it carried its cash failed. The association's cash was tied up and too often it was simply wiped out. Some who were closely acquainted with the troubles of numerous associations in depression years are convinced that their losses from deposits in closed banks mounted larger than any of their other losses during the long period of troubles. Certainly even the tying up of the deposits that associations customarily kept in their local banks spelled major trouble for the normal operations of institutions so involved.

Furthermore many associations had borrowed money from the banks to pay the periodically large maturities of systematic savings; they usually repaid the loans out of the next few months' receipts. On December 31, 1931, the associations owed $300 million to commercial banks. As soon as a bank got into trouble, one of its first steps was to call on all borrowers for payment of short-term advances; these borrowers included, of course, savings and loan associations. The repaying of these loans siphoned off a large part of the current receipts of associations. Thus to the limited extent to which associations were indebted to banks they had a second large worry whenever a bank "went under."

Making matters much worse, however, was the psychology of fear which the troubles of the banks engendered. Apprehension was general among the people in the area of any commercial bank failure; and no matter where anyone had money invested, he became increasingly interested in trying to get it out. People "hoarded" money in their safety boxes and in hiding places at home to a degree which sounds incredible to the present generation. Currency in circulation in February 1933 reached a peak of $6,258,-000,000, of which $284 million was in gold coin—the chief medium for hoarding before it became illegal to own gold coin—and $3,405,000,000 in Federal Reserve Notes. Between the beginning of 1930 and the crisis month of February 1933, *the circulation of gold coin tripled* and the circulation of Federal Reserve Notes doubled, all of this at a time when business indexes were steadily declining. This was the measure of the increasing skepticism about banks and financial institutions generally and the rush to keep cash in hand, preferably gold.

The problems of withdrawals

Coping with the situation of a general public rush to get cash challenged all the ingenuity, as well as the human sympathies and good intentions, of the men and women operating savings and loan associations. Long before state laws came to their help, they devised systems of rationing the money available to pay out to savers. They made every effort to take care of distress cases, becoming skillful in seeing the difference between a hard-luck story which was obviously untrue and a genuine hardship case. Coupled with such decisions, which had to be made very frequently, were the secretary's efforts to counteract rumors about the association's inability to pay. All too often an institution that was in a relatively good condition saw its cash siphoned off by savers who had been stirred by rumors. It was this situation, more than anything else, which created withdrawal lists and led to the paying out of only part of the saver's funds at a time.

Lengthening withdrawal lists and other complications ensuing from the commercial bank disasters of 1930-1933 and the worsening unemployment levels led to a condition generally referred to in those days as "frozen." This was the term for that unhappy state in the middle ground between a going concern and one terminating operations. A "frozen" association was simply one through which money was no longer flowing. People were not putting new money in; few were getting any out except in dribbles; and no applicant could get a loan because there was no money to lend.

There were, to be sure, many smaller towns and a few cities never hit by commercial bank troubles, where the savings and loan associations continued to pay all withdrawals promptly. There were also some states unaffected by the troublesome non-liquidity problem which plagued too many spots in the nation. New

York and New England were the principal areas that escaped the general "frozen" situation. The banking situation was more nearly in hand in those areas than elsewhere.

The associations also moved to their own defense in several different directions. Two state government arrangements were effected in Massachusetts, a central bank in 1932 and a share insurance fund in 1934. Already in existence before the depression was the Land Bank of the State of New York, owned, controlled and operated by the savings and loan associations of that state.

In the early stages of trouble, emergencies in individual associations were sometimes met by the helpful collaboration of managers of other associations. For instance, in New York state, a small group of savings and loan men took the responsibility of rescuing institutions at the very first hint of a problem, thus preventing any real loss of public confidence. Familiarly known within the business as "flying squadrons," these men made their volunteer help available to any manager who was likely to have to go "on notice." News of an impending problem was quickly communicated to them by the state league. They worked on the telephone and by personal visits hither and yon to arrange a loan to tide such an institution over so that it could maintain public confidence in its ability to pay promptly. Above all they helped maintain the morale of the manager in such a situation—one of the truly great problems of the times. Savings and loan people, as a whole, were unaccustomed to major business crises, and the sense of being alone in such unprecedented dilemmas was often almost overwhelming.

Since loss of confidence in savings and loan institutions was not universal, this determined somewhat the decisions made later in the correction of savings and loan difficulties. There was a difference, for instance, in procedures in the insurance of accounts in commercial banks from those used in insuring savings and loan associations; but this story belongs more properly in Chapter 6.

Even without too much dependence on the new federal agencies which were created from 1932 to 1935, many savings and loan institutions managed to reduce their withdrawal lists; "panic" withdrawals substantially subsided after the correction of the bank troubles in Washington in 1933. Numerous associations which had once been in deep trouble managed at least to keep their heads above water, even if they were not doing business on anything like the old scale, either in taking in new money or in making loans.

Solution of "frozen" situations

You will hear savings and loan people who lived through that period say "we had a hard time saving that association," and the remark gives an insight into the spirit with which leaders in the business and public supervisors as well worked on the problem. From the vantage point of almost a generation later, it seems surprising that so small a toll of the number of associations was taken in these extremely discouraging early 1930s. But the fact is that by 1935, the "frozen" situation was pretty well a thing of the past. Only 1,500 of the 12,000 associations in existence at the start of the 1930s had gone out of legal existence. In percentage and numerical terms, the mortality rate, in the actually "depressed" years, was markedly less than that in the commercial banking field.

The associations had the advantage of a legal framework which permitted a gradual return to normal operations, if there was a reasonable expectancy that this could happen. Many adopted a procedure which put part of the institution back in business as usual, while waiting out the liquidation of the "frozen" assets. This was the device generally referred to as "segregation of assets." Once the segregated association started operating normally and paying withdrawals, it could advertise for savings with a fair hope of getting its share of even the curtailed savings flow of the time.

On the other hand, many associations very gradually liquidated entirely over the next five to 10 years. The "Grass Roots Progress" described in Chapter 7 includes a more detailed account of the process of segregation of assets and of other reorganization steps by which some associations emerged into new life and others went out of existence.

Troubles with borrowers

The "frozen" assets referred to in the preceding paragraph were largely the result of the second stage of savings and loan troubles. The growing unemployment level in the United States impaired many a borrower's ability to pay off his loan. Associations seeking to meet the emergencies of borrowers permitted more and more of them to make interest payments only; eventually sizable parts of the loan portfolio of many associations were characterized by serious delinquencies. Most of the borrowers kept up the monthly payments during the first months after they lost their jobs; people ordinarily cling to the obligation to pay for a home as long as they can meet the payments and still have money enough for the other necessities of life. This attitude was, of course, no whit different in the 1930s from that with which this generation is familiar.

When delinquency was inevitable because of joblessness, the association typically met the problem with a tideover arrangement. It rewrote the loan, postponing the maturity date and allowing smaller monthly payments. Of course some loans were hopelessly delinquent and foreclosure lay at the end of the road. An accumulation of such arrangements with unfortunate borrowers sharply curtailed the normal inflow of money from loan repayments. Thus an association already having difficulties because its cash was tied up in a closed commercial bank not infrequently experienced the tapering off of its remaining monthly flow of money from the borrowers.

The troubles of the savings and loan associations with borrowers lasted much longer than those with the savers. As unemployment continued, the problem of the borrower who could not pay became more insistent. Foreclosure became the only remedy—especially in cases where the problem was other than a home owner in financial trouble. There were real estate speculators among the borrowers. There were—as always—cases where the family unit had been broken up and responsibility cast to the winds. There were many instances where clear title to an abandoned property could be obtained only by realizing on the security.

Foreclosures were a necessary remedy in certain areas because of the investments made by the associations beyond the range of prudent lending on residential property. In Pennsylvania, savings and loan associations were permitted to make second mortgages and had done so in substantial volume. In New Jersey, income properties had been a lucrative investment for many of the associations over some years; they were not the kind of loans which could be nursed along when depression came and the properties were standing idle. These are just two examples of "problem" situations that arose from borderline lending.

Over the years of coping with foreclosed real estate, managers came to some significant conclusions about some of the lending practices which had contributed to their troubles. One of the first answers which a symposium at a nationwide savings and loan

19

meeting gave to the question, "What kind of homes have you been taught to avoid in the future by your foreclosure experience?" was "lending on poor construction." There was also a definite revulsion against lending on multiple dwellings—and as already indicated, on income properties.

All these reactions are reflected in the arrangements which were made to help the associations move into safer operations. The Federal Home Loan Bank System was set up with definite limitations on the size and nature of the property on which a mortgage would be acceptable as collateral by the Federal Home Loan Banks; one-to-four family homes were made the basis of all lending transactions in the Federal Home Loan Bank System. Associations entered a major new phase of activity in the 1940s when they began to devote as much as a third of their lending funds in some years to new construction; always closely tied to this operation is a careful system of inspection of the construction. Reflected in that safeguard was the memory of the detriment poor construction had been in the "salvage" operation of the 1930s.

Problem of "real estate owned"

In the backwash of the mortgage foreclosure and delinquent mortgage situation, the associations found themselves deeply in the real estate business. An almost nonexistent item on most association financial statements in previous years, the "real estate owned" vaulted in the early 1930s to about $1.2 billion. By 1935 real estate "owned" constituted about 20% of the total assets of the associations. And this burden continued in nearly the same ratio until the early years of World War II. Table 1 shows the grave incidence of real estate owned in the composition of total assets.

Association managers found the handling of real estate, which became a larger and larger part of their total assets, a time-consuming and irritating phase of the work day. Deciding whether to wait for a better market or get rid of the property promptly was a basic operating problem. Many held that the only answer was to hold the property and rent it, claiming one could not sell the foreclosed property at any price. There were localities where associations held auctions to dispose of the foreclosed properties and start with a clean slate. In Milwaukee, a bureau was set up by the associations to dispose of foreclosed houses.

Table 1. Real estate owned by savings and loan associations
in relation to total assets, December 31, 1930-1941
(in millions of dollars)

Year	Real estate owned	Total assets
1930	$ 238	$8,417
1931	370	7,737
1932	642	7,018
1933	828	6,406
1934	1,012	5,875
1935	1,163	5,772
1936	1,160	5,682
1937	1,026	5,632
1938	901	5,597
1939	689	5,733
1940	499	6,049
1941	332	6,150

Source: Federal Home Loan Bank Board, annual reports and
United States League, secretary-treasurer's reports

The unfamiliar bulk of real estate assets was much more of a problem because it was acquired in a very weak market. The depression of the 1930s was accompanied by a drastic decline in all prices. Property values in real estate were among the earliest and longest enduring of the victims of this decline. A typical $5,000 house in 1926 was worth about $3,300 by 1932. And even as late as the mid-'30s, it had gained back, in the average case, only about five percentage points of its initial great drop in value. The "down" side of the real estate cycle was in full command.

Any potential home owner hesitated to buy a house because he had seen the experience of his friends who had lost their homes. He naturally feared further deflation might come in the years ahead, even if he got what looked like a bargain. Furthermore it was a common occurrence in many cities for apartment buildings to be in receivership, and thus to be available at extremely low rentals. In the atmosphere of the times even the low prices at which homes could be bought did not tempt people who could purchase their rented shelter so inexpensively. The continuing shortage of mortgage money inside and outside the savings and loan field further discouraged home ownership and kept many prospective customers from being able to take advantage of the bargains among the vacant houses.

The real estate on the asset side of the financial statement was a poor earner. The rental income from a foreclosed home was meager enough; it did well to cover the taxes on the property and the expense of managing it. A large block of real estate owned was thus a substantial deterrent to increasing the earnings distributed by the association—a distribution so necessary for reviving confidence.

The earnings position was, in itself, still another dilemma for savings and loan management in the depression. In the early days of withdrawal problems the associations commonly cut off distribution of earnings to any shareholders who listed themselves for withdrawals; this device was intended to retard the rush to withdraw money, where it was believed the withdrawals were dictated more by fear than by need. The more serious remedy of complete abandonment of earnings distribution required the courage almost of despair, for this step destroyed the one remaining reason for people to leave their money with the association; and no association took it until its problems reached crisis proportions. When this step was taken it gave rise to another word descriptive of the times and unknown to the present generation: This was "passing dividends," all distributions of earnings being commonly referred to at that time as "dividends."

Effects on distribution of earnings

Such a step was by no means prevalent, however, even in the worst of the depression. While many associations reduced the rate of earnings paid to savers even as low as 1%—unheard of before 1930—the average continued at 3%, or above, through the 1930s. And the mere reduction of the rate of distribution of savings and loan earnings was not too hard a stumbling block in dealing with savers, since competitive rates on savings were not particularly remunerative. The yield on government bonds, for instance, had gone down almost a full percentage point from that of the early 1930s.

Many associations continued to pay a rate of return which they did not earn; often the complicated bookkeeping procedures failed to reveal too clear a picture of the income earned. There was, in fact, much wider variety in the rates paid by savings and loan institutions in the early 1930s than at any time before or since; the element of competition did not enter in, since new savings were so relatively scant. The result was that every institution was able to deal with its own particular situation as far as distributing earnings was concerned. And, the fact that each could do so without having to consider what its neighboring institutions were paying enabled many to make the sound decision which might not otherwise have been possible.

The association had to think about the borrower as well as the saver in deciding what to do about distributing earnings. The vast majority of the 2,200,000 loans which savings and loan institutions had on homes in 1930 were written on what was known as the "share accumulation plan" or "sinking fund mortgage," a pattern inherited from 100 years of operation. It had never run into any trouble until the depression of the 1930s and the consequent decline in earnings. Under this arrangement the borrower subscribed for shares equal to the face amount of the loan at the time that he borrowed the money. When he made his monthly payments, the part which was not interest was paid into these shares instead of being directly credited to the indebtedness. Earnings were credited to those shares just as to the shares held by savers (the so-called "free shares"); but throughout the life of the loan the interest payments of the borrower were figured on the full amount of the money he had borrowed in the beginning. When the amount of the shares plus earnings reached the face value of that loan, the indebtedness was cancelled. Obviously, when an association cut the rate of earnings distribution, the borrower did not accumulate the full amount required to offset his loan as rapidly as he had contemplated.

The reputation of the business suffered at the hands of borrowers who found themselves paying on their loans several months longer than they had anticipated. Management became increasingly concerned, too, about the plight of borrowers caught in this situation. Thus in the years of reformation and rehabilitation of the savings and loan business, there was little opposition to abandonment of the old pattern of loan repayment. But, for the depression years, the loan plan was a definite liability. The reputation of the savings and loan business as a means of paying for a home suffered for some years.

Impaired, rather than mere nonliquid, assets posed to many associations the ultimate problem of staying alive. It was—as already seen—possible for an association to pull out of its troubles by the segregation method, if its chief ailment was "being frozen." But an institution became definitely a case for the supervisors when a substantial depreciation of its assets was its main trouble. The pessimistic outlook for real estate values was a great problem in the maintenance of asset soundness. Losses on cash deposited in closed banks were another problem and have already been discussed at some length. In addition, "other investments" of associations in those days often included municipal bonds and not infrequently bonds for local improvements; and such obligations suffered the fate of most securities in the depression. When the association sold the bonds, the loss was apparent; even if it did not sell them but evaluated them realistically on its books, it still had to incur a loss.

Insufficient reserves

Reserves which should have enabled the associations to take substantial losses in their stride were too frequently insufficient to provide this cushion. In 1931 the total surplus and undivided profits of the associations—they were listed thus in supervisory practice at the time—amounted to only 3.26% of total assets. Even accounting for the overstatement of assets which came about as a result of the widespread use of the sinking fund type of loan, this small cushion meant little when the associations already held 10% of assets in real estate, with prices on real estate declining steadily.

Comprehensive statistics on reserves are of limited value, since there was wide variety in practice as well as in legal requirements on reserves at that time. Ohio, for example, had surplus and undivided profits in 1931 far greater than the real estate owned, when the associations were looked at in the aggregate. On the other hand, Pennsylvania associations had reserves equivalent to less than a third of the real estate owned in 1931. Florida, where nearly all the associations were in trouble in the depression, had reserves equivalent only to one-tenth of the real estate owned at the end of 1931. In other states the two items were more nearly in balance. A few states—such as Ohio, Massachusetts, New York and the District of Columbia—had built the kind of reserves which could stand considerable shock.

But the reserve figures quoted are for all the associations in a particular state; and since reserves are not transferable from one institution to another, they serve mainly to show a trend and to indicate a more far-sighted approach to reserve policy in law and in management practice in one state than in another.

Losses and involuntary liquidation

The losses which eventually resulted from the real estate debacle and depreciation of other assets in those years took many years to be reckoned. Long after the troubles were over the research department of the United States League undertook an exhaustive analysis of the records of 539 associations which were in operation in 1930 in Milwaukee and Kansas City, Mo., and in the states of Michigan, Indiana, California and West Virginia. It found that 85 associations with assets of 24.4% of the total assets of the group had losses equivalent to more than 20% of their 1930 mortgage loan balances; 138 with assets of 34.4% of the group had losses in excess of 15%; and 191 associations with assets of 48.3% had losses in excess of 10% of their 1930 mortgage loans. The data include the losses of associations which weathered the storm without drastic rearrangement of their affairs, as well as of those which went out of business, reorganized or merged with another institution. In most jurisdictions factual data on the actual losses were impossible to develop.

But as early as 1932 the thinkers in the business everywhere knew that lack of reserves had been the Achilles heel of earlier savings and loan policy in preparing for a stormy day. The building of reserves had not only been de-emphasized, it had frequently been looked at askance. The theory of paying out earnings at as high a rate as possible was a natural concomitant of the system of offering a definite maturity of savings shares and relying on the maturity of pledged shares to pay off the loan. The business swiftly changed its attitude on reserves. State legislatures as early as 1930, '31 and '32 enacted new laws for reserve requirements. And after the bitter experience of the early '30s, one heard no more of the argument that an association should pay out all of its earnings to the shareholders.

The new set of practices which established the flourishing system of the 1950s was reserve centered above all else. Safety became more important than return in a business which had learned this truth in the hard school of experience.

Whether the association had to face up to its impaired situation because of a suit instituted by shareholders or because the supervisor himself took the matter in hand, it faced, in such a situation, "involuntary liquidation." Although it has been noted that the depression took a relatively small toll of the number of associations, it is still true that the number of involuntary liquidations during the early 1930s was so much greater than any previous experience of the business that it was a profound shock.

In 1933, a larger dollar amount of savings and loan assets was involved in involuntary liquidations than in any year before or since; the 88 associations that failed that year had $215,516,812 in assets. The report of the United States League secretary-treasurer states that 64 of these failures were attributed by the state supervisors to existing economic conditions; the rest to mismanagement, defalcation and making bad loans. It is, of course, a question where the supervisors drew the line between a failure caused by existing economic conditions and one due to bad loans. Twenty-one out of the 48 states were represented in the list. Table 2 shows the rise and decline in the amount of money involved in involuntary liquidations.

Table 2. Savings and loan failures, December 31, 1929-1935

Year	Total number of associations	Total resources	Number failed during year	Total liabilities of failed associations
1929	12,343	$8,695,154,220	159	$ *
1930	11,777	8,828,611,925	190	80,437,508
1931	11,442	8,417,375,605	126	61,908,529
1932	10,997	7,750,491,084	122	52,818,387
1933	10,727	6,977,531,676	88	215,516,812
1934	10,919	6,450,424,392	68	34,727,616
1935	10,534	5,888,710,326	239	31,946,235

*This data not assembled prior to 1930
Source: United States League, secretary-treasurer's reports

The fact that the peak of savings and loan mortality occurred in 1933 is noteworthy; the new Washington aids—the Federal Home Loan Bank System and the federal chartering of associations—were too new at that time to exert leadership in pulling associations out of their troubles. It was too soon for the new state laws, designed to help savings and loan institutions survive the depression, to be fully implemented; many of them were just in the making.

The problems of many savings and loan institutions in the depression were augmented by amateur management. Very often those who managed institutions were accustomed to working in them only a few hours of a week. During those hours much of their time was heavily occupied with other matters. Not deeply versed in mortgage lending, but quite willing to do tedious and time consuming work in handling the association, they got along quite well until the troubles of the depression became so many as to demand full-time concentration on the association's affairs. It must be remembered that thousands of part-time associations were responsible for the savings of several hundred thousand members of savings and loan associations. Had they had greater knowledge of the intricacies of the mortgage market and the possible effect on that market of a downtrend in the business cycle, they might have found it easier to survive. No one can say for sure, since many associations operated by keen businessmen working on a full-time basis had troubles along with the rest. The limited time, however, which amateur management could give to the association in trouble was a real problem. In the final analysis it may be considered remarkable that the part-time amateur management came through as well as it did in averting major losses to the savers and maintaining the confidence of many communities in the savings and loan institutions.

Depression problems of savings and loan associations were not confined to their operations. As members of the business community and more particularly as financial institutions, they faced a growing hostility to private business on the part of influential segments of the public. Questions were raised about the validity of profits; and the position of the interest rate in the whole system was subjected to the kind of scrutiny which had not been heard in the land since the late 19th century and the Populists' emphasis on the wickedness of money lenders.

When the campaign of castigation against business was in its heyday, it seemed possible indeed that the American public might get an entirely new and totally experimental set of values—to the detriment of many institutions hitherto respected and accepted. So the savings and loan man had a psychological problem just as did the banker or the securities underwriter or the manufacturer. In the final analysis, however, this propaganda found less acceptance by the people as a whole than the businessmen of the times feared it might.

To be sure, the whole realm of so-called social legislation, including the Fair Labor Standards Act, the Wage and Hour Law, the Social Security measures, the Securities Exchange Act, and even such arrangements as the Federal Deposit Insurance Corporation and its sister institution, the Federal Savings and Loan Insurance Corporation, rode onto the statute books on the wave of this kind of public thinking. As it turned out, the highly adaptable American businessman, in whichever of the major fields he was engaged, learned to live with these strange new federal laws. But in learning to live with them he had to change many of the less-than-basic, but accepted, facets of his day-to-day activities.

Public attack on thrift

The savings and loan world was confronted, among other problems, with a broad attack upon the principle of thrift itself. In high places there was wide subscription to the theory that "he who spends his money contributes most to his country's welfare"; such an attitude seemed an ominous threat to the future of institutions dedicated to savings. One economic school dismissed the time-tested "rainy day" principle with the smart aleck statement that "saving for a rainy day only makes it rain." This school certainly attracted that part of the population which favored staying with the newly discovered thrift substitute, namely, a paternalistic government. Even in the dreary days of the depression, however, only a relatively small, although highly vocal, sector of the American people ever substituted a paternalistic government for their own individual thrift. Be that as it may, savings and loan leaders of the 1930s foresaw a formidable future in which savings would have to be fought for with much sharper weapons and much subtler appeals. This apprehension played its part, also, in the lines along which the newly developing savings and loan business proceeded.

Despite the refusal of the American people to accept the saving-is-useless theory, one far-reaching development of this emphasis during the depression years embedded itself definitely in all 20th century thinking. Practically a 180° turn in the people's concept of the government's place in the economy dates from the 1930s. The "hands off private business" posture, heretofore almost traditional, now was supplanted by a clamor for government action at the national level. While this was more of a "do something" appeal than a call for specific legislation, one trend emerged clearly: a mounting feeling that the economy could no longer be trusted to run itself.

Savings and loan leaders and observers of the political scene in those days were concerned by the development of so much government activity in the area of housing. Like other organized business groups, the savings and loan leaders took positions—and testified before congressional committees—for or against provisions of many proposals for new forays of the government into home financing and the building and subsidizing of housing. Where they could not hope to have a deciding voice in preventing the adoption of what was believed to be unfortunate legislation, they offered and often obtained passage of ameliorating amendments in order to limit the unfortunate consequences of the new legislation. The United States League consistently opposed the granting of uncircumscribed powers to newly created government officials—powers which might be used to harass the businessman and hamper business practices in the building, home financing and allied fields.

Lending in the depression years

But the best way in which savings and loan executives combatted the impression in the community that the government should take over all of the home financing function was by continuing, to some extent, in the lending business. Even in the worst depression years dollars were flowing out of savings and loan associations into the hands of people buying, repairing and refinancing homes. A continued plodding activity was theirs, putting out a little money here and a little money there. It tends to be overlooked, when the depression of the 1930s is recalled, but the fact that the associations were still making home loans in the worst years of money scarcity emphasized even then their unique position in the home lending field in the United States.

But it was not easy in the 1930s to stay in the lending business. Table 3 shows the mortgage lending activity by savings and loan associations for the years 1930-1936.

In a large number of associations lending came to a virtual standstill. Conditions in 1933 (the leanest year in loans) may be glimpsed in the reports from the state savings and loan leagues

Table 3. Mortgage lending of savings and loan associations, 1930-1936
(in millions of dollars)

Year	Mortgage loans made
1930	$1,300
1931	900
1932	530
1933	435
1934	463
1935	642
1936	755

Source: United States League, secretary-treasurer's reports

made each year at the annual convention of the United States League. Of about 20 state leagues commenting specifically on new loans in 1933, seven reported that "few to very few" were being made; three said that about half the associations in the state were making some loans; one, that most associations were doing "some loan business."

However spotty the situation and however few the associations making any large volume of loans, the first crucial test of the times was met favorably by the savings and loan business. A sufficient volume of loans was being made by associations to justify the establishment of permanent new federal instrumentalities, based on the savings and loan principle, as one way to combat the shortage of home owner credit. Had lending from this source come completely to a standstill the chances of getting the Federal Home Loan Bank System started or of chartering federal associations would have been virtually nonexistent.

Chapter 3

Federal
emergency legislation

T wo predominant forces were brought to bear on the problems of the savings and loan associations to hasten and facilitate their rise above the problems of the 1930s and their transformation into the savings and loan system as the mid-century knows it. The larger role was that of the business itself; the instrument which it used was the United States League, with the support and collaboration of many of the state leagues. The other force was the United States government; it moved into an entirely new sphere of economic concerns during the Great Depression and stayed there for the succeeding generation.

But the moves of the government assisted these associations mainly because the leaders of the business worked diligently to bring that help within the reach of their institutions. Thus the story of the two forces cannot well be separated in any recounting of the recovery and transformation of the savings and loan institutions.

The Great Depression brought a gargantuan assignment to the United States League which the savings and loan business had providentially strengthened in 1929. There were many sides to the task. Among them were the re-creation of confidence on the part of the public, the planning of a vastly revised legislative framework under which the institutions might operate more safely, and the rallying of the manpower within the associations to arduous, discouraging, often displeasing, but eventually rewarding, work and decisions. The method of achievement was as complex as the goal. Leadership with a capital "L" is one way of describing it simply.

But what was accomplished by the mere handful of people involved in the actual leadership is the most startling fact of the period. The almost ceaseless activity, both mental and physical, required of the United States League's leaders cannot be re-created by the imagination of any person who did not live through those days. The League's executive vice president spent practically as much time in Washington as in Chicago headquarters, because lobbying with lawmakers and conference after conference with busy men heading new, experimental and always urgent federal government programs were necessary. Frequently in Washington, too, were the key men on the Legislative Committee of the United States League and top leaders of one or two other committees which happened to be dealing with phases of the business that dovetailed with the emergency program. These trips were made by train, principally, in the 1930s, this being the period before frequent air travel was prevalent. This method of travel added one more ingredient to the toughness and sacrifices of personal energy required of those relatively few men who provided the leadership.

Stimuli to savings and loan action

But they had to do other things besides persuade men in Washington to include savings and loan ideas in their thinking. They had to stimulate action in the savings and loan business by convention speeches, by talks to specially called meetings of county or city leagues, by letters, telephone and wire. They had to burn midnight oil to work out educational courses in how to use the new instruments of law and regulation. They often had to sit in with a committee of the League in a far-into-the-night session to reach a decision on some emergency that was at hand because of a surprise pronouncement from the White House or from Capitol Hill in Washington, or because a competitive threat had suddenly come to the fore, or a sudden gust of public opinion was blowing the wrong way as far as savings and loan was concerned.

Some of the lines along which the League led the savings and loan business to a better day make clear-cut pictures. The four chapters immediately following this one will concentrate on these portraits. Other approaches, contributing almost as much in the final analysis, cannot be described so concretely as can new laws, additional organizations and professional societies. In the realm of building up morale, the League's leadership was, of course, intangible; but the consensus of the men operating associations in this time of doubt and perplexity gives the credit for a new *esprit de corps* unquestionably to the programs stemming from the United States League.

The job done is the more remarkable in view of the frequently hurried answers which had to be found. The legacy from the savings and loan leaders of the previous generation has already been cited. But it was a limited legacy in view of the propensity of the 1930s to spin problems from an ever-whirring wheel. Leaders of the business in the 1930s had to be both long-term planners and short-term solvers of problems, when crises became their weekly bread. They had to shape a sound course from the contact of the electricity of the new thinking with the sturdy metal of experience, tradition and judgment. And the challenge to bring these qualities to light—in the service of the business as a whole—was most pronounced in the area of contacts with government.

The most spectacular of all the achievements of the savings and loan leaders was the bringing into being of the Federal Home Loan Bank System. But this achievement was so far-reaching and so basic to the other recovery measures which followed in its wake that it needs special treatment; the next chapter will give appropriate space to that development. This present chapter enumerates the ways in which savings and loan associations benefited from programs which the government in Washington worked out as general measures in order to take the sting out of the depression for many different types of business enterprises and people. It also tells of one emergency program created for the savings and loan associations that had its small but significant part in recovery.

From the general emergency programs of the federal government—one in the Hoover Administration and one in the days of President Franklin D. Roosevelt—savings and loan associations received two different kinds of assistance. To sum it up, a few hundred associations got loans from the Reconstruction Finance Corporation—the first of the "alphabetical" agencies which appeared on the Washington horizon, since it came generally to be called the RFC. Several thousand associations turned delinquent loans over to a later and almost equally famous alphabetical agency, the HOLC—officially the Home Owners' Loan Corporation.

Loans from the Reconstruction Finance Corporation

The RFC was the first major federal government effort to thaw the assets of business and finance in general. It came into being in January 1932, being modeled upon the War Finance Corporation of 1917 which had been successful as a temporary buttress for the domestic economy. When its work was performed it meant to abandon the scene to the better ways and devices of private enterprise. The RFC was thus designed for temporary life; estimates pointed to five, or at most 10, years for its activity.

Its original capitalization by the Treasury was $500 million, with a potential debenture issue up to $2 billion. It was to deal strictly with business entities, never with people. In the first six months of its existence, days of real panic, the RFC made about $2 billion worth of loans, principally to commercial banks. The urgency with which it had to act will be realized when the reader thinks back to the multitudinous bank failures described in Chapter 2 and their devastating effect upon so many communities.

Savings and loan associations would probably not have become eligible for RFC loans in the ordinary course of events. It should be recalled that they were a relatively small ($8.8 billion) part of the financial system of the nation. Including them among the rescue operations of the great new government corporation would probably not have occurred to anyone in Washington had the leaders of the savings and loan business not been on hand to get them included. Furthermore the RFC's need to get started pouring out financial succor was so insistent that a savings and loan program might have been sidetracked indefinitely if leaders of the business had not been on hand in Washington to see that the technicalities were worked out for a swift utilization of funds by the associations. There was a close personal relationship between the United States League leaders and the RFC top echelon which generated remarkable confidence in the prospects for a savings and loan program to be sound and worthwhile. As is often the case in human affairs the existence of this mutual respect between persons without official ties was the key to the assistance which RFC offered and provided the savings and loan business.

One of the experienced full-time state league executives went to Washington on a leave of absence from his major job in order to help set up the savings and loan section of the corporation's activities. Among the jobs which had to be done were: preparing the loan application forms; detailing instructions for the selection of collateral mortgages and preparation of forms for their listing; and highly important, the setting into motion of state government machinery to remove the restrictions at the state level upon associations borrowing from the RFC. For, as pointed out earlier, all associations were operating strictly under state laws.

The United States League made a quick survey of the credit needs of all associations in the United States. (Since the individual enrollment of associations in the League had not reached even 50% by early 1932, the organization did the practical thing of including nonmembers in all its strategic planning.) Partly upon the results of this survey the plans of the RFC to advance credit to the savings and loan sector were made. Representatives of the United States League in Washington saw this as the first opportunity for the business to avail itself of temporary aid; it would be a stop gap, they reasoned, while work was going ahead to bring to the statute books the far more significant legislation that had already been introduced in the form of the Federal Home Loan Bank Act. At first the RFC money was destined to be channeled to associations that needed it to repay money borrowed from banks. Later, it became possible for them to get RFC money to meet maturities and withdrawals and thus make some headway toward getting thawed from their "frozen" status.

RFC loan terms

Savings and loan total borrowing from the agency was around $118 million. This credit became available to associations more than six months before the Federal Home Loan Banks were advancing funds. Thus it filled a pressing need, as far as the men operating associations saw it. Loans were granted on six-month terms; they could also be renewed for a longer period if circumstances demanded. This was the kind of borrowing which made sense to association leaders whose previous experience had been to get money from banks on a short-term basis.

The RFC rate of interest was 5½%. Substantial collateral had to be put up. This latter provision is quite understandable in view of the relatively unknown risk involved in making the loans, but it also proved to be a deterrent to the use by many associations of the RFC credit. Loans began to be made as early as March 1932. Within three months, RFC loans had been made to associations in at least 18 states. The United States League staff was called upon frequently to help associations avail themselves of this credit. Sometimes where there was delay and actual by-passing of the requests by the very new government servants who were engaged in processing these matters, the League staff smoothed the way.

Most of the credits granted in early 1932 were refinanced by the Federal Home Loan Bank System soon after the System actually got into operation. This was the desire of the RFC officials and the policy urged by leaders of the business. By the end of 1937, savings and loan associations had paid back all but $2 million of the total.

But the experience was far more important to the future Washington relations of the savings and loan institutions than the dollar volume of loans would indicate. It had afforded officials of great influence in the nation's capital their first opportunity to see the economic role of a savings and loan association. The institutions had not shown up adversely when viewed alongside the commercial banks. The RFC program had helped enhance their reputation as reliable units in the financial structure.

Home Owners' Loan Corporation

The other general emergency program of the federal government which helped restore savings and loan institutions to active operations was the Home Owners' Loan Corporation. Early in April 1933, President Roosevelt called for legislation to provide "immediate and direct relief of individual home owners." The program launched in response to this call was one of the largest—and one of the most interesting—domestic emergency undertakings in the history of the federal government. It was the mortgage refinancing operation known to many millions as the HOLC.

There was a somber backdrop for this undertaking. It was estimated that the total $20 billion home mortgage debt was already 40% in default. A staggering epidemic of mortgage foreclosures was in full swing. Before the depression, urban real estate foreclosures had averaged about 75,000 a year; in 1932 they reached their annual peak of 273,000, and by 1933 they had broken all monthly records, rising in June to more than 26,000. This rate, it will be seen, was the almost unbelievable average of 1,000 a day.

Savings and loan associations were not so deeply involved in the foreclosure situation as were some other lenders on home mortgages. It must be understood that outside the savings and loan institutions the overwhelming part of the home mortgage debt was in the form of unamortized loans secured by short-term mortgages written for from one to three years—sometimes up to five years. The borrowers expected automatic renewal for a similar period as long as the appraisal remained satisfactory, and without any need to reduce the principal. This had been the easy pattern of the era when real estate values were rising and mortgage money was plentiful. When depression came, the holders of these mortgages—the banks, the insurance companies, the mortgage companies and individuals—needed their money.

A much larger part of the mortgage debt was held by individuals at that time than has ever been the case since. Such mortgage holders had no public relations policies to restrain them from foreclosure when the loan came due and the borrower could not pay; their need for cash in hand was likely to be determining. They were not at all interested in renewing the mortgage. Borrowers in these straits found no other lenders with sufficient money to renew their loans; foreclosure was inevitable. Many authorities lay partial blame for the depression itself on the wide use of the straight, short-term mortgage and the way in which it aggravated the problem of home owner delinquencies during the early 1930s.

Whatever the validity of this claim, borrowers and lenders alike by 1933 needed immediate and decisive aid. With no private agencies in a position to undertake the huge task, HOLC was created. Moving into the gap, the corporation refinanced $2.75 billion worth of home mortgages (more than a million in number) formerly held by private lenders during its three-year lending life, June 1933 to June 1936.

Nature of HOLC relief

The HOLC actually advanced nearly $3.1 billion in all, including reconditioning loans, refinancing for taxes and assessments, and closing costs—and this in the days before billion dollar figures became commonplace. The principal recipients of this relief, by category, are shown in Table 4, with the dollar amounts of assistance which went to each category.

Table 4. Home Owners' Loan Corporation disbursements
(in millions of dollars)

Mortgagees:		
Commercial banks	$525.0	
Mutual savings banks	410.0	
Savings and loan associations	770.0	
Insurance companies	165.0	
Mortgage finance companies	196.0	
Estates, trusts, etc.	110.0	
Individuals	575.0	$2,750.0
Others:		
Taxes and assessments		230.0
Repairs and reconditioning		70.0
Miscellaneous loan expense		43.5
Total amount of closed loans		$3,093.5

Source: Federal Home Loan Bank Board

The agency did not please everybody; and many lending institutions, including savings and loan associations, encountered some difficult and annoying problems in adjusting to its methods. But there is general agreement that without HOLC's broad contributions, foreclosures would have risen to even more tragic levels, real estate prices would have shown an even greater decline, and there would have been a serious threat to the capacity to "carry on" of virtually all mortgage lending institutions.

The operation was fairly simple in concept. Lenders turned over their distressed mortgage loans to the corporation and received HOLC bonds in exchange. The loans were refinanced by HOLC

38

on more liberal terms—monthly payments that would amortize the loan, including the relatively low 5% interest, in a 15-year period. These terms may sound extremely moderate to a mind accustomed to the mortgage lending activities of the 1950s. But let it be remembered that a loan with even as long as a 12-year maturity, such as the savings and loan association made in the early 1930s, was confined almost exclusively to these institutions, that amortization was almost exclusively a savings and loan practice, and that a rate of at least 6% on such a long-term loan as a mortgage was taken for granted.

Under the new arrangement, for the first three years of the Act a moratorium was granted on discharging the principal, and interest payments only were required. The borrower's debt was a direct one to the goverment—the first time in the history of the United States that such an arrangement had been made on any large scale. The precedent set thereby is still having its effects on legislative proposals in Washington, nearly 30 years later. In 1933, for an individual to borrow money from the federal government, either through an agency or direct, was to establish a completely new relationship between the citizen and his government. And it remains to be seen in the light of much longer history whether or not the precedent can be judged as desirable.

The original bonds which HOLC exchanged for mortgages yielded 4%, and only the interest was guaranteed by the United States Treasury. An amendment the next year refunded these bonds for 3% and added a government guarantee of the principal. Subsequent issues bore even lower interest rates—2¾% and 2¼%. Many lending institutions preferred the relatively low yielding bonds to the alternative assets of uncertain loans and devalued real estate. Even the writing down of the face value of loans to qualify them for the 80% loan-to-value ceiling of HOLC became almost palatable in the light of the fact that HOLC bonds could be sold and cash—the most treasured entity of depression years— procured. In the case of savings and loan associations, cash meant ability to pay withdrawals.

At the peak of its operations, the corporation was a conversation piece in all corners of the nation. In 1934, 458 offices (regional, state, etc.) were being maintained in the field. Concurrently, the agency was employing a small army of 20,811 persons—2,762 in the home office and 18,049 in the field—to handle the 1,886,000 applications for $6.2 billion worth of loans that ultimately were processed.

Clamor for foreclosure moratoria

The reaction of savings and loan institutions to the HOLC was colored in each individual case by its particular experience; where thousands eventually found its assistance extremely valuable, others remembered it chiefly for the harassments to which the existence and operations of the HOLC gave rise. Heightening the troubles of mortgage lenders, from quite early in the depression, had been the clamor for temporary statutory suspension of mortgagees' rights to foreclose. Thirty years later the reader may well wax incredulous trying to realize the temper of the times. But the fact that the farmers in one middle-western state organized a mob to lynch a mortgagee's collection agent in their effort to save their farms from foreclosure indicates the emotional atmosphere.

In many states moratoria on foreclosure were enacted. Most of these moratoria had to do with farm property and were not immediately detrimental to the ability of savings and loan associations to foreclose when they had to. But the public psychology created by legal arrangements to postpone any foreclosure was detrimental to general borrower observance of contract. Newspaper accounts of the moratoria, for instance, seriously affected the volume of regular payments in some localities. The demands of political demagogues for debt scaling and further mortgage moratoria led many people to delay their payments when they had the capacity to pay.

It was against this background that many of the problems which the HOLC created for savings and loan institutions must be seen. Obviously there was a hazard that the mortgagor would deliberately default. Armed with the information that only distressed loans were eligible for the more favorable federal financing, hundreds of thousands of borrowers from savings and loan and other private institutions merely refrained from making payments in the hope that their cases would meet legal stipulations (in the original legislation only mortgages in default were exchangeable). Besides undermining an already shaky collection situation, this development had a more pernicious side effect: It further corrupted the sense of debt obligation which had begun to waver with the first moratoria laws.

An even more serious source of HOLC's unpopularity with private lenders was a purely human frailty—overeagerness of its officials to get off to a good start. Many associations protested, during the heat of the corporation's early operations, that they had been politically pressured into surrendering some of their choice loans for the comparatively low-earning HOLC bonds. (When an association transferred to HOLC a loan which could be expected to pay out without difficulty, it sacrificed nearly half of the normal earnings.) The principal temptation to the borrower to get his loan switched to HOLC stemmed from the attractiveness of the loan terms, 5% interest and extended time to repay.

These are some of the problems which influenced some managers in those days to think that the HOLC was more of a liability than an asset.

Although the legislation limited the loans to genuinely distressed borrowers, in actual practice many unqualified persons were able to take advantage of the windfall. Preference for the government loans was based on more than the generous written provisions. Many people instinctively felt that a citizen could always expect Uncle Sam to be more lenient than the private lenders.

Savings and loan institutions transferred 13% of their total mortgage holdings to the HOLC. This percentage was smaller than that which prevailed with regard to the mortgage indebtedness of the nation as a whole: The $2.75 billion in bonds which HOLC issued in exchange for mortgages represented 14% of the home mortgage debt of the country at the end of 1932. The largest proportion of home mortgage loan portfolio turned over to the HOLC was that of commercial banks—26%. The 13% of the savings and loan associations was matched by individual and miscellaneous lenders, while mutual savings banks and life insurance companies exchanged the lower percentages of 12% and 9%, respectively. These latter two groups had usually confined their home mortgage lending operation, before the depression, to fairly low percentage loans of the most unassailable character, and their superdiscrimination doubtless influenced their depression experience.

The $770 million of HOLC bonds received by savings and loan associations in exchange for their "slow" mortgages served as a significant hypodermic. Eventually they became good earning assets to retain on the books or to sell for cash. In many ways the United States League helped associations avail themselves of the privilege of switching mortgages to HOLC. Many needed information on how to proceed, hundreds wanted more precise explanations of some of the very complicated requirements, and still others sought advice on how to handle the more difficult public relations problems which arose from the presence of a vast and unprecedented federal government relief organization in the community.

The United States League had a simple information piece printed at the time of the great excitement created by the inauguration of the HOLC. It was designed to help savings and loan institutions give out the facts about what the HOLC did, and did not, do. Associations placed this in the hands of their borrowers and also made it available to chambers of commerce, newspapers, civic clubs and other molders of public opinion in the community.

Safeguards in Home Owners' Loan Act

Fortunately the final draft of the legislation had incorporated many of the suggestions of the leaders of the savings and loan business. One prime example of an inconspicuous but farsighted amendment included in the law—at the instance of savings and loan leaders —was that which prohibited any person, partnership, association or corporation from making any charge in connection with a loan by the corporation or any exchange of bonds or cash advance under the Act, except ordinary charges authorized and required for services actually rendered. A criminal penalty was provided for violation. Its objective was to take the profit out of any plan to promote the switching of mortgages for bonds.

In view of the propensity of all human beings to see where advantages can be turned into dollars, it is not too extreme to say that this amendment protected the existing mortgage institutions from wholesale raiding of their good mortgages and from having them switched into the Home Owners' Loan Corporation on improper grounds. All institutions which held mortgages in 1933 could have been destroyed if the purse of Uncle Sam had not been tightly closed against the opportunist.

Also at the suggestion of the savings and loan representatives a provision was placed in the Home Owners' Loan Act (Section 4(k)) to thwart empire-building on the part of the personnel administering the giant relief program and to pave the way for automatic liquidation of the corporation. It required all payments upon principal of HOLC loans to be applied to the retirement of the bonds of the corporation. Observers have since remarked that it was a miracle for this subsection to have been included in the Act and a still greater miracle that no attempt was ever made to amend it out. History records the termination of the activity of the HOLC on schedule—when its job was done—as a rare happening in government. Without this provision there might have been no such record.

The HOLC went down in history as one of the few federal government emergency operations which closed activities without cost to the taxpayer. It acquired this golden reputation despite some years in which its experience with delinquent borrowers led to a mounting number of foreclosures—the type of thing it had been inaugurated to prevent.

It was after the suspension of lending activities—in mid-1936— that HOLC foreclosures reached their peak, averaging around 8,000 a month for a three-month period. In all, slightly more than 200,000 properties were foreclosed—approximately one for each five loans. The HOLC reconditioned foreclosed properties and sold them, taking back a mortgage from the buyer on a 15-year maturity at a high percentage of value. In a five-year period sales on these terms brought in around $1 billion dollars. But nearly all the properties were sold before the real estate upturn and the official annual report shows losses exceeding 30% of the amount of loans foreclosed.

The HOLC had a subsidy in the use of government credit; but it returned a small profit to the Treasury. That it did so must be traced to the original 5% and later 4½% loan rate and to the low cost of its money—an average of about 2½%—traceable to the government guarantee of its bonds. Part of its success in getting low-cost money was due to heavy reliance on short-term obligations.

The liquidation of the HOLC was finally speeded up by the repurchase of its remaining mortgages in large blocks by savings and loan associations and other lenders in the late 1940s and early 1950s. The corporation went out of existence in 1951.

Federal investments in savings and loan associations

Another federal emergency program of temporary character was especially designed for savings and loan associations. It had its impact on the business a little later than did the RFC and HOLC. This was the investment of federal funds in the accounts of savings and loan associations. It took its cue from that part of the RFC program wherein federal funds had been invested in the stock of banks which needed more capital in order to survive. While the first legislation authorizing such federal disbursements was adopted in 1933, with only federal associations eligible, the program achieved its highest popularity and usefulness when funds had also been authorized for investment in state-chartered associations. The technical source of the later funds was the HOLC rather than the United States Treasury, but this is a bookkeeping distinction rather than an actual difference in the source of the funds; all these dollars were obtained by the use of the credit of the United States.

This activity was relatively so small and spanned so brief a period of time that it was not long remembered among the major federal government aids to the business. The great boon which it bestowed upon the savings and loan institutions still struggling to get their breath was that it was money actually invested in the association— not a loan. Many associations were hesitant about borrowing money and being obligated to pay a contract rate of interest for money. Furthermore there was a stern limitation in the form of a maximum percentage of assets which could be borrowed. The assistance the Federal Home Loan Bank System could render ran up against these problems. Quite often associations needed more money than they were permitted to borrow under these limitations. Investment of federal funds in their savings accounts was the partial answer.

The arrangement with the government was that the money would stay with the association for five full years without any call for its repayment. After that only 10% of it would be called for repayment in any one year. Here was stability of a most marvelous kind, especially to institutions which still had vivid memories of their great withdrawal problems. Savings from the public had begun to trickle back in many communities by 1935, but the flow was not substantial enough to permit the associations to make loans at anything like their old-time pace and these were new times when more money was needed.

Flow and ebb of federal funds

Between 1933 and 1942 approximately $275 million of federal funds were invested in some 1,400 savings and loan associations. The sum was well over 5% of the total assets of all the associations at the time. One who looks back from the 1960s must continually remind himself that a dollar amount which looks insignificant now was quite significant then; a business only 1/12th the size of today's giant savings association system would obviously be affected substantially by the injection into its veins of $275 million. This is true, although this sum is less than the net savings flow in any one month, even a month of relatively poor showing, in the late 1950s.

The idea of authorizing temporary investment of federal funds in the accounts of savings and loan associations was put forward in the first draft of the Home Owners' Loan Act of 1933. In this initial proposal a national program for distressed mortgagor relief would have relied as a mainstay upon a vast investment of federal funds in savings and loan institutions instead of the mortgage exchange program using federal funds directly, which was eventually adopted as the basis of the relief program of HOLC. Although rejected for the main job of mortgagor relief the idea remained intact in that title of the Home Owners' Loan Act authorizing the chartering of federal savings and loan associations. The stipulation was that $1.00 of federal funds would be invested in the federally chartered associations for each $1.00 of local savings so invested. A limitation of $100 million was placed upon the program in the 1933 Act. This sum was not exhausted in the first year, as will be explained in Chapter 5, where the history of the federal system of savings and loan associations is delineated. In 1934 the law was changed to permit $3.00 of federal investment for each $1.00 of local savings in a federal association. The United States League had worked for the inclusion in the 1934 statute of a provision for state-chartered associations to be similarly eligible for such investments. In 1935 Congress gave the state associations this privilege.

In the largest year of the move of federal funds into savings and loan accounts, 1936, more than $100 million was invested. The flow declined precipitously in 1938, by which time nearly $3 million had been repaid ahead of schedule. The stream had started back into the Federal Treasury from many of the associations which had been successful in re-establishing public confidence. Table 5 reveals the year-by-year data on investments, repurchases and balances outstanding.

All the money invested in savings and loan accounts by the United States government was repaid long before the end of the 10-year period over which the repayments were scheduled to stretch. War intervened, savings became plentiful and the federal government sought through various programs to reclaim some of the lar-

Table 5. Investment in savings and loan accounts by United States Treasury and Home Owners' Loan Corporation, 1933-1942

(cumulative by years)

Year	Original investment			Repurchases			Balance outstanding		
	Treasury	HOLC	Combined	Treasury	HOLC	Combined	Treasury	HOLC	Combined
1933	$ 18,000	$	$ 18,000	$	$	$	$ 18,000	$	$ 18,000
1934	10,725,400		10,725,400	10,725,400		10,725,400	10,725,400		10,725,400
1935	49,300,000	19,846,500	69,146,500	27,500		27,500	49,272,500	19,846,500	69,119,000
1936	49,300,000	125,621,300	174,921,300	309,000		309,000	48,991,000	125,621,300	174,612,300
1937	49,300,000	206,619,570	255,919,570	1,249,300	144,500	1,393,800	48,050,700	206,475,070	254,525,770
1938	49,300,000	215,541,310	264,841,310	2,246,800	740,000	2,986,800	47,053,200	214,801,310	261,854,510
1939	49,300,000	219,926,310	269,226,310	9,621,300	8,473,000	18,094,300	39,678,700	211,453,310	251,132,010
1940	49,300,000	221,645,710	270,945,710	22,552,000	27,361,900	49,913,900	26,748,000	194,263,810	221,011,810
1941	49,300,000	223,259,210	272,559,210	28,016,200	48,092,150	76,098,350	21,283,800	175,167,060	196,450,860
1942	49,300,000	223,856,710	273,156,710	31,752,100	71,545,500	103,297,600	17,545,900	152,311,210	169,867,110

Source: Federal Home Loan Bank Board

gesse it had poured out in the lean years in assisting business and financial institutions. The savings and loan associations responded promptly and in 1943 completed the repayment of all U. S. funds invested in their accounts. The government funds had earned a substantial return—rates of earnings distributed were typically between 3½% and 4% in those days. All in all, the arrangement was concluded as one of benefit to both parties. As a more or less silent aid in the rehabilitation of the savings and loan business, it justified the confidence of its sponsors.

In retrospect, the highest tribute to all the emergency programs of the federal government in their impact upon the savings and loan business was that they are generally forgotten. The leaders of the business who had been influential in making available to the savings and loan institutions at least two of the three major emergency aids described in this chapter did so with profound conviction that their emergency needs were for something only "to tide them over," and they were proved right. All the leaders of the business saw the emergency programs as of only secondary importance. Consistently and to a man they were working toward far-reaching structural and psychological changes in the institutions and those who manned them. The next four chapters will describe the procedures developed and the successes achieved.

Chapter 4

Federal
Home Loan Bank System

The federal government was a fairly simple operation a generation ago. In 1929 the President of the United States had to do much of his own worrying about the business recession and about the doleful statistics which came across his desk from the Departments of Commerce and Labor. President Herbert Hoover, having been Secretary of Commerce in a previous administration, understood all too well the meaning of figures indicating a persistently lower rate of business activity. Furthermore the fall-off in construction, and in home construction particularly, seemed deplorable to him not only from a social point of view but also because it contributed so heavily to the unemployment that afflicted the United States.

Herbert Hoover knew more about savings and loan associations and their value to a community than any other person who has ever lived in the White House. He believed in the savings and loan business as a significant, though small, link in the nation's financial system, and he saw some of its potentialities for becoming something greater. He recognized the wisdom of the amortized home loan, which at that time was almost exclusively a savings and loan lending trademark. By one of the more fortunate strokes of chance he was President of the United States when savings and loan leaders saw that something had to be done, and done right away, to assure any real future for their institutions.

As early as his election campaign, Herbert Hoover had pledged the sponsorship of a regional banking plan to promote better-developed facilities for the nation's home mortgage financing. In May of 1930 he said in a major speech that one of the "most inadequately organized areas of credit" was the flow of funds to the home builder. As the slump became more serious he was frequently made aware that this flow had become a mere dribble.

By the fall of 1931 relief from the stringency of mortgage funds became the objective of many different proposals for government assistance. On November 13 Mr. Hoover publicly announced that he would propose to Congress the establishment of a system of Home Loan Discount Banks. Among the points which he listed in favor of this proposal as a remedy for the emergency was "to strengthen and support the building and loan associations." Mr. Hoover proposed that the federal government furnish the initial capital for the system but that it should be owned eventually as a "co-operative institution between the building and loan associations, the savings banks and other home loan agencies."

Two and a half weeks later the President's Conference on Home Building and Home Ownership convened in Washington. It was a widely based aggregation of real estate men, mortgage lenders of all types, architects, building supply dealers and man-ufacturers, and many other businessmen with an interest in sustained home building activity. The conference had been planned months before the mortgage money crisis of that autumn. Coming when it did, however, it was a natural proving ground, as far as businessmen were concerned, for the President's discount bank proposal. The plan was referred for detailed study to the conference's Committee on Finance. Some savings and loan repre-sentatives, including the then-president of the United States League, were members of this committee; commercial bankers and life insurance executives, however, constituted a more numerous bloc and they succeeded in their efforts to keep the committee from endorsing the President's proposal.

But the full conference heard the story direct from the savings and loan representatives in open session; and by a rising vote the conference went on record in favor of President Hoover's "home loan discount banks." The date of that approval, December 4, 1931, is important in the story of the Federal Home Loan Bank legislation. It marked the first serious public support for the proposal outside the President's circle and the savings and loan business. From this date forth, it was clear that the plan had merit in the eyes of a wide cross section of persons interested and experienced in home financing and home building.

Introduction of legislation

President Hoover recommended passage of such legislation in his State of the Union Message to Congress, December 8, 1931. Subsequently, bills to create a Federal Home Loan Bank System were introduced by Republican Representative Robert Luce of Massachusetts and Republican Senator James Watson of Indiana. Mr. Luce, a distinguished legislative and parliamentary authority, carefully supervised the original drafts of the legislation and in doing so worked closely with savings and loan leaders. Some of the wording of the Federal Home Loan Bank Act reflected, for instance, ways to avert some of the problems into which the RFC had run in adapting its lending operations to savings and loan associations operating under state charter.

The writing of practicable legislation was facilitated by the fact that the United States League Committee on Reserve Credits had readied a detailed plan, after careful sessions earlier in the fall. This League committee had turned its attention to the task as soon as it had become known that there was serious discussion in Washington of a government-sponsored mechanism to enlarge the flow of funds to home building. The idea of having the federal government advance the capital for the system had come, however, from President Hoover. The savings and loan leaders eagerly supported the provisions written into the Act for automatic retirement of the government funds as soon as eligible member institutions were able to supply sufficient capital.

Extensive hearings were held by subcommittees of the House

and Senate Banking and Currency Committees. The arguments for the legislation were naturally shaped to appeal to the mood of the times. Some of the troubles which the Bank System faced later in getting started stemmed from the definite "relief" flavor which its advocates in Congress emphasized, in time-honored political fashion. Obviously the best way to get any legislation through Congress in 1932 was to show how it would help the victims of the depression. People who were losing their homes were among the most easily dramatized of the unfortunates. So the possibility of the proposed new Bank System alleviating foreclosure problems was given decided emphasis.

The strongest testimony in support of the measure related it to the need for revival of home construction, with its massive impact upon the unemployment problem. While the long-range benefits were always a cardinal consideration to the savings and loan leaders and to the President, Congress thought in more immediate terms. National elections to choose a new Congress and a President would be held the following November; and if there was ever a time when votes were determined by economic considerations, it was 1932. Congressional leaders made their support of the Federal Home Loan Bank System part of the campaign talk about their efforts to alleviate human misery.

Opposition from competitors

The main opposition to the measure came from lenders competing with savings and loan associations. The commercial banks, insurance companies and mortgage bankers (mainly those which placed loans for insurance companies) looked with disfavor on legislation that would give savings and loan associations a new place in the economy. A spokesman for the Chicago Mortgage Bankers Association was the most prominent and frequently heard witness against the Bank System. A full-time lobby was maintained in Washington for the express purpose of preventing passage of the bill; thus there was a major tug-of-war between nongovernment forces in those crucial months of 1932, with savings and loan representatives working full time for enactment and the spokesmen for the opposition no less vigorous and persistent.

The competitors' dislike for the whole idea of newly invigorated savings and loan institutions lay back of their outward contention that the System was not needed, and that the proposed obligations of the Bank System were unsoundly devised and would be a miserable failure in the capital markets. Another opposition argument, which was picked up in many places and endorsed, was the claim that the Federal Home Loan Bank System would lead to overbuilding; this warning found some response among the more conservative members of Congress. It is not surprising that the competitors in the lending field took a stand against the Bank System, but in retrospect the intensity of their opposition is quite amazing.

The support of the savings and loan business for the Federal Home Loan Bank bill was felt not only in the testimony given by its representatives but also in the generalship by the United States League of the whole campaign to line up supporting witnesses. Many businessmen concerned about home construction and about the markets for home furnishings and building supplies were enlisted to testify in behalf of the Bank System. The National Association of Real Estate Boards was an able ally. There was then no organized home builders' group on a nationwide basis, but individual builders testified for the legislation and made clear to the congressional committees that there was indeed a lack of funds to finance new construction.

Some of the prominent Republicans—although members of the President's party—were not totally committed to the measure. This circumstance gave pivotal importance to the active push for passage of the bill coming from outside Capitol Hill. The Hoover Administration did not have the large staff of congressional liaison personnel which came to be commonplace in later administrations. Thus without the determined effort of the savings and loan business to get the legislation passed, it probably would have failed of enactment.

Savings and loan representatives maintained headquarters in some unpretentious suites in the Willard Hotel in Washington— a spot from which the dome of the United States Capitol is visible and from which the Capitol itself was less than 10 minutes' ride. Across an open square was the Department of Commerce, whence derived much of the administration support for the measure. The White House was only two blocks to the west. The comings and goings of savings and loan representatives from far and near, with assignments to see this person or that person of influence in the legislative or executive branch, were part of the fascinating pattern of those days.

Speaking before the League convention six weeks after the bill became law, Representative Michael K. Reilly of Wisconsin, chairman of the subcommittee which handled the bill in the House of Representatives, said: "The reason you have a Federal Home Loan Bank Bill on the statute books today is largely the effort put forth by this organization as represented by your officials and others interested in the building and loan movement."

The 71st Congress was one of those rare ones split as to party control; the Senate was under Republican control and the House of Representatives had just come under Democratic leadership with the elections of 1930. It was a situation in which a measure strongly sponsored by the Republican President might have become a veritable political football. But there was really no period in the course of the legislation when party lines were drawn upon it. Staunch supporters for the proposal came from both sides of the aisle in both houses of Congress, a witness to the inherent merits of the bill and a measure of the care with which savings and loan representatives worked at the task of obtaining support. Somewhat prophetic was the salutary bipartisan endorsement of this first large endeavor of the savings and loan business to perform its task more ably. Throughout subsequent years bipartisan support for savings and loan propositions to improve the legislative framework for these institutions has been the rule.

The bill which came out of the House Banking Committee (May 25, 1932) was a new draft introduced by Democratic Representative Reilly, replacing the original, which had been sponsored by Republican Luce. But this change was a result of parliamentary technicalities rather than of any real partisan split. Prominent in the floor fight for the measure was Democratic Representative Frank Hancock of North Carolina.

On the Senate side, Senator Watson, chairman of the subcommittee handling the bill, let week after week pass without bringing it up for a subcommittee vote. The intervention of the chairman of the full Banking Committee, Republican Senator Norbeck of South Dakota, was finally responsible for the Senate Banking Committee's favorable reporting of the bill on June 14; savings and loan representatives had their part in persuading Senator Norbeck to act.

Approval by Congress

The legislation was approved by the Senate July 12, 1932, and by the House of Representatives July 15. Differences which had to be ironed out in conference numbered 147. Many times in the last days of that session the measure, even this close to enactment, seemed to have been lost in the hectic rush to adjournment.

Congress had already worked past the adjournment date it had set for itself and was trying to attach amendments of all sorts to whatever bills were before it. Some irrelevant ones, such as that legalizing 3.2% beer, almost got included in the Federal Home Loan Bank Act and might have doomed the legislation. An irrelevant provision to expand the note issues of national banks did get included and may have been responsible for a few supporting votes. By the time the Federal Home Loan Bank Act got through conference, many of the lawmakers had already departed, including the Speaker of the House, the Honorable John N. Garner.

One final crisis had to be resolved the very last day of the session: There was no appropriation to get the new Bank System started. The House suspended its rules to earmark $250,000 for the purpose. Senate proponents of the measure got the appropriation approved by attaching it to a District of Columbia bill which was on the calendar and sure to come up for action. Loud cries of "foul" rose from opponents of the Bank System when this maneuver succeeded.

The Federal Home Loan Bank Act had earned a special distinction. Its enactment had come in the last hour of the last day of a congressional session which had lasted over seven months. It cleared Congress on July 16, 1932. President Hoover signed it on July 22.

What actually did the new law provide? It set up a system of regional Federal Home Loan Banks to be wholesalers of funds to member mortgage lending institutions in order to supplement the funds available from their own investors and savers. The lending institutions eligible for membership were "any building and loan association, savings and loan association, co-operative bank, homestead association,* savings bank and insurance company."

---

*Author's note: The first four were the savings and loan type of institution.

The law provided for not fewer than eight nor more than 12 regional Banks; the original Federal Home Loan Bank Board decided on 12 Banks. An eligible institution was to be served by the Bank in whose geographical district it was located. The cost of membership was stock subscription equivalent to 1% of the home mortgage loans the institution had outstanding. The regional Bank was to pay dividends on this stock out of its regular earnings. It was to set up reserves and surplus and follow orthodox banking standards for maintaining a solvent, going concern.

These Banks were set up in business to make two types of loans: 1) unsecured, short-term; and 2) collateralized, long-term, amortized over a period of up to 10 years. For collateral a member institution was required to provide home mortgages. Evidence of the way in which the legislation had to make allowances for other than savings and loan eligible members is the fact that non-amortized mortgages were acceptable as well as the characteristic savings and loan amortized mortgage. The Banks could, however, lend a higher percentage on the security of amortized mortgages of eight years or more maturity. The outside limit which a member institution could borrow was 12 times the amount paid in on its stock subscription.

The major source of funds for the Federal Home Loan Banks' operations was to be the sale of obligations in the financial market, backed by mortgages which the Banks held as collateral from the member institutions. The maximum of outstanding obligations of any Bank was to be five times the amount of paid-in capital. Thus at the start the Federal Home Loan Banks could have issued $600 million of debentures on the basis of the original $125 million capital subscription by the Treasury which was authorized; and it was confidently anticipated by the leaders of the business that there would be early resort to the sale of obligations of the System.

The original law looked to a marked degree of autonomy for the regional Banks such as was then adjudged to be the case with the 12 Federal Reserve Banks. Policy in each was to be determined by a board of 11 directors, nine representing the member institutions and two appointed as "public interest" representatives—a parallel with the Federal Reserve Bank directorates.

The supervisory body for the regional Banks was to be an independent agency in Washington, the Federal Home Loan Bank

Board, consisting of five members to serve full-time in this responsibility, appointed by the President of the United States with the consent of the Senate.

Pleas for participation

The day after the Federal Home Loan Bank Act was signed into law the United States League dispatched a bulletin about the new legislation to every savings and loan association in the United States. Printed copies of the law were not yet available, but the bulletin analyzed its substance in order that all association boards of directors might immediately be aware of the procedures and the benefits of affiliation. Through this communication, the League urged immediate steps to join the System and backed up its pleas and persuasion with that highly important and practical ingredient, instruction on how to do it.

The savings and loan leadership realized that despite some of the grave problems which the business faced in the autumn of 1932, a scramble to climb aboard the new vehicle was not likely. Even had the choice been up to the executive officers of the associations, such immediate reception of the idea, without urging, would have been unlikely. By this time many associations had adjusted to the most shocking encounters with the depression. Furthermore several thousand associations were neither members of the United States League nor of their state leagues; they had received League bulletins from time to time telling them of the efforts to get the Federal Home Loan Bank System authorized, but it is doubtful if many outside League membership had taken much interest in the legislation or were even remotely aware of the long-term advantages it provided.

So far as League member associations were concerned their directors—not their executive officers—were now the key men. The board of directors had to make the decision as to whether the association should become a Federal Home Loan Bank member; a resolution of the board was required for an association to subscribe to the stock of its regional Bank. And—most difficult in a time of scarce cash—the directors had to authorize purchase of Federal Home Loan Bank stock equivalent to 1% of the unpaid principal of the association's mortgages. When a $3 million association had to disburse $30,000 for stock in the Federal Home

Loan Bank System there were bound to be questions; the authorities made it more palatable by allowing the initial application for stock to be accompanied by a check for 25% of the total stock subscription, with the remainder to be paid in equal installments over the ensuing nine months.

Furthermore the association directors had to learn about the new Bank System almost from zero. They had not—in most cases— been the association people most active in the struggle to get the Federal Home Loan Bank Act adopted. Except where they had a particular interest in the idea or had been enlisted because of their strategic contacts with Congress, the directors had not been close to the month-to-month developments. Finally, the directors of many savings and loan associations disapproved of borrowing money. Although the associations as a whole had piled up a substantial indebtedness to commercial banks during 1931 and 1932, as related in Chapter 2, only some of the associations were involved in this kind of debt; the rest of them had never borrowed any money. And the directors who disliked borrowed money naturally regarded it with even more skepticism when they considered what had happened to those institutions which had borrowed money from commercial banks in recent years. In Nebraska the savings and loan institutions were forbidden by law to borrow.

It was against this skepticism in the savings and loan business that the leadership fought a battle to get the System started, as difficult in some ways as getting the legislation through Congress. And it won this battle in a surprisingly short time. While the first 30 days during which stock subscriptions were open— September 15 to October 15—brought in capital subscriptions of less than $1 million, the ensuing three months brought the subscription within sight of $6 million.

Launching of the system

On the "plus" side was the fact that President Hoover had appointed two savings and loan leaders among the five members of the newly constituted Federal Home Loan Bank Board, the United States League's president and executive manager. The new Board members took the oath of office on August 9. The first offices of the Federal Home Loan Bank Board were in the Department of Commerce Building at Fourteenth and D Streets,

N. W., Washington. For some months they continued there in quite limited quarters. So simple was the operation of the System then contemplated that the first funds of the organization, that hard-struggled-for, last-minute appropriation to get started in operation, were deposited in a newly opened account in one of the better-known commercial banks in Washington. There was not at the time any commingling of the funds of the Federal Home Loan Bank Board with the federal budget or any of the other symbols of a vast bureaucratic operation. There can be little doubt that the expeditious manner in which the System got started was due to the sense of urgency on the part of the savings and loan members of the Board. The swift pattern of the Federal Home Loan Bank System launching is noteworthy. The timetable reads thus:

August 24 . . . . The 12 Federal Home Loan Bank districts established.

August 28 . . . . Location of each Bank announced.

District One: Cambridge, Mass.
District Two: Newark, N. J.
District Three: Pittsburgh, Pa.
District Four: Winston-Salem, N. C.
District Five: Cincinnati, Ohio.
District Six: Indianapolis, Ind.
District Seven: Evanston, Ill.
District Eight: Des Moines, Iowa.
District Nine: Little Rock, Ark.
District Ten: Topeka, Kan.
District Eleven: Portland, Ore.
District Twelve: Los Angeles, Calif.

September 15 . . . . Banks' stock subscriptions opened to member institutions at 65 Chambers of Commerce in leading cities throughout the country.

September 20
    to
October 10 . . . . Directorates for each Federal Home Loan Bank announced.

October 5 . . . . Washington meeting of chairmen, vice chairmen and presidents of the

12 Federal Home Loan Banks. Committees appointed to study internal organization, lending policies, admission standards and legal interpretation of Act.

October 12 ....First meetings held by Banks' directorates.

October 15-22 ....Federal Home Loan Banks opened in preparation for lending activities.

In the autumn of 1932, the savings and loan world as a whole was caught up into the excitement and responsibility of getting the Bank System going.

That fall and winter the United States League activities continued to mingle urgent persuasion with carefully set forth information on procedure. A mass opportunity to spread information about the new program came in the 40th Annual Convention in 1932. By a happy circumstance the convention dates were at the beginning of September. Since subscription books for membership were slated to open September 15, the convention was made-to-order as a "workshop" for the Bank System. All five of the original Board members and two of the members of Congress who had sponsored the bills were speakers. Immediately after the convention the League made a brochure of these addresses for the use of all associations.

A League bulletin on September 17 instructed associations how to fill out the application for membership and subscription to stock, line by line and question by question. It told the associations what to do in those states where enabling legislation had not been passed. By the time subscription books opened, such large savings and loan states as Pennsylvania, New Jersey, Illinois and Indiana had adopted enabling legislation, as had Arkansas, Kentucky, Michigan, Wisconsin and Texas.

Another League bulletin, dated October 13, brought all associations up-to-date on the happenings of the previous four weeks. It carried a last-minute note predicting that the Banks would make money available at 4½% to 5% interest. This was a very favorable rate at that time, and it was a factor which was highly important to the savings and loan institutions trying to see whether the new mechanism would truly benefit them.

However the largest hurdle of the individual associations in becoming part and parcel of the Federal Home Loan Bank System was still ahead. Before admitting an applicant association to membership in the System, the district Federal Home Loan Bank had to have from each institution a completely executed "Form 7."

Devising of "Form 7"

Form 7 was a truly pioneering device for the assembly of the pertinent financial facts about institutions whose operations varied widely, as pointed out in Chapter 1, and whose condition, after a year and a half of depression difficulties, had to be appraised for a purpose which never had existed before. The mammoth task had been tackled by the Federal Home Loan Bank Board with few preconceived notions of what the forms should reveal. Two members of the Board, the general counsel and some of the Board staff knew how the associations operated as a practical matter. They drew up a tentative Form 7 and circulated it among 100 state savings and loan supervisory officials—top responsibility men and those down the line—to see what they thought about it, what else should be included and which of the included items should be dropped. What emerged was the minimum which this group of people, experienced in the savings and loan situation, thought was necessary to give an adequate idea of an association's condition, policy and management.

The League issued a bulletin on November 18 explaining, line by line, how to execute this form, defining terms, and suggesting just where an association would find in its books the particular figure asked for in each blank space. This time-saving, informative communication was crucial for expediting the associations' affiliation with the new Bank System.

Prospective officers and directors of the Federal Home Loan Banks had been minutely informed on how to process an application for an advance from the time it came into the office from the member savings and loan institution until it was forwarded to Washington, D. C. This preparation meant that from the day the Banks opened they were ready to go to work. By the end of the year loans were under way to associations from the Banks of Winston-Salem, Newark, Cincinnati, Indianapolis, Evanston, Des Moines, Pittsburgh and Little Rock.

Despite the progress of the new System in getting started and the benefits which were already beginning to be realized by member institutions, more trouble for it lay ahead. Misunderstandings of the purpose and functioning of the System from the public point of view were rife. There were genuine threats that it would be quickly repealed out of existence as soon as Congress returned to Washington in December 1932.

Most of the misunderstanding of, and impatience with, the System came from the famous Section 4(d), which provided for direct loans to individual borrowers by the Federal Home Loan Banks wherever the home owner in difficulties could not get financing from a member institution of the new System. Many members of Congress were irate over the inability of the Federal Home Loan Bank System to "save the homes of the people." The business groups which had opposed the System in the first place helped whip up the dissent which they saw whirling around the new establishment.

On the second day of the congressional session in December 1932, a bill was introduced in the House of Representatives to expand the direct loan provisions. Success of this proposal would have turned the whole System away from its focus on savings and loan institutions and from its permanent status in the financial world. On the other hand, Senator Borah of Idaho proposed a resolution for outright repeal of the legislation.

Rescue of the Federal Home Loan Bank Act

Again the savings and loan leaders themselves had to do their best to rescue the System. The chairman of the Federal Home Loan Bank Board told a conference of savings and loan people in April 1933 that the efforts of the United States League and the concentrated publicity which it gave to the accomplishments of the Federal Home Loan Bank System were largely responsible for averting repeal. Again savings and loan leaders found themselves testifying at congressional committee hearings—this time in opposition to the resolution to repeal the Federal Home Loan Bank Act, the legislation enacted after so many hurdles only five months before.

They were outspoken in their contention that the only suitable course was the repeal not of the Act but of the direct loan section. Abolition of this thorn in the flesh had to wait a few months, but the Senate Committee, in its wisdom, pigeonholed the resolution to repeal the Federal Home Loan Bank Act. Within a few months the Congress had passed the mammoth and highly successful Home Owners' Loan Corporation Act to deal realistically with foreclosures, and the Federal Home Loan Bank System was left free to do its main job of strengthening the savings and loan institutions.

After some three decades of operation, the Federal Home Loan Bank System is too well known and understood to require exposition of its structure and functions in a volume devoted only to historical aspects. On the other hand, some reasons for certain of its characteristics are a notable part of its history.

The original number of 12 Federal Home Loan Banks was a parallel to other reserve credit systems already in existence. In the beginning the System was widely thought of as the third part of a well-balanced central credit system, the Federal Reserve System and the Federal Farm Loan System being the other two-thirds; and each of the latter two functioned through 12 regional banks.

Since the Federal Home Loan Bank System had potential membership from the savings and loan institutions, life insurance companies and mutual savings banks, the original measurement of the capital needed in the System was based on the total home mortgage holdings of all these potential members. An attempt was made to equalize the home mortgage holdings of the potential member institutions in the respective districts, and the boundaries of the districts were drawn accordingly. However, during the first 30 years there never was any major participation by either life insurance companies or savings banks. This attempt at equalization thus went awry. The result was a wide variance in the size and in the volume of business done by the several banks.

The original Federal Home Loan Bank Board was careful to avoid placing a Federal Home Loan Bank in a city that already had a Federal Reserve Bank. When the original sites were chosen, the Board was subjected to great pressure by the chambers of commerce and representative businessmen from numerous cities. In a time of depression, any new institution with a prospect for bringing more business to a city was naturally sought after. Thus the original District One Bank was located in Cambridge, Mass., instead of Boston, the Second District Bank in Newark, N. J., instead of New York City, and the Seventh District Bank in Evanston, Ill., instead of Chicago. Later these anomalies were corrected and the Federal Home Loan Banks which were operating on the edge of such great financial centers eventually moved into the financial districts, to the greatly increased prestige of the System.

The short time required to launch the Federal Home Loan Banks was always a matter of justifiable pride to the members of the original Board and their aides. The urgency of the savings and loan situation and the increasing effort of competitors and political opponents to undo the System before it could get under way were doubtless influential in getting this new entity into operation in only half the time it had taken the 12 Federal Reserve Banks to get started in 1914.

Uniqueness of FHLB beginnings

Its launching was unique, in retrospect. It must be remembered that here was no big government agency, staffed mainly from Washington, but rather a group of 12 Banks being originated because men in business, uncompensated (except for regional Bank directors' fees, which were not substantial), took the time and made the effort to accomplish it. Of the original directors of the 12 Banks, 91 represented savings and loan associations. Guided—and perhaps often prodded—by a vigorous and enthusiastic Board in Washington they had to do many tasks in those early months which their successors on Federal Home Loan Bank directorates have been spared.

In a majority of cases one of the savings and loan men out of the 11 directors was the president, or, if not president, the chairman of the board of the district Bank. The men from outside the savings and loan business on those original directorates represented savings banks and life insurance companies, and also a very wide cross section of business and public life. Their affiliations included the oil, paint and chemical industries, newspaper publishing, an academic institution and the federal judiciary, to name a few. Among them were a former Assistant Secretary of Commerce of the United States, an executive of the Scottish-Rite Masonic bodies, a lumberman and a department store magnate. Their part in getting the System into operation was substantial; their faith in the new System was one of the fortunate and significant circumstances of the launching.

Starting with the second fiscal year of the Banks, nine of the directors were elected by member institutions and only two—the so-called public interest men—continued to be appointed by the Board. In the course of the years contests for district Bank director-ships incited lively competition among candidates within the savings and loan business. That first year the directors had more headaches than glory.

A first duty of the directors was to choose someone to operate the district Bank. Three of the first Bank executives were men who had managed savings and loan associations; they included two members of the Reserve Credits and Banking Relations Committee of the League, which had worked out so many details of the Sys-tem. Another of the new Bank executives had been a newspaperman and a state savings and loan league executive and had had savings and loan supervisory experience in his home state. Another had a large hand in supervising savings and loan associations in his state while primarily responsible for bank supervision.

Staff for the Federal Home Loan Banks—on down the line from the executive vice president (the title for the full-time executive was later changed to president)—continued to be a problem in some Banks for several years. Close observers of the first years of the Banks' history were well aware that the holding of some posts of key significance by men not thoroughly familiar with the home mortgage process was a handicap to the full use of the System's potentialities. Such things have a way of righting themselves in time—men often grow up to jobs which are too big for them at the start. But a proper recording of the feeling of the times inside the business must include mention of this disappointment and frustra-tion here and there in the Bank System.

Nor was all rosy with those original savings and loan directors —in at least one district Bank there was a director who never succeeded in getting his own institution to apply for membership! There were some men on the initial directorates who didn't believe in the System and there were several outspoken savings and loan men, not on the directorates but influential and persistent, who continued to oppose it openly and vociferously.

The Bank staffs in the larger cities spent much time in the first few months explaining what the Banks were *not*. Due to an ill-advised statement from Washington that all foreclosures would be stopped in 90 days, and to the unworkable section for direct loans from the district Banks to distressed borrowers, the Banks had a stream of inquiries to which they had to say "no." Later, the Federal Home Loan Bank Board estimated that $136,000 of its first year's appropriation was spent explaining what could not be done under Section 4(d). No wonder the leaders in the business were anxious to get this unworkable section repealed.

Federal Home Loan Banks and the bank "holiday"

The great bank "holiday" of March 1933—long remembered because it brought such a shortage of currency in circulation that it affected the lives of everyone in the United States—gave the regional Banks their first opportunity to make a real impact on the community's thinking. Even before the "holiday" there had been banking troubles of ominous proportions in Michigan. The Indianapolis Federal Home Loan Bank (in which district Michigan was located) had surveyed the possible currency needs of its members in the immediate future, with the hope of keeping them all in "till currency." When the banking troubles affected the whole nation and President Roosevelt dramatically shut down banking operations, savings and loans were released from the order within a week. Meanwhile, the Federal Home Loan Banks had $40 million of currency to make available to their members, and this was the largest amount of currency available in the United States at the time. The Banks let their members have full access to it. The customers of those member institutions would long remember that they laid their hands on some needed paper money because the new Banks existed. Although few really understood the complicated transaction which made it possible, they had many a kind word to say for savings and loan associations because of it.

The Federal Home Loan Bank Board had instructed the district Banks to make advances to institutions which would use the money in the following order of precedence: 1) loans for the purpose of repairs, remodeling and other activities leading directly to employment; 2) loans to assist borrowers in paying taxes; 3) loans to institutions with the particular responsibility of accepting such loans as qualified under Section 4(d); 4) loans in cases where mortgagors were being pressed for payment by present holders; and 5) loans to pay withdrawals, maturities and existing debts. By April 1933, however, the district Banks were authorized to make such loans as they saw fit, with no priorities as to purpose; this was found to be the only practical way to operate the System.

The interest rates at which the Federal Home Loan Banks were to lend became one of the most important concerns of the member institutions. Let it be recalled that 1933 was not a particularly "low" interest-rate period; money was scarce and the price thereof reflected the scarcity. People in the business generally regarded it as fair enough when the district Banks offered money at 4½% to 5%; they believed their associations could pay that rate and still benefit. They were paying 5½% to the Reconstruction Finance Corporation. The Federal Home Loan Banks not only were able to offer a lower interest rate; their collateral requirements also were less onerous than those of the RFC.

The refinancing of mortgages held by other institutions was the main lending activity of the savings and loan institutions in 1933. They used some Federal Home Loan Bank funds for that purpose. But mainly, those first years, they used Federal Home Loan Bank funds for clearing up withdrawals. Few people wished to borrow money to build new houses or to remodel old ones in 1933 and 1934. Consequently it was a period of relatively little demand. Because of this circumstance the associations could concentrate their newly available funds from the Bank System on withdrawals.

In the early days of the Roosevelt Administration the Federal Home Loan Bank System ran into its first partisan complications. Partly because the legislation had been used by Republicans in their unsuccessful fight to win the 1932 elections, influential persons in the new administration thought of the Federal Home Loan Banks as "Hoover creations" and used their most persuasive methods to get them discontinued. The first move which many believed was to "ease out" the banks was the appointment by President Roosevelt of an entirely new five-man Federal Home Loan Bank Board, none of the original five members having had an opportunity to be confirmed by the Senate and all having thus served "interim" terms.

But the functioning of the Federal Home Loan Banks in the banking "holiday" predicament, plus the start of a significant outflow of funds into the hands of people who had savings temporarily frozen in savings and loan associations, came early enough to impress the practical-minded advisers of the new administration who knew a really good thing when they saw one. It began to be clear that the Federal Home Loan Banks were not just "relieving" savings and loan institutions but were pumping money into a sick economy. By the end of June 1933, $48,816,812 had been advanced by the Federal Home Loan Banks, and $1,237,932 had already been repaid. This was a going operation and it was obviously too important to lose.

The Bank System had $88,441,000 outstanding to member institutions by the end of 1933. Moreover some of the Banks had begun to measure up to that indispensable standard of any going business concern, making a profit. The Cincinnati Federal Home Loan Bank paid a dividend of 2% on its stock (government-held and savings-and-loan-owned) at the end of its first year of operations, October 15, 1933. The Banks of Indianapolis, Chicago and Little Rock followed suit in January 1934. It could not yet be seen what volume of business the new Banks would be doing in the next few years, but it was now clear that they could succeed as banking institutions.

Acceptance by savings and loan associations

Table 6 shows the first year's (1933) progress in bringing the eligible savings and loan institutions into the membership of their respective Federal Home Loan Banks. It will be seen that at the end of this crucial year, at least two of the 12 had enrolled better than half of the total assets of all eligible savings and loan associations. The 12 combined had gone over the one-third mark.

The anticipated first trip of the Federal Home Loan Banks to the financial markets for additional funds, so confidently anticipated by the sponsors of the System, did not come until 1937. Aside from the lack of mortgage loan demand which prevented the associations from needing the money, another factor entered the situation when Home Owners' Loan Corporation bonds were widely distributed in exchange for mortgages. These bonds were marketable by 1934, when Congress decided that the government should guarantee the principal as well as the interest on them. Money was easing; and interest rates reflected it. The Federal Home Loan Banks were keeping their old interest rate levels. Hundreds of savings and loan associations used their arithmetic. They sold their Home Owners' Loan Corporation bonds and paid off their loans at the banks.

By December 31, 1960, when the Federal Home Loan Bank System had passed its 28th anniversary, advances outstanding to member institutions amounted to $1,980,775,216; the combined

Table 6. *The number and assets of savings and loan members of FHLB System, and number and assets of all savings and loan associations, December 31, 1933*

FHLB Districts	All savings and loan associations*		Member institutions		Percentage of members to total	
	Number	Assets	Number	Assets	Number	Assets
No. 1 Boston	358	$ 632,893,698	103	$ 240,802,272	29%	38%
No. 2 Newark	1,852	1,569,785,058	227	318,971,035	12	20
No. 3 Pittsburgh	3,061	1,096,178,774	312	165,110,709	10	15
No. 4 Winston-Salem	1,682	489,041,710	230	204,012,733	14	42
No. 5 Cincinnati	963	1,233,388,708	359	576,975,218	37	47
No. 6 Indianapolis	454	423,791,067	93	260,976,911	20	62
No. 7 Chicago	1,089	697,810,211	237	219,843,057	22	32
No. 8 Des Moines	427	298,008,252	110	97,818,192	26	33
No. 9 Little Rock	364	331,006,843	112	153,671,724	31	46
No. 10 Topeka	374	392,193,542	121	132,674,444	32	34
No. 11 Portland	163	168,606,515	79	92,914,852	48	55
No. 12 Los Angeles	210	417,786,706	103	143,536,159	49	34
Total	10,997	$7,750,491,084	2,086	$2,607,307,306	19	34

*As reported for 1932

Source: *Federal Home Loan Bank Board, first annual report, Dec. 31, 1933, p. 10*

Banks had a membership of 4,694 savings and loan institutions and the combined resources of the Banks were $3,315,700,188. All the government capital had been retired some 10 years before, and the member institutions owned $989,315,075 of capital stock in the System. While some believe that the System is capable of doing much more in the years ahead to assist the savings and loan institutions than it has done in the past, the fact still remains that today's stature of the System is impressive; and there could be no more integral part of the savings and loan operation than the services supplied by the Federal Home Loan Banks.

It is now nearly a quarter of a century, too, since 1937, the date already mentioned as the Federal Home Loan Banks' first test of their ability to attract relatively large sums of capital for their purposes. The billions which have been advanced to, and repaid by, member institutions over these years were the result of the sale of Federal Home Loan Bank obligations in the open market, without reliance on any government guarantees as to either principal or interest. A total of $12.6 billion of obligations had been sold in the financial markets by the Bank System as of December 31, 1960.

But the financing of the System has had to be done in an atmosphere quite different from that anticipated by the founders of the System. Since 1930 there have been marked changes in the government bond pattern, a result of the major concern of the United States Treasury with the management of a government debt of proportions never dreamed of by anyone in the early days of the Federal Home Loan Bank System. The financing of the Bank System has had to be done in close coordination with the United States Treasury. This was one of the unanticipated challenges, but it has been met successfully, and that success is one more instance of the ability of the savings and loan business and its instrumentalities to adjust to the complexities of changed conditions.

Significance of Board in Washington

All in all, the creation of the Federal Home Loan Bank System in 1932 had a far-reaching result apart from the establishment of 12 Federal Home Loan Banks and the marshalling of thousands of the savings and loan units of the country into a coordinated system. Installed in the nation's capital as an independent agency of the federal government, the Federal Home Loan Bank Board consisted of five persons who were to give their full time to the job of supervising the Federal Home Loan Banks. This Board dealt with savings and loan managers and directors and with lawyers and accountants experienced in savings and loan work. From the start it was clear that people with this experience would determine the success or failure of the Federal Home Loan Banks. It is doubtful if even the best prophets among those who watched the System and the Board come into being—and there were several prophetic souls among them—foresaw what the setting up of this Board meant. But it did mean this: For the first time there was an agency in Washington, part of the federal government, many of whose thoughts, decisions and acts—week after week and month after month—centered on the operations of savings and loan associations.

Along with its basic powers over the fortunes of savings and loan associations, the Board acquired another responsibility which was inherent in its pioneering existence. It became inevitably the first place of recourse for anyone in government who might be considering any further legislation dealing with savings and loan. It became *the* savings and loan agency in Washington, giving the institutions for the first time in their century of existence the prestige of an official establishment in the nation's capital. And in the year and a half between the adoption of the Federal Home Loan Bank Act and the enactment of the National Housing Act which created the Federal Housing Administration—from the fall of 1932 to the summer of 1934—the Federal Home Loan Bank Board was the one place where legislative and executive leaders turned for advice on what to do about any and all emergencies in home mortgage operations. For this brief period of glory, the Federal Home Loan Bank Board occupied somewhat the position of arbiter on housing matters which the Housing and Home Finance Agency was to have in another 15 years.

The point to remember is that those years were crucial for the development of the new savings and loan pattern, for out of these years came the system of federally chartered associations and the Federal Savings and Loan Insurance Corporation.

Chapter 5

Federal charters
for savings associations

The system of federal savings and loan associations, which by 1960 accounted for 53% of the assets of the savings and loan business, came into being under provision of the Home Owners' Loan Act, enacted June 13, 1933. Section 5 of the Act authorized establishment of "local mutual thrift institutions in which people may invest their funds" and provided for $100 million to be immediately available out of the United States Treasury for investment of up to $100,000 in a single association; the Treasury funds were to match dollar for dollar the investments of local citizens and were to be repaid gradually, after they had remained intact in the associations at least five years.

The only strictly 1933 idea in this package was the provision for federal associations to accept investment of taxpayers' funds—an emergency program described more fully in Chapter 3. The possibility of federal charters for associations had been churning around in the minds of some advanced thinkers in the business for many years. The idea was traceable naturally to the dual charter system which had been characteristic of commercial banking since 1863. The United States League's Committee on Reserve Credits and Banking Relations had recommended at the League's Philadelphia Convention in August 1931 that the idea of federal incorporation of savings and loan associations be discussed within the business. It was the first part of the twofold program the committee suggested for study at that time, the Federal Home Loan Bank System being the other.

One of the speakers at that convention was a former League president who believed strongly in the possibilities of federal charters and made his address, entitled "Savings and Loan Statesmanship," a half-hour argument in favor of establishing such a federal system alongside the existing state-chartered institutions. He suggested letting state associations convert to federal charter as well as the chartering of new associations under the aegis of the federal government. The Philadelphia Convention, however, rejected the proposal.

However since the proposal had been made at a convention attended by more than 1,000 savings and loan executives the idea of a federal system was put into the minds of many. There it could be incubated. Federal incorporation of savings and loan associations was formally recommended by a majority of the United States League's Reserve Credits Committee in December 1931 to the savings and loan representatives attending President Hoover's Conference on Home Building and Home Ownership (see Chapter 4). But the savings and loan representatives there, just as the larger group in Philadelphia four months earlier, saw too many undesirable features in federal incorporation to urge further consideration at that time.

Reporting some nine months later at the 1932 United States League convention in French Lick, Ind., the chairman of the Reserve Credits Committee said the majority of the committee still believed federal incorporation was desirable and urged the League to seek legislation authorizing it. He predicted that the practical working of the Federal Home Loan Banks would emphasize more and more the necessity of standards of practice and claimed that federal incorporation would be especially helpful in achieving uniform supervision. There was still heated disagreement with this view. Opponents held that new emphasis on federal incorporation at that time would divert attention from the possibilities of the newly born Federal Home Loan Bank System and would dampen enthusiasm for making the Bank System work. They also held that federal chartering would be antithetical to the local character of the savings and loan association. The convention voted to "receive" the report and have it printed. But the assembled savings and loan representatives went no further.

Changed Washington situation

The events of the following winter and spring, however, were calculated to change the views of savings and loan people on this much-considered matter. President Franklin D. Roosevelt took office on March 4, 1933, and before a month had passed (April 2) the Secretary of the Treasury, Henry S. Morgenthau Jr., met with the five newly appointed members of the Federal Home Loan Bank Board to talk about proposals for relieving individual home owners in distress over their mortgage loans. Obviously the new President had in mind to do something swiftly effective and spectacular.

Out of the several approaches advanced from the Federal Home Loan Bank Board at this conference, two appeared in the legislation which was subsequently introduced. One of these approaches was to authorize the Board to incorporate "national home loan associations in local communities" and provide for an appropriation by the United States to be invested in stock in these new associations. The other approach was to charter a Central Home Mortgage Corporation to issue bonds up to $3 billion for long terms and to trade interest-guaranteed bonds for existing home mortgages. These two ideas eventually emerged as the Federal Savings and Loan System and the Home Owners' Loan Corporation.

The proposal for the incorporation of "national home loan associations in local communities" was of course a suggestion for federally chartered savings and loan associations. Back of this proposal were several influences. The most important of them was that the Federal Home Loan Bank Board was staffed mostly with persons who were steeped in savings and loan thinking and who had already struggled with many of the depression problems of the savings and loan business. The general counsel of the Board was a man who in his own state had done more than anyone else to revive the savings and loan business during the 1920s. These circumstances helped assure that the bill which the Board originally sent to the White House, providing for mortgagor relief, should contain some such proposal as federal charters for savings and loan institutions.

The thinking in the savings and loan business veered gradually but surely toward substantial support for federal charters. The heavily charged government-action atmosphere of the new administration suggested that it would be well to have a major new proposal which would keep existing institutions at least in the area of the vast relief program for mortgages. The experience with the banking "holiday" immediately after Mr. Roosevelt took office had underscored the seriousness of the situation which the nation faced and converted many savings and loan leaders to the idea that something in addition to the Federal Home Loan Bank System was needed.

One glaring gap in the potentialities of the Bank System was the shortage of savings and loan institutions in some areas. Since the System had to function through such institutions, its ability to help relieve the mortgage problem was obviously curtailed by the lack of existing associations in areas of need. At least a third of all the counties in the United States were estimated to be without adequate savings and loan facilities in 1933; and there were a thousand or more counties in which no savings and loan association existed. The first annual report of the Federal Home Loan Bank Board, December 31, 1933, pointed out that the need for new associations was intensified by the withdrawal from the field of many financial institutions of other types hitherto engaged in making home mortgage loans.

Origin of the proposal for federal associations

The savings and loan leaders worked with the Federal Home Loan Bank Board and its staff in shaping the proposal for federally chartered associations. The two United States League officers who had been members of the original Board (which went out of office with the advent of the Roosevelt Administration) were in Washington more than they were away from the capital city during March and April. The practical details of the plan for federals were of great concern to the entire business, and these men had much experience to offer. The new administration was not too ready to accept ideas directly from men who had held office under the preceding President, but the savings and loan representatives had many friends in Washington who were willing to listen.

On April 13, 1933, President Roosevelt sent his Message to Congress urging the passage of "legislation to protect small home owners from foreclosure and to relieve them of a portion of the burden of excessive interest and principal payments incurred during the period of higher values and higher earning power." Although the message omitted reference to setting up new federal associations, the bills which were immediately introduced in both the Senate and House (by Senator Robinson of Arkansas and Representative Steagall of Alabama) contained the federal charter provisions. The United States League president issued a call for a meeting of the Executive Committee in Washington on April 24 and also asked the Reserve Credits Committee to consider, without delay, the proposals in the newly introduced administration bill.

The League sent the text of the bill to all member institutions and issued a blanket invitation to all savings and loan managers to attend this open meeting of its Executive Committee where the far-reaching proposals in the mortgage relief bill would be considered. (It should be pointed out that the Executive Committee of the United States League was during this period the larger body which was later known as the Board of Directors. It consisted of a representative from each state in the Union plus the smaller group elected from eight districts, and also all League officers and past presidents, as well as chairmen of the League divisions and the president of the American Savings and Loan Institute.) The invitation to the meeting commented on the initial reaction from insurance companies and savings banks that the President's proposal means "that building and loan associations are to become the major, if not the only, small home financing agencies in the country." That prediction took some decades to come to pass, but it had a strange ring of credibility by 1960. As a result of the April 24 meeting, savings and loan leaders urged amendments to perfect the proposal for a system of federally chartered savings and loan associations.

One of the moot questions in the savings and loan discussions was the administrative agency for the federally chartered institutions. There was a body of opinion in favor of an instrumentality to supervise them entirely separate from the Federal Home Loan Bank Board. Whether or not the HOLC as proposed should be under the Federal Home Loan Bank Board was also a subject of discussion. The prevailing opinion was that it would be better to keep the "whole package" under the one existing agency which was at that time dealing with savings and loan institutions. Therefore, full savings and loan support was given to this phase of the proposed legislation. The far-reaching consequences of this decision need hardly be elaborated; most observers nowadays concede that it was well for the savings and loan business that the machinery was set up in this fashion.

Savings and loan reactions

The relatively swift legislative course of the new proposal was a pattern to which the thinking of the majority of savings and loan managers had to adjust. There were fears on the part of association managers that new and competitive associations would be organized in localities already adequately served. After the House of Representatives had passed the bill including the federal chartering provisions, the United States League issued a bulletin to assure its member institutions that the Federal Home Loan Bank Board did not intend to grant charters with a lavish and unwise hand.

The same bulletin called attention to the probable need for enabling legislation in many of the states before the associations could convert to federal charter, for there was already much talk among the savings and loan managers about the possibility of conversion. The League had the twofold task of keeping those not minded to convert from being concerned about competition from the new system and also of cautioning the enthusiasts against expecting miracles immediately.

When the Act had been signed into law League leaders urged every savings and loan manager to read it carefully. As early as the League convention in Chicago, September 1933, scarcely three months after the adoption of the law authorizing the establishment of federal associations, a leading League official predicted that the advent of federally chartered savings and loan associations would develop into an event of great significance in the savings and loan world. He emphasized the need for existing institutions to begin to function again and for new home financing units to be established where there were none. He believed that the alternative was "the government in the home mortgage business."

𝕾𝖊𝖛𝖊𝖓𝖙𝖞-𝖙𝖍𝖎𝖗𝖉 𝕮𝖔𝖓𝖌𝖗𝖊𝖘𝖘 𝖔𝖋 𝖙𝖍𝖊 𝖀𝖓𝖎𝖙𝖊𝖉 𝕾𝖙𝖆𝖙𝖊𝖘 𝖔𝖋 𝕬𝖒𝖊𝖗𝖎𝖈𝖆;

𝕬𝖙 𝖙𝖍𝖊 𝕱𝖎𝖗𝖘𝖙 𝕾𝖊𝖘𝖘𝖎𝖔𝖓,

Begun and held at the City of Washington on Thursday, the ninth
day of March, one thousand nine hundred and thirty-three.

AN ACT

To provide emergency relief with respect to home mortgage indebtedness, to refinance home mortgages, to extend relief to the owners
of homes occupied by them and who are unable to amortize their
debt elsewhere, to amend the Federal Home Loan Bank Act, to
increase the market for obligations of the United States and for
other purposes.

*Be it enacted by the Senate and House of Representatives of the
United States of America in Congress assembled,* That this Act may
be cited as the " Home Owners' Loan Act of 1933."

DEFINITIONS

SEC. 2. As used in this Act—

(a) The term " Board " means the Federal Home Loan Bank
Board created under the Federal Home Loan Bank Act.

(b) The term " Corporation " means the Home Owners' Loan
Corporation created under section 4 of this Act.

(c) The term " home mortgage " means a first mortgage on real
estate in fee simple or on a leasehold under a renewable lease for not
less than ninety-nine years, upon which there is located a dwelling
for not more than four families, used by the owner as a home or held
by him as his homestead, and having a value not exceeding $20,000;
and the term " first mortgage " includes such classes of first liens
as are commonly given to secure advances on real estate under the
laws of the State in which the real estate is located, together with
the credit instruments, if any, secured thereby.

(d) The term " association " means a Federal Savings and Loan
Association chartered by the Board as provided in section 5 of this
Act.

REPEAL OF DIRECT LOAN PROVISION OF FEDERAL HOME LOAN BANK ACT

SEC. 3. Subsection (d) of section 4 of the Federal Home Loan
Bank Act (providing for direct loans to home owners) is hereby
repealed.

CREATION OF HOME OWNERS' LOAN CORPORATION

SEC. 4. (a) The Board is hereby authorized and directed to create
a corporation to be known as the Home Owners' Loan Corporation.

*The Home Owners' Loan Act of 1933 provides the legal basis for the charter-
ing of federal associations*

Within 10 weeks after the enactment of the Home Owners' Loan Act of 1933, a set of rules and regulations for the federal associations had been drawn up. By September the Federal Home Loan Bank Board had directed the HOLC well into its lending program and was ready to turn some major attention to making a success of the program for federally chartered associations.

The statute provided that the federal associations were to follow "the best practices of local mutual thrift and home financing institutions in the United States." But it contained few of the details for operation of the institutions and implied heavy reliance on the rule-making wisdom of the Federal Home Loan Bank Board. In this respect the federal statute was a departure from nearly all state legislation covering savings and loan supervision.

Implementing the statute

In drawing up the first rules and regulations the Federal Home Loan Bank Board and its staff had one very welcome precedent. Work which the leaders of the savings and loan business had already done toward an improved legislative framework was the key to interpretation of this provision. An ideal system of state law for savings and loan institutions was in the process of being drawn up by the United States League's Advisory Committee on State Legislation; it was familiarly known as "The Model Code." Some of the state legislatures had adopted some of its tentative provisions verbatim. Besides this meticulously put together draft, the Federal Home Loan Bank Board and its staff had the freely available and often aggressively proffered aid of the savings and loan leaders watching the Washington scene. Some of the association managers who had no intention of ever seeking federal charters wanted, nevertheless, to see this parallel system started properly for the benefit of the entire business; the guiding policy of the savings and loan leadership was to go all the way in helping the federal system do a good job.

The United States League was definitely committed by its Executive Committee to cooperate in that part of President Roosevelt's mortgage relief program which asked for establishing federal associations in localities not then served by any thrift and home financing institutions. The League, however, always meticulously maintained its neutrality with regard to federalization of *existing* institutions. In the early weeks following the passage of the law, its communications pointedly referred querying savings and loan managers to Federal Home Loan Bank Board officials if they wanted actual advice about whether they should convert to federal charters.

But the League threw the influence of its publicity department into the breach to spread information about federals, explaining the purposes of the proposed new system and reporting periodically on progress made. Savings and loan leaders were keenly aware of the importance of keeping the public apprised of the value of this phase of the President's mortgage relief program, for this was the one sector of it which relied essentially on business-type institutions instead of on government-operated programs.

In the fall of 1933 a Federal Savings and Loan Division was set up within the Federal Home Loan Bank Board. Its first chief was a man who had helped organize savings and loan associations in the 1920s under the sponsorship of the lumber dealers of the Southwest, and who had helped bring the American Savings and Loan Institute into being. As time went on, the division mapped out what was tantamount to an enrollment drive spearheaded by a corps of some 30 field organizers. They were all experienced savings and loan executives with a thorough knowledge not only of the objectives of the new system but also of the differences of operation which "going federal" would entail for existing associations. Directed from Washington, these field men worked out of the 12 Federal Home Loan Banks. They spoke at stockholders' and directors' meetings; they helped institutions complete the forms and reports required for Federal Home Loan Bank membership, for federalization and for other government assistance as it became available; and they suggested procedures by which the institutions could help themselves.

The existence of the framework of the Federal Home Loan Banks by the time the federal charters came into being was one of the circumstances which made possible a fairly early utilization of the new law in many communities. With the advent of the federal system the Federal Home Loan Bank Board tended to devote much more time and thought to federal charters than to the Federal Home Loan Bank System. To many observers it was quite clear that some of the vigor that might have gone into expanding the lending activities of the Banks was diverted into the System's supervisory responsibilities over federal institutions. The turn of events had at least some influence on the tardiness with which the Bank System became a major factor in supplying funds to savings and loan institutions, both state and federal.

The League's affiliate, the American Savings and Loan Institute, collaborating with the basic League policy of "all-out assistance in getting the federals off on the right foot," supplied an essential ingredient for putting the federal system into operation. Its staff helped draw up the accounting system for the federals and performed the tedious task of developing accounting forms to be reproduced in quantity. The director of education for the Institute was retained temporarily as a consultant to the Federal Home Loan Bank Board to expedite the matter.

These forms were a *sine qua non* for operation under the new type of charter. There was no firm of office suppliers or printers anywhere which could offer these necessary workaday items, and part of the romance of the story of getting the federals started lies in the means by which they were first provided. A firm which had been doing the principal printing business of the League for several years printed the first run of them at its own expense and thus enabled the Institute to start making them available to the federal associations.

Slow start of federal system

Despite these moves from Washington, from the Federal Home Loan Banks and from the savings and loan business, the system of federals was slow in getting started. The Federal Home Loan Bank Board, consisting in the latter half of 1933 of persons unfamiliar with the savings and loan business or with the thinking of the men who operated the associations, was surprised to find apathy about converting to federal charters. They had thought that there would be a rush by associations to avail themselves of the possible $100,000 of government investment in their accounts. Five months after the legislation was passed President Roosevelt was said to be greatly concerned over the fact that less than 25 new federal associations had been chartered.

But existing associations had several reasons for hesitation. A considerable number of them had already overcome their worst problems by mid-1933 and these neither needed nor wanted the $100,000 of government investment. There was genuine uneasiness about what the new type of supervision might entail in trouble-some personal relations. Perhaps most influential of all the reasons for taking a very long look before leaping was the undefined but basic fear of "the government," by which was meant, of course, the federal government. Getting a federal charter meant coming under the "control of the government" in the minds of many savings and loan officers and directors, and this they did not want.

Of course part of the deliberate pace with which the federal system came into being was the old story of the time-consuming process of getting action where so many individuals and considerations were involved. Considerable resistance to the federal idea was evidenced by supervisors of state-chartered savings and loans. Associations in areas where state supervision was particularly good

Table 7. Applications for federal charter and charters issued,
July 1933 - December 31, 1934
(cumulative by months)

Month	Total		Conversions from state charter		New charters	
	Applications for charter	Charters granted	Applications for charter	Charters granted	Applications for charter	Charters granted
1933						
July	3				3	
August	3	3			3	3
September	11	4			11	4
October	26	8	2		24	8
November	58	29	2		56	29
December	77	59	3	1	74	58
1934						
January	131	82	8	1	123	81
February	182	130	32	2	150	128
March	237	190	50	5	187	185
April	319	250	77	12	242	238
May	391	286	128	27	263	259
June	502	369	175	48	327	321
July	579	441	214	78	365	363
August	653	480	264	91	389	389
September	747	534	304	112	443	422
October	800	577	334	124	466	453
November	842	601	360	134	482	467
December	886	639	393	158	493	481

Source: Federal Home Loan Bank Board, second annual report,
Dec. 31, 1934, p. 107

and where it was deemed adequate were not attracted to the new system and often found fault with it. Many years had to elapse before the feeling of cleavage between the federal system and the well-run state-chartered associations was forgotten. One reason why the program for insurance of accounts in savings and loan associations, embracing both federal and state charters, found ready acceptance and support just a year after the enactment of the federal statute was the desire of so many state-chartered associations to maintain their principal supervision at the state level.

These combined reasons postponed until well into 1934 the kind of speed in chartering federals which the President of the United States and the sponsors of the system wished to see. By February of that year, over 100 federal charters had been granted and by the end of December 639 were issued. Table 7 shows the progress of the federal system during the first year and a half after the law was enacted.

As already indicated the federal savings and loan system was authorized by a very short statute. Operating details were prescribed not only in the rules and regulations but also more irrevocably in the charter. This document could be amended only with consent of the individual institution's members and the Federal Home Loan Bank Board.

Contents of federal charter

The operating provisions of the original federal charter, designated by the letter "E," represented a halfway point between the more familiar type of savings and loan operation in the early 1930s and the modernized business as known some 30 years later. A notable feature was the reduction of the number of share types to four, in contrast to the fact that 13 types were being considered for inclusion when the legislation was nearing the final drafting stage. Direct reduction, monthly amortized loans were expressly provided for federals, with a maximum 75% loan-to-value ratio. Also, 80% loans could be made with the approval of the Federal Home Loan Bank Board.

An evidence of the transitional character of the original federal charter was authorization for the share account sinking fund as well as direct reduction loans. Another vestige of the old way of doing things was permission for a forfeiture of part of the earnings

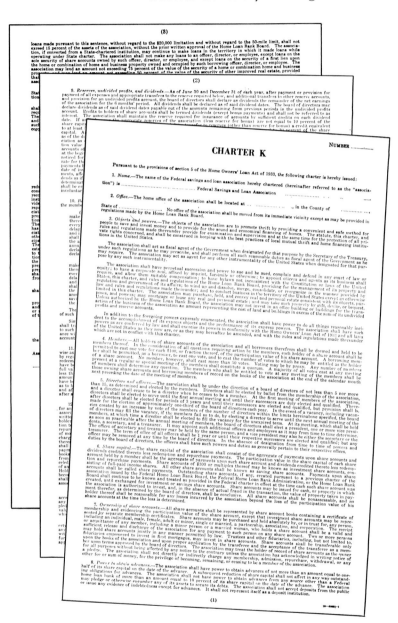

Charter K, promulgated by the Federal Home Loan Bank Board in 1936, provides the legal basis for modern federal savings association operations

on withdrawal before maturity. Reserves for the new institutions were set at 5% of net earnings to be allocated annually until 5% of total assets had been accumulated. A few voices had called for a substantially higher figure; but the business in general, depression notwithstanding, was still some distance from that kind of thinking about reserves in 1933. The old concept of shares instead of accounts was in this original charter; and most revealing of the "burnt child dreads the fire" complex of the day in regard to withdrawals was the concentration throughout on the term "repurchase of shares" instead of the prejudiced word "withdrawal."

When the first charter was issued, it was agreed that there was to be no comprehensive revision for a reasonable length of time. Charter K was promulgated in the fall of 1936, but even this date —representing a lapse of three years and some months—was earlier than leaders in the business had wished.

The United States League had appointed a Federal Savings and Loan Committee within a year after federal chartering of associations began. Thus the national organization had an instrument which could deal with the special problems of federals. A member of the League staff was assigned to serve as secretary to this committee, which later became the Federal Savings and Loan Division and still later the Committee on the Federal Savings and Loan System. Through this device the League was able to exert its best efforts for the federal associations during all of these formative years when so many of their concerns were peculiar to them and had no significance for state-chartered associations.

The final form of the new Charter K reflected the fruitful work of this committee. Committee members had painstakingly studied the original draft written by the Federal Home Loan Bank Board in February 1936. All federal associations were given an opportunity to study the draft more than once. Until near the end of the summer the new charter went through drafting and redrafting and committee conferences with the Federal Home Loan Bank Board. Finally the League committee agreed that the charter was in desirable form, and it felt justified in recommending its adoption by all federal associations in the "interest of the whole federal savings and loan program."

The 1936 version of Charter K represented several further steps toward the type of federal operation which was common by 1960 and which was based on either Charter N (1949) or Charter K (Rev.)

(1952). The improvements represented by these later charters, the reasons for their development, and their significance to the federal system are treated in Chapter 16 in connection with postwar developments. The 1936 Charter K meanwhile gave federal associations considerably greater attractiveness to savers and a definitely better break in the competition for loans.

Savings features included: 1) reduction of the savings and investment plans to two, those on which distributed earnings accumulate and those on which earnings are paid in cash; 2) provision for two types of bonus plans instead of one, with permission to the association to omit bonus plans if it wished; 3) elimination of the right of the association to retain any part of the earnings of a saver upon withdrawal; 4) clarification of the right to pay withdrawals on demand; and 5) permission for share loans up to 90%.

New features on the lending side were: 1) increased authority to borrow from the Federal Home Loan Bank; 2) elimination of the share sinking fund loan and a more detailed authorization for some of the protective provisions in the direct reduction loan; 3) increase to 80% of the loan-to-value ratio for home and combination home and business properties; and 4) privilege of making a limited volume of unamortized loans.

To many savings and loan people, the liberalized franchise was welcomed as a businesswide "go ahead" signal—an affirmation that the time was ripe for greater growth. In January 1937 the *Federal Home Loan Bank Review* pointed out that the business had been "hampered from the beginning by a tradition that quite small units are so natural as to be almost inevitable . . . which has never been conducive to strength, nor maximum service . . ."

Constitutionality litigation

Attacks on the system of federal savings and loan associations continued to be made by savings and loan supervisors in some states. Although it must be admitted that the element of jealousy for their own rights and prerogatives was a factor, many had also a sincere skepticism about the new system. In 1936 these opponents of the system challenged the constitutionality of federal charters. The actual case was an action brought in the Wisconsin Supreme Court by the state's attorney general and banking commission against a newly organized federal association in Milwaukee. The complaint was that the federal association was not acting under state savings and loan laws, that its existence would jeopardize the existence of established savings and loan associations, and that it was acting as a corporation without being duly incorporated.

The real issue was whether Congress had power to authorize and provide for the operation of federal associations. The case was transferred to the United States District Court (Wisconsin's Western District) which 1) ruled that the Act incorporating federal savings and loan associations was constitutional, and 2) restrained the Wisconsin authorities from hindering the business of the association in question.

The decision in favor of the system was upheld by the United States Court of Appeals in Chicago. An appeal to the United States Supreme Court was denied, and the system's constitutionality was not further contested. Thus the resolution of the case ultimately stood out as a positive justification of the system. The litigation continued for two and a half years and was perhaps the last major crisis which federal associations faced in their march toward permanence and respectability in the savings and loan business. As far as the public was concerned, the acceptance of the associations was no whit dimmed by the constitutionality litigation, and there was no setback in the growth of savings as a result of the cloud over their constitutionality.

Through its Federal Savings and Loan Division, the United States League had moved early to marshal the resources of the federals to fight the constitutionality case; a substantial defense fund was raised from voluntary contributions of several hundred of the federal associations to be sure that a complete record was developed in the litigation in Wisconsin so that the case for the federals might be in the best possible position in the event of an appeal to the United States Supreme Court. The counsel employed by the committee cooperated with the general counsel of the Federal Home Loan Bank Board which was defending the constitutionality in the Wisconsin case. The committee alerted all federals to the situation which might arise if the case did have to be decided before the Supreme Court and the possible need for financial assistance in fighting the case.

By the time the federal system had its tenth birthday—an appropriate point for looking backward—these troubles were largely history. In 1943 there was general talk of the contribution which the federals had made to the savings and loan business. Among these contributions were listed: the long-term blessing of standardization; the assistance in regaining public favor for the business which the word "federal" had supplied; and the providing of a "new look" at the bottom of the depression when it was most welcome. Chart 2 shows the trend in the number of federal associations and their relative position as compared to all savings and loan associations for selected years.

Chart 2. Number of federally chartered savings and loan associations and percentage to total number of associations, December 31, selected years

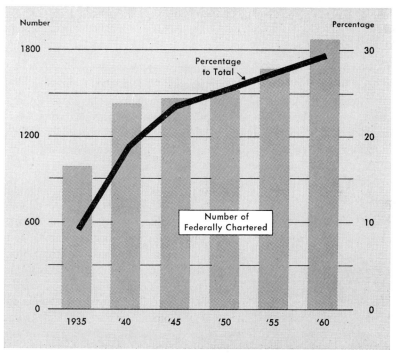

Source: Federal Home Loan Bank Board, annual reports

Although the period of numerous transfers from state to federal charter was roughly that of the decade of the 1930s, there was always thereafter a nominal number of cases of conversion to federal charter.

Conversions to state charter

A new era for the whole federal system came with the beginning of transfers from federal back to state charter, a development of the 1940s and thereafter. Legislation was passed by the Congress in 1948 clarifying any doubts that might have existed about the legality of conversions to state charter. With this enactment the dual system of savings and loan associations was well established, with freedom of the institutions to move from one type of supervision to the other as their officers saw the advantages of the statutory provisions in the one jurisdiction or the other. The dual system, in fact, meant that state and federal associations could compete in securing legislative and regulatory improvements to serve their communities better.

In many of the improvements in the powers of savings and loan institutions state statutes have led the way because of the relatively greater ease with which amendments to laws can be secured in some state legislatures as compared with the Washington process of amendment. A case in point is the power to make loans for the improvement of residential sites, which many of the state-chartered associations were able to do, and were doing, many years before federally chartered associations got the power in 1959. In summary, the existence of the dual system of charters—as in the banking world—is widely held to be one of the reasons for the continuing progress and modernization of the savings and loan system.

Chapter 6

Insurance of

savings and loan accounts

The idea of government guarantee of the safety of financial institutions is older in the United States than the first savings and loan association. Six states experimented with a guaranty of bank obligations in the 1829-1858 period, with varying degrees of success. A recurring pattern of bank failures and of repudiation of bank notes gave rise to these experiments. The enactment of the national bank laws of 1863 and 1864 and of a federal tax which made state bank notes impractical as a circulating medium brought this first phase of governmental bank guarantees to a close.

Again in the period 1908-1921, when a financial panic and bank failures raised the clamor for something to be done, eight states adopted state bank deposit insurance systems, the last of which terminated its operations during the rash of bank failures in the early 1930s.

Proposals for the federal government to enter the realm of deposit guarantees had been made in Congress as early as the 1880s. The Senate version of the Federal Reserve Act in 1913 incorporated a provision for bank deposit guarantees; but it was not acceptable to the House of Representatives. In May 1932 when the savings and loan people were busy trying to get the Federal Home Loan Bank legislation enacted by Congress, the House of Representatives approved a bill for federal guarantee of bank deposits, but this time the Senate failed to act on it.

These are some highlights of the long story back of the enactment of two parallel systems of government insurance—for bank deposits and for savings and loan accounts—during the first years of the Franklin D. Roosevelt Administration.

Both systems have attained high prestige and are synonymous with reliability. Now that more than a quarter of a century has passed, insurance of accounts is regarded as one of the major contributions of the Roosevelt Administration to a firmer structure for the chartered financial institutions in America. Both systems had, moreover, the good fortune to be launched at a time when at least 25 years of relatively high economic activity assured them of the necessary period to build up their strength—a boon which had not been granted most of the experimental state systems of earlier times. As of December 31, 1960, FSLIC insurance was carried by 4,098 savings and loan institutions, with 94.3% of the assets of all savings and loans in operation. The FDIC insurance was carried by 13,451 banks, with 97.6% of all bank deposits.

There was skepticism about the program in commercial banking circles up until the time it was enacted and for some time thereafter. Savings and loan leaders moved very cautiously in advocating such a device. They probably would never have pushed the idea at all in their own councils had not the insurance of bank deposits become a successful undertaking. Looking back one must attribute the emergence of these far-reaching and unprecedented pieces of legislation to the bank "holiday" of March 1933. That "holiday" was an extreme emergency; it was an experience of great consternation for those who had accounts in financial institutions as well as for the managers and boards of directors of financial institutions. Consequently the "holiday" drew a line of demarcation between all financial institution history which had gone before and any which would come after.

As pointed out in Chapter 4, savings and loan associations were momentarily caught up in the all-inclusive order which President Roosevelt issued for the closing of commercial banks practically as soon as he took the oath of office on March 4, 1933. The combined efforts of the leaders of the business and of the Federal Home Loan Bank Board succeeded in getting the associations released from the bank closing order within a few days. But their status remained a problem in certain jurisdictions, and many holders of savings and loan accounts were plagued with misunderstandings about the whole situation.

Almost immediately after the bank "holiday," rumors were rife about the prospects for a swift move for government guarantee of bank deposits. Savings and loan leaders at that time believed that any guarantee system which applied to the savings accounts in commercial banks would give banks a competitive advantage over their associations.

Reactions to deposit guarantee discussions

The United States League's officers and Legislative Committee used the weeks immediately following the "holiday" to watch the development of deposit guarantee plans for the banking world. On March 9, League officials addressed a letter to all members of Congress requesting that no legislation be enacted providing for guarantee of the noncommercial, interest-bearing deposits in commercial banks unless some protection of like character were provided for the accountholders in savings and loan associations.

In a bulletin to member institutions three weeks later, when the banking legislation was beginning to take some shape, the League summarized the outlook. It voiced the opinion that a federal guarantee of bank savings deposits would have a substantial effect on community savings institutions; it assured the member institutions that leaders of the business were studying the several guarantee plans proposed, discussing them with the Banking and Currency Committees of the two houses of Congress and "developing a policy." There was a hint that savings and loan associations might participate in the plan for the insurance of bank deposits, if it should be based upon a premium payment. (The plan eventually accepted for premium and assessments was only one of several under discussion; the premium plan was considered soundest by orthodox economic observers.)

It should be recalled that this first savings and loan grass roots discussion of the possibility of federal insurance of accounts took place before federal charters had even been officially proposed in Washington. Accordingly, the savings and loan business recognized that any program guaranteeing the savings accounts in the associations would be difficult "due to the exclusive state incorporation and supervision." All savings and loan association officers were asked to consider the matter and help those "on the firing line" with their views.

In considering the problem they were cautioned to recognize that the "whole trend in the banking structure is toward strong nationalization" and to ponder that "public confidence in *federal* banking enterprises may remain at a high point for some time."

Deposit insurance legislation

The first legislation for insurance of bank deposits reached the statute books in June 1933. Events had moved swiftly to consolidate Capitol Hill sentiment in favor of it. It is noteworthy that the plan did not receive early approval from President Roosevelt and that its most consistent and determined advocate was Representative Henry B. Steagall of Alabama, chairman of the Banking Committee of the House of Representatives (he had steered the legislation for this purpose in its successful course through the House the previous year). He felt that the dislike of bankers for the idea should not carry too much weight with lawmakers in the light of the banking debacle just experienced.

The League's Executive Committee had been called into session in Washington in April to consider the far-reaching mortgage relief measure sponsored by President Roosevelt (the HOLC), including the proposal for federal charters. By this time it was clear that savings and loan institutions could not fit into the pattern of federal insurance of bank deposits, since there was a close tie-in to the Federal Reserve System in the version then gaining favor. The sense of the Executive Committee meeting on April 23 was that members of Congress be requested to confine legislation providing guarantees for bank deposits to those deposits outside the savings department. The Congress, however, proceeded to write the type of banking legislation it felt necessary and made the insurance apply equally to all types of deposits. For several months, there-

94

fore, the savings and loan leaders were inclined more toward a wait-and-see attitude; they wanted to study the effect of insurance of bank deposits upon the inflow of money in savings and loan associations.

The bank legislation as it emerged provided a year—until July 1, 1934—in which all eligible banking institutions must become members of the Federal Deposit Insurance Corporation or forfeit membership in the Federal Reserve System. A temporary program of insurance of deposits would first become effective January 1, 1934. This initial date for the scheme and the July 1, 1934, final deadline afforded the savings and loan leaders more time for deliberation and consultation. Meanwhile they turned their attention to the prestige possibilities of the federal chartering of new and converted savings and loan associations, which was the major news of the summer of 1933.

There was one feature of the Banking Act of 1933 which gave savings and loan executives some reason to think the federal program for bank deposit guarantee might be less than disastrous competition; this was the ceiling which it placed on the payment of interest on insured time or savings deposits. The Federal Reserve Board was then—for the first time—given the right to regulate the rate of interest. Immediately the savings and loan leaders realized that the mutual savings banks would not hurry to avail themselves of insurance offered by the Federal Deposit Insurance Corporation, in view of the strait-jacket which it placed on their interest rate decisions.

In fact the deposit insurance legislation incorporated several features which would tend to discourage mutual savings bank participation. Thus many of the immediate fears of savings and loan leaders were diminished. As long as they felt the savings bankers would hesitate, savings and loan men could pursue yet further the wait-and-see game. Actually, mutual savings banks did not accept the guarantee of deposits principle until nearly 20 years later. By December 31, 1960, however, 325 mutual savings banks with 86.7% of the total deposits in such banks were insured. The continued opposition of the commercial banks, especially the strong ones, to the insurance of bank deposits was another factor which justified the leaders of the savings and loan business in their policy. Certainly the outlook in the immediate future was for less than universal acceptance of the plan.

Combined Board and League program

In late 1933, as the day approached for convening of the final session of the 73rd Congress, the United States League worked with the Federal Home Loan Bank Board to present a combined program to the Congress. The League and the Board were striving for proposals through which savings and loan institutions could play a continuing constructive role. The persistent business doldrums kept the atmosphere propitious for the enactment of any plausible projects which promised to help start the wheels of business and industry rolling again. There was grave and increasingly greater concern about the inactivity in home building. Accordingly, the position of savings and loan institutions was strategic, and the representatives of the business were quick to capitalize on the unique relationship of their institutions to the home building industry. Home building in 1933 had dropped to 93,000 units, the smallest number of new units since World War I.

Meanwhile the American Savings and Loan Institute was making a study of the guarantee of bank deposits and possible consequences for savings and loan associations. As the date of January 1, 1934, approached, when the guarantee of bank deposits would go into effect, the findings of the Institute's research were interesting reading indeed to the savings and loan world.

The Institute study focused upon the experience of state banking systems which had come into existence to guarantee deposits after the panic of 1907-1908. The study concluded that savings associations had grown satisfactorily despite the bank deposit guarantee systems. But this fact afforded little justification for thinking there would be a similar escape from competitive disadvantage in such a period as 1934; the two periods were significantly different.

The state guarantee systems had omitted any national banks from their membership; therefore, they had constituted a limited type of competition even when they were strongest and making the greatest impression upon the public. Furthermore many astute savings and loan leaders of the 1930s were well aware that new ingredients had entered the atmosphere in which savings and loans must compete in the future. One was the magic of the name of the federal government, which was being used in the Great Depression for the first time to build many business enterprises back to respectability in the eyes of the public.

Interesting, too, to the savings and loan observers were the reasons for the closing down of the various state insuring programs and the deficits which most of them had to encounter. Their collapse, the research study pointed out, was largely a result of inherent weaknesses in the form of the guarantees. Risks were concentrated in too few banks and the particular states in which the plans were tried had been especially dependent on one industry—namely, agriculture. Commenting years later on the earlier systems, the Federal Deposit Insurance Corporation pointed out similarly that the fundamental underlying factors in the failure of these systems were the impact of the deflationary monetary policy after the close of World War I and the accompanying business depression, plus the continued adverse economic situation in agriculture throughout the 1920s.

First proposal of savings and loan insurance

The Institute's research study included a skeleton plan for the insurance of accounts in savings and loan associations. This was the first detailed proposal to provide this new ingredient for public confidence in savings and loan institutions.

Early in January 1934 the chairman of the Federal Home Loan Bank Board publicly announced that the Board was studying the question of guarantee of savings and loan accounts. Significantly, the following October, when addressing the United States League's convention in New Orleans, he said: "The United States Building and Loan League is largely responsible for the establishment of the Federal Savings and Loan Insurance Corporation. It examined the possibilities and advocated the legislation. In our opinion it was a wise policy to support."

Back of the chairman's announcement that he was considering the proposal for insurance of accounts in savings and loan associations were some statistics gathered by the League. Among them were facts on the sources of home mortgage money: About 35% of the money supplied for loans on homes ordinarily came from savings and loan associations; about 15% from savings banks; about 15% from life insurance companies; and the remainder from commercial banks, mortgage companies and individuals. The commercial banks were not lending on real estate at that time. Mortgage companies were not functioning. Individuals were not making direct loans on homes. It was important, therefore, that savings and investment funds flow into savings and loan associations and similar institutions such as savings banks and insurance companies if there was to be a steady source of mortgage money.

The federal insurance of deposits was undoubtedly working to get money out of hoarding and back into banking institutions. Between April 1933 and March 1935, savings and time deposits of Federal Reserve System member banks (all insured) rose more than 16%; while the increase for nonmember banks (insurance optional) was slightly under 9%. But bank deposit insurance seemed to be draining funds from home financing institutions into commercial banks, which lent the money for purposes other than homes. The Federal Home Loan Bank Board was reminded by savings and loan leaders that normally half of the funds advanced by savings and loan associations were put to work in building new houses or in home improvements, which create employment—the great demand of early 1934 in the minds of public leaders. If savings and loan associations were to be enabled to attract funds to resume this activity, the insurance of their accounts was an answer worth considering.

Several drafts of legislation to create a Federal Savings and Loan Insurance Corporation were made at the Federal Home Loan Bank Board. On February 9, 1934, one of these was circulated among administration leaders for consideration and comment. On February 27, one group of inner circle advisers to President Roosevelt went on record as favoring legislation for insurance of the accounts of savings and loan associations and mutual savings banks (both in the same corporation).

That same month the Executive Committee of the United States League met in Washington with the legislative proposals of the administration as its chief business. Previously the Reserve Credits Committee had been asked to submit its comments on the draft of legislation prepared by the Federal Home Loan Bank Board to provide for insurance of savings and loan investments. The League's Executive Committee ended by giving a back-handed endorsement to a legislative draft by stating that, "if we must have an insurance corporation, this is the right approach." There was no enthusiasm and much skepticism. However there was an underlying awareness that events were marching relentlessly.

The basic decision that the savings and loan leaders had to make about their approach to insurance of accounts was whether or not all going savings and loan institutions should be blanketed under the insurance, as had been the policy with respect to banks. A difference in the conditions under which the two insurance systems were launched had to be considered. The FDIC temporary insurance had been imposed upon all national banks which were to reopen. Through the further requirement that all member institutions of the Federal Reserve System must finally be insured, control of the federal government over adoption of insurance by most state banks was possible. By contrast, thousands of savings and loan associations were open and doing business at the time when insurance of their accounts was being considered, and only a few associations were then under federal charter.

Savings and loan leaders had a very live fear about the blanketing of savings and loan institutions into insured status; it arose from their anxiety about the solvency of the new Corporation. It must be remembered that the savings and loan business had not experienced a trial-and-error period, such as the state guarantee systems of bank deposits provided.

The savings and loan leaders also had a rather clear understanding of the state of mind of many state supervisors in the business. These supervisors were increasingly concerned about the savings and loan difficulties in their jurisdictions and the blot which some of these not-yet-solved problems might leave on their reputations as public servants. If all the savings and loan institutions had been blanketed into membership of the Insurance Corporation, it would have been a fairly easy step for the state supervisors to put the troubled associations into involuntary liquidation and let the FSLIC pay out. The fear of such a widespread "dumping" of associations on the FSLIC militated against adoption of any plan for providing all operating associations with this protection. Despite the realization that federal insurance for every savings and loan association would have given a tremendous lift to public confidence, the leaders of the business decided against it.

The proposal for insurance of savings and loan accounts met some opposition after the savings and loan leaders came to their conclusions about whether, and in what form, it should be supported. The introduction of legislation to create the Federal Savings and Loan Insurance Corporation was delayed. It was not until May 14, 1934, that President Roosevelt transmitted to Congress suggestions for legislation to improve conditions "for those who invest in houses." This was the National Housing Act, the original FHA statute. It was a four-point program, the President's message explained, and point four was "the insurance for share and certificate holders in building and loan associations similar to the insurance provided for bank depositors."

Introduction of legislation

Mr. Roosevelt elucidated by saying that these institutions are custodians of the savings of thousands of small savers and it is essential that they be given every reasonable protection. He believed insurance of this type was necessary in order to arrest any further drain from these institutions and to put them in a position to resume their normal, useful functions. On the same day, Representative Steagall, chairman of the Banking Committee of the House of Representatives, introduced the National Housing Act with its provisions for the FHA and the Federal Savings and Loan Insurance Corporation. The mutual savings banks had been omitted from eligibility in the Insurance Corporation when the legislative draft reached the stage of being introduced on Capitol Hill; from this time forth there was no more discussion of their inclusion.

But when the insurance plan was introduced in Congress as part of the administration measure, it had been changed drastically from the draft with which League representatives had worked in early February. Widespread participation by savings and loan associations appeared unlikely if the program enacted carried the proposed premium rate, one much heavier than commercial banks paid. An astonishing and disturbing degree of "control" of insured institutions by the Federal Home Loan Bank Board was implicit in the proposal. Furthermore whole states would have been barred from participation by some of the provisions. As the League bulletin to its members in June stated, "had it been passed as it appeared in the administration bill, we could not have honestly urged a single association in the United States to participate." It developed that an official of the United States Treasury, after one or two days of study and without any previous knowledge or experience on the subject, had made these vital changes from the original draft.

By laborious effort and by careful testimony before the committees of Congress, League officials succeeded in getting the meas-

Seventy-third Congress of the United States of America;

At the Second Session,

Begun and held at the City of Washington on Wednesday, the third
day of January, one thousand nine hundred and thirty-four.

AN ACT

To encourage improvement in housing standards and conditions,
to provide a system of mutual mortgage insurance, and for
other purposes.

*Be it enacted by the Senate and House of Representatives of the
United States of America in Congress assembled*, That this Act
may be cited as the " National Housing Act."

TITLE I—HOUSING RENOVATION AND MODERNIZATION

CREATION OF FEDERAL HOUSING ADMINISTRATION

SECTION 1. The President is authorized to create a Federal Housing Administration, all of the powers of which shall be exercised by
a Federal Housing Administrator (hereinafter referred to as the
"Administrator "), who shall be appointed by the President, by
and with the advice and consent of the Senate, shall hold office for
a term of four years, and shall receive compensation at the rate of
$10,000 per annum. In order to carry out the provisions of this
title and titles II and III, the Administrator may establish such
agencies, accept and utilize such voluntary and uncompensated
services, utilize such Federal officers and employees, and, with the
consent of the State, such State and local officers and employees,
and appoint such other officers and employees as he may find necessary, and may prescribe their authorities, duties, responsibilities, and
tenure and fix their compensation, without regard to the provisions
of other laws applicable to the employment or compensation of
officers or employees of the United States. The Administrator may
delegate any of the functions and powers conferred upon him under
this title and titles II and III to such officers, agents, and employees
as he may designate or appoint, and may make such expenditures
(including expenditures for personal services and rent at the seat of
government and elsewhere, for law books and books of reference,
and for paper, printing, and binding) as are necessary to carry out
the provisions of this title and titles II and III, without regard
to any other provisions of law governing the expenditure of public
funds. All such compensation, expenses, and allowances shall be
paid out of funds made available by this Act.

*The National Housing Act, passed by Congress in 1934, provides the legal
basis for the insurance of savings accounts of savings and loan associations*

ure amended so that it was in a "shape in which it could be used." Such battles may appear remote and inconsequential to a generation which has seen the smooth workings of the Federal Savings and Loan Insurance Corporation and its overwhelming acceptance by the savings and loan business. Yet experience with legislation dealing with business and finance has demonstrated over and over again that the technicalities are often equally as important as the basic objective of a statute. This is especially true where a program is being set up which involves the voluntary cooperation of a group of persons, or of financial institutions primarily policy-determined by a local board of directors.

The statute, Title IV of the National Housing Act adopted June 24, 1934, created the Federal Savings and Loan Insurance Corporation, with $100 million capital stock to be supplied by the Home Owners' Loan Corporation (through bonds guaranteed by the U. S. government—in short, federal funds). It was to insure the accounts —up to $5,000 each—of savings and loan associations which became members and which paid an annual premium amounting to ¼ of 1% of insured accounts and creditor liabilities. Membership was mandatory for federals and optional for state-chartered associations. The members of the Federal Home Loan Bank Board were to constitute the board of trustees of the Corporation.

Very significantly an insured association was required to build up a special insurance reserve—a reserve exclusive of all other funds of the reserve type—to 5% of insured accounts and creditor obligations by the time it had been insured 10 years. In case of default of an institution, the holder of every insured account was to be repaid in one of two ways: 1) by an account of like amount in a going, insured association; or 2) a 10% payment in cash, and the remainder in one-year and three-year debentures of the FSLIC.

The necessary haste of the conference between the House of Representatives and Senate versions of the bills had left several confusing and almost unworkable provisions in this first FSLIC legislation. The leaders of the savings and loan business worked closely with the Federal Home Loan Bank Board to arrive at practical solutions of the problems created by these last-minute compromises. They thought it was important to work out most of the problems in advance, for they were well aware that the associations applying would want to know exactly what was involved when they committed themselves to insurance.

102

Interpretation of the new statute

The United States League was once again, for the third year in a row, in a position where its staff had to devote its major attention to interpreting the problems of a new, potentially beneficial statute to the individual member associations. Institutions which applied for membership in the Federal Savings and Loan Insurance Corporation had to accept rules and regulations. Hence the rules and regulations which the Corporation adopted at the start were a key development in the sucess of the venture.

The Federal Home Loan Bank Board worked with the League officers on its drafts of the regulations. Members of those League standing committees concerned with the provisions of the FSLIC statute were also consulted. A formal hearing with the Federal Home Loan Bank Board was then held.

The crux of the position taken by the League that crucial summer of 1934 was that the regulations should permit every honorably conducted, solvent association to have the benefit of the insurance. Furthermore the admission of an institution to insurance should be determined by persons well informed and sympathetic with the savings and loan program. Leaders in the business sensed that substantial harm could be done through any program of insurance of accounts which was not vigorously and "generously" administered.

They contended that the regulations should deal only with interpretations of the law and matters "absolutely essential to the sound functioning" of the Corporation. Most decidedly they held that care should be exercised that supervision by the FSLIC over insured state-chartered associations not be tantamount to federalization.

On September 17, 1934, the League mailed to every association in the country the rules and regulations which the Federal Home Loan Bank Board had promulgated for insurance of accounts. Its letter of transmittal characterized them as constructive and in keeping with advanced savings and loan thought "in many particulars." Though disagreeing with some of the provisions, the League officials emphasized that the savings and loan business was embarking upon a new enterprise, could accumulate substantial capital through the assistance of the insurance of accounts, and could invest it in the traditional savings and loan areas. Summing up the situation as the regulations went into effect, the League said to its members, "There are hundreds of associations which should immediately seek insurance of their investments. There are thousands which should study and weigh and discuss the matter carefully before final action is taken."

Now it was that the associations had to deal with the true significance of an application for insurance. They had to supply a formidable volume of information about their financial condition. They became subject to the Corporation's wishes as to fees charged, lending areas and some of their advertising practices. Those institutions which had any choice in the matter were certainly not going to accept it overnight. Fortunately, for the good showing which the FSLIC naturally wanted to make at the very beginning, there was the nucleus of federals, slightly over 500 of them by this time, which had to insure. This very fact gave the state-chartered associations time to catch their breath before making the big decision and yet not imperil the program's entire future by their delay.

As in the case of federalization, the United States League's stand was neutral insofar as the conditions of the times permitted. The leaders were aware that much needed to be done to bring the savings and loan institutions back into complete public acceptance and to establish them once again as a source of as much as a third of the home mortgage credit of the country. But they had to lead and counsel with savings and loan institutions rather than "sell" or "push" the idea. Whereas the League had generally taken the stand that affiliation with the Federal Home Loan Bank System was "necessary unto salvation," its stand as to federalization and insurance was "use it if you need it."

The brighter mood of 1933 and 1934, as compared with 1932, had something to do with this change. Also, let it be remembered, by this time the business had begun to realize some of the problems which dealing with a federal instrumentality created for management. They were increasingly convinced that the federal government's assistance to the business was to be bought at the price of some loss of independence of action.

Improvements in statute

The United States League lost no time in laying plans to improve the statute. In May 1935, less than 11 months after the first law was passed, three important changes were made in the FSLIC law.

The most patently significant was the reduction of the premium rate to ⅛ of 1%, the rate which the commercial banks were then paying as a result of provisions of the Banking Act of 1935.

An insured association was allowed 20 years to accumulate its 5% insurance reserve instead of the 10 in the original statute.

The section which had prohibited the payment of dividends if any losses were charged to the insurance reserve was amended; the new provision gave the trustees of the Corporation discretion in permitting an association to pay dividends under such circumstances.

Also, a most important technical change in the Insurance Corporation's powers to deal with a "sick" institution came in the 1935 legislation. This was the right of the Corporation to make cash contributions to restore the solvency of an institution—later the most frequently employed solution.

After these amendments the League moved without delay to suggest that "the insurance of accounts by the Federal Savings and Loan Insurance Corporation should be obtained by all institutions suffering from lack of public confidence or not having a flow of savings sufficient to permit active lending operations."

Then began the slow upward climb of state-chartered memberships in the FSLIC. The problem of getting qualified, once the application was in, became graver than the decision to apply. A League staff executive who had been largely responsible for the initial study of the whole idea concluded about this time that the real test of insurance of accounts as a significant factor in the savings and loan business was: Will at least half of the total assets of the business be brought into the plan? If not, he confided to a few associates, the scheme would eventually die a natural death without having accomplished very much. It took five years for the insurance program to reach that testing point. By December 31, 1940, insured assets represented 51% of the total; 1,437 federals were insured and 840 state-chartered institutions.

Looking back, one can observe, however, that as early as 1937 the good points of the program had carried the field against skepticism. Insured associations, on the average, had already shown that their growth was likely to be more rapid than that of the noninsured. Also, savings and loan managers found that insurance of accounts led almost immediately to a decrease in withdrawal notices. So potent was the new tie-in to federal prestige created by insurance of accounts that withdrawals by 1937 actually fell below the predepression norm in some areas.

First tests of insurance

The first test case of the value of insurance to the insured accountholder came early in the Corporation's history. In December

Table 8. Savings and loan associations in the membership of the Federal Savings and Loan Insurance Corporation, December 31, 1935-1960 (in millions of dollars)

Year	Number of insured institutions			Total assets of insured institutions	
	Total	Federally chartered	State chartered	Amount	Percentage to total of all associations
1935	1,117	987	130	$ 711	12.1%
1936	1,575	1,200	375	1,281	22.2
1937	1,884	1,318	566	1,758	30.9
1938	2,098	1,357	741	2,127	37.8
1939	2,199	1,398	801	2,509	44.8
1940	2,277	1,437	840	2,926	51.0
1941	2,343	1,460	883	3,353	55.4
1942	2,398	1,467	931	3,643	59.2
1943	2,447	1,466	981	4,173	63.2
1944	2,466	1,464	1,002	4,995	67.0
1945	2,475	1,467	1,008	6,123	70.0
1946	2,496	1,471	1,025	7,294	71.5
1947	2,536	1,478	1,058	8,528	73.0
1948	2,616	1,485	1,131	9,715	74.6
1949	2,756	1,508	1,248	11,278	77.1
1950	2,860	1,526	1,334	13,644	81.0
1951	3,020	1,549	1,471	16,146	84.3
1952	3,172	1,581	1,591	19,582	86.7
1953	3,304	1,604	1,700	23,498	88.2
1954	3,433	1,640	1,793	28,243	89.3
1955	3,554	1,683	1,871	34,075	90.6
1956	3,666	1,739	1,927	39,243	91.5
1957	3,772	1,772	2,000	44,375	92.2
1958	3,881	1,804	2,077	51,311	93.1
1959	3,979	1,841	2,138	59,547	93.8
1960	4,098	1,873	2,225	67,430	94.3

Source: Federal Home Loan Bank Board, annual reports

1935, FSLIC received the case of an insured association which was voluntarily liquidating. The Corporation 10 months later sent a contribution to the association to make it possible for the account-holders to receive 100¢ on the dollar. It handled two other such cases in 1938, and that year also saw two troubled associations enabled to continue in operation, thanks to the FSLIC's hand in their affairs and to an FSLIC contribution to make them solvent under a new management.

Table 8 shows the annual growth in insured associations, total assets insured and percentage to total of all assets, 1935-1960.

In 1939 the Corporation arranged for three mergers to solve the problems of insured associations which got into financial difficulty; also, that year it handled four other trouble cases, making a

Chart 3. Savings and loan assets of FSLIC-insured and noninsured associations, with percentage distribution, December 31, selected years

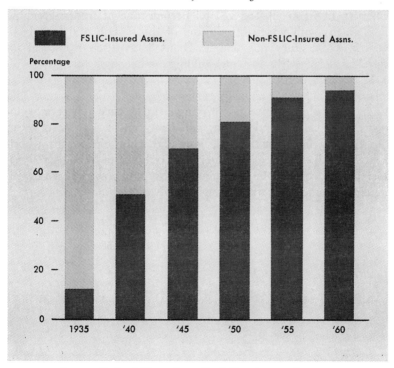

Source: Federal Home Loan Bank Board, annual reports

107

contribution to assets and bringing about a change in management. In every instance, the entire proceeding was so orderly and without fanfare that no disturbance of public confidence resulted. These first 12 "proofs of the pudding" of insurance of accounts before 1940 added the final testimony to the workability of the program.

But the need for insurance of accounts was by no means unanimously felt. The depression was over; thousands of associations had recovered public confidence to some degree, at least, without paying an annual ⅛ of 1% of their liabilities as an expense for insuring them. The commercial banks got a lower insurance premium for FDIC in 1937, 1/12 of 1%. From 1938 on, the United States League's legislative program asked for a similar reduction in the savings and loan premium. When this was effected in 1950 the number of insured institutions among the state-chartered started to rise significantly.

The great usefulness of the FSLIC in rehabilitating associations needing reorganization and other financial assistance is described in Chapter 7. All in all, the FSLIC became one of the far-reaching implements with which the destiny of the savings and loan business in mid-century was shaped. Chart 3 reveals the place of insured associations in the total savings and loan sector.

Men may argue another 25 years—and probably will—over whether or not the leadership exercised by the Federal Savings and Loan Insurance Corporation through supervisory power was indispensable to a sound savings and loan system. But no one can question the fact that the little blue and white circle with a horizontal red bar across its center—the insignia of the insured association—succeeded in becoming to the public a trademark with much the same force as "sterling" on silver.

Chapter 7

Grass roots
progress

At first blush the dramatic assistance which the savings and loan business received from Washington through legislative enactments in the period 1932-1935 tends to overshadow all else. But other things were happening across the country to revive the business and to make it possible for it to utilize the several Washington aids. They were happening in the offices of state savings and loan supervisors, in the state legislatures, in the headquarters of state leagues, in the Chicago office of the United States League and in the places of business of literally thousands of associations. They are facets of the savings and loan story that must be added to the headline events recounted in the preceding four chapters in order to round out the account of how the system was revived, reshaped and set on its path to greater size, strength and usefulness.

It must always be emphasized that the state-chartered system of savings and loan institutions is as proud a component of the whole in 1960 as that ushered into being for the first time under federal charter in 1933. The preponderant number of savings and loan institutions has always been, and will be in the foreseeable future, under state charter. The survival of a vigorous state-chartered system adapted to new ways and new public attitudes is traceable to several happenings. Most basic, perhaps, was a wholesale revision of state laws.

The reshaping of state laws to provide for more adequate supervision and more modern, flexible practice was in many ways a more difficult accomplishment than the adoption of the spectacular federal laws. Obviously it required a larger number of specific enactments, and thus it meant persuading many more lawmakers of the need for change. Amendments to existing laws, such as those in the several states, often ran into severe prejudices as well as the ever present resistance to change—an inherent characteristic of human nature. South Carolina adopted its first savings and loan law in the depression era. By mid-century only Maryland and Alaska had no state supervision of savings and loan institutions.

Amendments of state laws

The putting of new wine into old bottles of supervision was the great accomplishment in the state legislatures in the 1930s. As early as 1931, 37 of the 48 states made some changes in their savings and loan laws. In that year nine states adopted complete new codes. The prevalence of the custom of state legislatures to sit in only alternate years complicated the task of the savings and loan leaders and inevitably prolonged the process of getting more adequate statutes enacted. But during the depression years there were many special sessions, and the associations through their state leagues used them to good advantage.

Prior to 1933 the direction of the main stream of amendments to state laws was set by the accomplishments of the United States League's Advisory Committee on State Legislation. From the first years of its establishment as a standing committee of the League the group had worked toward greater uniformity among state supervisory laws. As already mentioned in Chapter 5, it developed "The Model Code" as a logical approach.

This Model Code of 1933 paved the way for amendment of the various state laws in the direction of a flexibility in basic association operations far beyond that provided by any then-existing state laws. For example, this code placed the concept of optional savings, which had hitherto been acceptable in only a few states, on a par with the universally accepted installment, systematic savings accounts as the principal avenue through which an association could serve the saver who wanted to accumulate funds. The Model Code also placed full-paid income accounts on a par with these other forms of raising the association's capital. These accounts were already acceptable in a number of states. They became one of the principal methods by which the savings and loan association of the 1950s raised its capital.

The other major advance towards savings and loan operation of the mid-20th century variety was the provision for the repayment of the loan by the crediting of payments directly on the principal of the mortgage. It was still the most common practice in the early 1930s for a savings and loan mortgage loan to be repaid by the "share accumulation" method (see Chapter 2). The Model Code of 1933 recognized both systems of loan repayments—again in order to permit flexibility on the part of the associations.

In a majority of the states there was need for even further work with the state legislatures than the amendment of savings and loan codes for the supervision of state-chartered associations. The significant new federal enactments required enabling legislation in many states, and the state league leadership rallied to the task of bringing this legislation to pass. Sometimes where the federal legislation required long months of debate and maneuvering before it reached the statute books, some of the states already had their enabling legislation passed by the time the federal law was in force.

Role of state leagues

A contribution to the strengthening and revitalization of the state-chartered system totally incapable of adequate evaluation was the activity of the state leagues. As the years went along the federally chartered associations found the services of the state leagues indispensable for the most part; and of course the state-chartered associations which converted to federal charter already had their close contacts of several years' standing with the state league. They usually maintained these ties. Certainly on the doorsteps of these leagues the depression left a variety of work so great as to defy description. And by and large the demands of the hour found an intelligent and helpful response in the state league offices.

Naturally those leagues which had equipped themselves with full-time executive staffs (usually one man and a few stenographic and clerical assistants) by 1930 were in a better position to meet their responsibilities than were those which still depended on the part-time efforts of savings and loan executives who had to do the league's work in their spare time. In 1930 the full-time executive of the state league office was an established position in 10 states. A few others quickly equipped themselves with this necessary vehicle to fight the depression. They numbered 15 by the end of the '30s.

The full-time executives of the state leagues had already formed, by the time the depression began, a confidential relationship with the managers of the institutions. They knew the basic financial situation of most of the associations in their respective states. As economic conditions worsened, they kept in yet closer touch with individual situations. As a result, much of the state league work with member institutions in the time of trouble was a matter of sitting down with the manager or with some of the board and talking over what could be done. A fairly close liaison was usually maintained between the state supervisory department and the full-time state league office. Both geography and previous relationships gave the state league efforts with the savings and loan associations in the early 1930s practicality and effectiveness.

Local leagues

At the grass roots level, in cities and counties and in groups of counties, savings and loan associations had local organizations which played their part in keeping many associations in operation and helped them to avoid some financial difficulties. Many state leagues fostered the creation of such units during the depression years for the first time. The times of trouble created a need for savings and loan men to ask advice of each other as they had never done before. The competitive compulsions of prosperity became dormant in those days and the "help each other" instincts of people in trouble came into the ascendancy. These local vehicles of common action depended in nearly every case on voluntary leadership and were demanding on the time of many of the men in the business. But all would have agreed it was time well spent.

Meetings of such groups presented ready-made opportunities for the state league leaders and national leaders in the business with a message of hope and practical help to explain and discuss the new programs and the new devices. They were the only gatherings where any sizable number of directors could be brought together, and the only occasion when an hour or two of their time could be concentrated on what was new and what was needed. They were the only meetings which even a great many of the savings and loan managing officers ever attended. In Allegheny County, Pa., for instance, an attendance of well over 1,000 could be counted on for the annual banquet; this was a figure in excess of attendance at United States League conventions in those years.

The local organizations did not exist everywhere, and the savings and loan areas which lacked them were the poorer. Just to mention a few, the more active city leagues included those in New York City, Portland (Ore.), Birmingham, Indianapolis, Terre Haute, New Orleans, San Francisco, Louisville, St. Louis and Kansas City, Mo. In Pennsylvania and New Jersey the normal local vehicle was the county league. The very populous Ohio counties, such as Cuyahoga and Hamilton, also had their county leagues. There was a definite pattern of district and group organizations—consisting of several counties—in the Midwest, particularly in Indiana and Illinois and the less thickly populated parts of Ohio.

The specific projects of these groups varied as widely as their geography and their immediate problems. As early as 1932 many of them were carrying on cooperative advertising campaigns—the local league has always been the normal unit for this endeavor. The metropolitan league in New York City had its special interest in the standardization of practices among its members; Chicago's foreign language savings and loan groups adopted a code of ethics, paving the way for the rebirth of the business along sounder lines. When foreclosed properties became the problem in any area, there was a ripe field for cooperative action through the local league. Some local groups were so organized that they sent regularly to members instructive bulletins on phases of savings and loan operation.

Supervisory attitudes and actions

The supervisory personnel in the state savings and loan departments played their difficult and many times thankless role in reviving the state-chartered system. As in all human endeavors, some did outstanding work, some mediocre and only a few did a poor job. On the whole the oft successful efforts of these men to avoid the costly, time-consuming and confidence-diminishing process of receiverships for associations in trouble was one of their noteworthy services to the business. Their willingness to act in collaboration with the federal agencies was often paramount in their success. Such efforts achieved monumental results in "saving" hundreds of associations.

Of the essence of the work in this complicated area was the lack of any public spotlight on it. The public records of it are, therefore, scant, but the memories of all who were connected with it bear strong witness to the indispensability of some of the major state leagues and the attitudes of some of the state supervisors of savings and loan associations.

As the 1930s went along it became evident that the work of the Federal Home Loan Bank System, the Federal Savings and Loan Insurance Corporation and of federal charters in resuscitating the savings and loan business would be along some lines which had not been in the center of their sponsors' thinking. The powers, personnel and financial resources of these programs played a conspicuous part in the successful rehabilitation, or inconspicious exit, of many associations in the 1934-1943 period. The supervisors could scarcely have been in a position to cope with the problem had they not had access to some of the tools—and money—which Washington legislation had made possible. They worked closely with the officials of the Washington instrumentalities, especially the Federal Savings and Loan Insurance Corporation, to evolve a savings and loan system that could go once again to the people for funds, offering reasonable assurance of safety, of ability to pay adequate earnings and of returning their money to the savers when they needed it.

Statistics alone—the dip from 10,500 associations in 1935 to 6,500 in 1943—give a sweeping view of what happened. Behind these statistics is the detailed story; it includes broad structural changes brought about by reorganizations and consolidations, and subsequent insurance of accounts or conversion to federal charter. These activities created several hundred new savings associations, even where the place of business remained the same, the management changed only partially and some part of the old assets were retained.

114

Piecemeal rehabilitation

The commercial banks had solved their problems before their permanent insurance of accounts went into effect. As Chapter 6 indicated, the conditions surrounding the inauguration of the two insurance systems were different and made different approaches advisable. As already shown the savings and loan leaders themselves had favored doing the savings and loan rehabilitation job the more difficult, piecemeal way. It was a much more trying approach, taking a great deal more time because it had to be done locality by locality or state by state. This solution also meant that the newly repaired fabric of the savings and loan business in one city could be displayed and start meriting public confidence at a time when this had not yet been accomplished in some other area. New Orleans and Kansas City, for instance, got around to doing the job early. Newark and other New Jersey industrial cities came along a little later in this progress. Chicago and its metropolitan area struggled long and hard to get the financial rehabilitation program going. Pennsylvania, which had one of the most serious and widest spread problems, was still working on it in the early 1940s. These are just some geographical variations in the chronological table.

The remedies represented many possible combinations. Segregation of assets and share accounts was the earliest approach to solving the problem of a "frozen" association. Of course, it was never the case that all the assets were "frozen." Part of the association, therefore, could be put back into business as usual, while waiting out the liquidation of the truly "frozen" assets. To accomplish this the association was divided into two corporations.

One was the savings and loan association which was to continue in business; on the assets side it kept all the good mortgages and liquid assets. By the ratio of these good assets to total assets, the dollar amount in the account of each saver was written down from his original account. The other corporation contained all the "frozen" assets; the shareholders were given certificates of participation in this second corporation for the balance of their original accounts. As the "frozen" assets were "thawed," they received periodically "liquidating dividends." For example, if only 50% of the assets were in good mortgages and cash, the newly emerging association was only half its former size and the shareholders' accounts were only 50% of the balance shown in the old passbook. But the liquidating

115

corporation which held the other 50% might eventually pay out so that the saver lost nothing.

The association which emerged from this operation was in a position to pay withdrawals immediately and to accept savings accounts without any question. The same board of directors ran both the liquidating corporation and the new, or segregated association. It was responsible to the state supervisors for the operation of both. The decision to "segregate" was made by a meeting of the shareholders, and thus confidence in the new, although smaller, savings and loan association was restored. The shareholders having had the situation explained to them thoroughly and having accepted the proposal for the remedy, overcame their major suspicions and fears. Once the segregated association started operating normally and paying withdrawals, it could advertise for savings with a normal expectancy of getting its share of even the curtailed savings flow of those years.

The liquidating corporations of many segregated associations ended by remitting to the saver who had waited more than 100¢ on the dollar. It was several years before real estate improved to the place where such assets could be liquidated to advantage, but in the long run the savers' participation certificates turned out to be valuable assets.

In 1936 the Federal Home Loan Bank Board reported the case histories of 26 associations that had undergone this operation. In these cases the "good" assets were used to form the nucleus of new federally chartered associations, and the combined assets of the new federals in these cases represented less than 50% of the combined assets of the associations before segregation. In other words, there were several extreme cases in the group. Yet in six months they were able to resume lending and were getting new money. These associations demonstrated an ability to revive public confidence comparable to that of 50 other associations in the same state which had been federalized and had taken 100% of the old assets into the newly chartered institutions.

Or an association might undergo "reorganization." Typically in such instances insurance of accounts by the FSLIC was applied for on the basis of a specific plan. For example, the plan might encompass cancellation of all outstanding "stock," with accountholders accepting a voluntary write-down of their original holdings. The percentage of write-down would depend on the amount of "bad"

116

assets the association had. The accountholders voted on the plan. If there was a sufficient majority for it, the plan would go through. The institution would then be reorganized on the basis of unrestricted withdrawals. Some state laws permitted a write-down of the liabilities simply by vote of the accountholders. In such jurisdictions this pattern of reconstruction was popular. Where the courts had to approve any such write-down, this particular approach was less often used.

In the larger cities—which were the main trouble spots—rehabilitation was often accomplished through a "program" involving the entire community, participated in by the state supervisors, the state league—especially if it was a league with a full-time staff—and representatives of the Federal Home Loan Bank of the district. If associations were in trouble this team would determine (along general lines) what had to be done. The team was made up of those who could advise and had power to offer assistance of a substantial nature. The men on it had to persuade the directors of the association involved to carry out the plan, either to consolidate, liquidate or reorganize. Persuasion was even needed in some cases to convince a board of directors of a going association that it could afford to take over part of the assets—the good loans—of one of the less fortunate brother institutions in the neighborhood. It was a massive undertaking, involving political powers, wisdom in dealing with people and unfaltering conviction that something had to be done to save the situation.

A tedious succession of work was also involved. Whenever an association had a large volume of nonproductive assets and/or capital impairment, it became necessary to find out more details about the association than had ever been lined up in any single docket before. The judgment of the public on these institutions had been formed on a cursory impression of their being "frozen"; the men who operated them had to act on much more detailed information. Appraisal of doubtful assets by disinterested appraisers, examination of the institution and very often an audit by an independent accountant were among the first steps. Wherever there was to be any segregation of assets, a careful classification of the assets was involved and, of course, some exercise of arbitrary judgment.

Customarily a reorganization committee would be functioning either from the association's board of directors—or with membership from both the board and the shareholders. Early they sought approval of the reorganization plan by the Federal Savings and Loan Insurance Corporation and, if possible, some commitment from the Home Owners' Loan Corporation for investment in the accounts of the rehabilitated association. Since the Federal Home Loan Bank Board governed both the Home Owners' Loan Corporation and the Federal Savings and Loan Insurance Corporation, the dovetailing of these two programs for any one institution's betterment was not a difficult task. But the whole process required many months to consummate. The fact that some of this activity was still on the agenda by the time World War II began, bringing a completely different set of economic circumstances, cannot be surprising in the light of the practical factors involved.

No one could claim that the major surgery of these eight or nine years was accomplished without leaving large amounts of scar tissue. But the health of the savings and loan body as a whole owes much to the decisions that were made all along the line—by account-holders, by boards of directors, by those in authority and those in advisory capacity. Somehow, the combined wisdom of all of these—or at least the net margin of good choices over bad—gave the management of thousands of associations the right to hold their heads high once again. And it gave the associations the urge to move onto the main streets of communities; they were no longer looking upon their often obscure office locations as a blessing because they were not easily found by dissatisfied customers. They took to Main Street with a belief that the satisfied customer could once again become the norm.

The United States League provided a clearing house for information on what was being, and could be, done where associations were in trouble. Sectional meetings at its national conventions—particularly the meetings of Supervisors and the Insurance Section and Attorneys Committee—had speakers and round tables discussing ways and means of accomplishing effectively and equitably these critical reshapings of the savings and loan structure. In day-to-day operations the legal staff of the League furnished considerable consultative service. The *Legal Bulletin* which the League started publishing in 1935 was a continuing source of information on litigation in both the federal and state courts and on new legislation. At this time all these developments were especially important to the programs of liquidations, consolidations and reorganizations.

United States League membership

But much of the United States League's part in the rehabilitation of the whole savings and loan business depended on the success of its efforts to get individual membership enrollments. It had sent information about the Federal Home Loan Bank System and its possible benefits to all savings and loan institutions. Of the 11,000 associations in existence when the Federal Home Loan Bank System opened for business, the United States League members totaled only 2,700. This was more than twice the number of members the League had a year earlier, but it was far from the kind of membership support that was needed.

The relatively low percentage of associations that belonged to the League at the beginning of the depression was a result of the fairly late development of the concept of individual memberships. Until 1924 this League had been only a federation of state leagues. The majority of the existing associations had an indirect affiliation with the United States League through their state league membership. It became apparent to all leaders of the business, however, that in an emergency such as the early 1930s the direct affiliation of an association with the League was highly important.

In presenting the position of the savings and loan institutions before congressional committees, the League already had faced the problem that it could boast only a relatively small percentage of the total number of savings and loan institutions in its membership—a fact which could weigh against the significance of its testimony. It was obvious, too, that without a direct link between the individual association and the United States League headquarters, such as membership afforded, the League was limited severely in its ability to counsel with and assist associations on federal aids.

Finally the League was branching out into a much more costly type of operation in contrast to former years. Typically only one legislative proposal, at the most, had hitherto concerned savings and loan associations in any given session of Congress. Now it became apparent that not one but many bills in every Congress would carry savings and loan concern. The only hope for an adequate budget to support the kind of activity which the crucial depression years were calling upon the League to perform lay in the wide expansion of individual association memberships.

119

So it was that from 1930 to 1934 the membership rolls of the United States League were increased by 3,000 associations. Back of this amazing achievement were the voluntary efforts of savings and loan men who took it upon themselves to ask others to become members. It was the result of drives sometimes patterned after financial drives for charity and other philanthropic endeavors. Teams were organized and individual association members were given lists of associations to solicit; successful solicitors of members scored points for their team. There were also reciprocal membership arrangements with some of the state leagues; in these cases all members of the state leagues were required to join the United States League. Finally a new member of the League staff was added in 1931 who went up and down the country calling on associations, offering information. The wide enrollment of the business in the nationwide organization was accomplished by use of the automobile, the train, the telephone and the United States mail.

United States League services

There were a great many other things which the United States League—growing in membership and in the effectiveness of its staff—did day-by-day, week-by-week and month-by-month to revive the spirit of the savings and loan business from the blows dealt it by the depression. It operated a news bureau to supply to the newspapers and wire services facts about savings and loan activity. Using a fine-toothed comb, it found encouraging signs in such developments as improvement in loan repayments and good dividend paying records and made news items for the nationwide press. These were not days when the newspapers were clamoring for statements from savings and loan officials—except in cases of trouble where the association officers were reluctant to say anything.

A timely assist to the program of disseminating good news about savings and loan institutions came in the League's reaching out for fairly frequent, up-to-date figures on the performance of the associations. The only official statistics of the business in 1930 were the annual reports of the League secretary-treasurer, in which were consolidated the data from each of the state supervisors. These were the official figures carried every year in the *Statistical*

Abstract of the United States, with due credit to the United States League. But they were at least six months old when completed and made public; they reflected balance sheet items rather than current transactions with savers and borrowers; they provided no way for making month-to-month—even quarterly—comparisons on inflow and outflow of money.

Chapters 9 and 10 will describe in the proper perspective some of the League's special efforts to find out what was going on in the business, nationwide, in order that the performance of the savings and loan institutions might be made known in high places. But even before these efforts took place, at the beginnings of the recovery stage, the League headquarters was doing new things to fill in the gaps on statistics.

Some of the state leagues were cooperating with the United States League by sending in monthly report forms, getting figures every month from a sizable number of their members on balance sheet items, number of loans made and number of new savers added; the state leagues would then make a projection for the whole state on the basis of the sample and send the data to the United States League. These were rudimentary data but they furnished badly needed clues.

From time to time the American Savings and Loan Institute conducted research into operations; it developed the first estimate, for example, of the number of persons employed in the savings and loan business, getting its local chapters to make their findings and report. Everywhere in every business in 1932 and 1933 more statistics were being demanded; many had convinced themselves that there would have been no depression had they had more facts and had them in time; so the League moved to meet this need for savings and loan institutions until such time as there were governmental sources for the information.

The United States League and state league communications to members were among the most important single approaches to a better-informed, better-able-to-act savings and loan business. To provide the increasingly important national point of view, frequent *Confidential Bulletins* went out from headquarters to all members; the publication which began as the *Journal* of the American Savings and Loan Institute—*Savings and Loans*—was gradually expanded to serve as a monthly review of those savings and loan practices being found most effective. The long-established independent savings and loan publication, *The American Building Association News,* served for many years as the League's official printed periodical for conveying its news to the members; every month it carried scores of pages of news of the business gathered by the United States League headquarters. It also incorporated special supplements for the news of some state leagues.

The relish of the savings and loan members of those days for information and for comment on the rapidly moving national economic and politicial developments can be understood only if one realizes how few communications of this kind there generally were in the business world. The average small businessman lived in virtual isolation from the facts of life at the Washington level; he had never had to pay much attention to them before 1931. There were a few four-page "Washington Letters" covering the scene generally, but the development of the numerous private business ventures of informing and assisting businessmen by regular bulletins was still far in the future. In the 1930s the savings and loan men were not as yet complaining that their desks were so full of material they did not have time to read it!

Standard Accounting System

The grass roots progress of the savings and loan business in accounting was one of the spectacular developments of the first half of the 1930s. It was the combined work of many people and organizations, but the United States League was responsible for focusing attention on the problem and for bringing together the principal elements for its solution. For many years there had been concern on the part of savings and loan leaders about a major standardization of practice in the business. They knew, furthermore, that in order to achieve any material result they would have to reform the accounting methods of the savings and loan institutions. One of the things with which the staff of the Federal Home Loan Bank Board had to work so tediously—at the start of the Bank System—was the multiplicity of accounting methods used in 48 different state jurisdictions in 1932. There were other variations for different localities within each state. No wonder the launching of the Standard Accounting System in 1936 was hailed by the League president as "the most significant nonlegislative work accomplished by the organized savings and loan business in many years."

The League had created an Accounting Division as early as 1930. It first analyzed and reconciled the great variety of reporting forms in use by state supervisors in the several states; by 1935 a system of standard report forms for associations to render to the supervisor had been completed. Not only the Federal Home Loan Bank Board and its related agencies, but also many state supervisory departments adopted the standard form. Universal adoption came within a relatively few years. A standard method of presenting the financial position was thus achieved. The standardization embraced the balance sheet, the statement of operations, the statement of expense and the reconcilement of the undivided profits account. Following naturally in its wake was the highly important development, from the public relations point of view, of a uniform presentation of the published financial statement.

This, however, was only the preliminary job. The development of a Standard Accounting System required the cooperation of many groups inside and outside the business. The exacting work of producing it was given a head start by the American Savings and Loan Institute which had already created the accounting system for the federal associations. With the aid of highly proficient accountants who were working for savings and loan associations and of some managers who were themselves certified public accountants, the Institute was able to move into new ground in creating a system that could be fitted into the state-chartered pattern as well. The supervisors in the several states and in the Federal Home Loan Bank System were called on for advice. The Accounting Division, made up of managers of savings and loan associations with a flare for accounting and an absorbing interest in it, continued in an advisory capacity as the motive force behind the entire undertaking.

Through its efforts a standing committee was created by the American Institute of Accountants to develop greater uniformity in CPA audits of savings and loan associations and to relate them more definitely to the Standard Accounting System. It was manned principally by CPAs who had numbered savings and loan institutions among their clients. Its work was one of the completely necessary steps to implement the bravely launched new system. When, in 1940, the American Institute of Accountants published its bulletin on auditing procedures for savings and loan associations, it was breaking new ground, having never before taken such a step for a particular industry.

The Standard Accounting Manual was published in 1936. Its adoption was hastened in hundreds of associations by the expansion of the American Savings and Loan Institute's business service of printing and selling forms. It will be recalled that the Institute had done this in connection with the federal savings and loan accounting system in 1933-1934. With quantities of newly made up accounting forms it was now able to step into the breach for the service of all associations which were ready and anxious to adopt the standard system. This practical step put the finishing touch on the accounting revolution of the 1930s in savings and loan offices.

From the supervisory point of view there was one final step in the rounding out of the standard system. This was the adoption of standard examination forms for use by the examiners. Because so many different jurisdictions were involved the work took time. But the Accounting Division pursued it, and the forms developed under its sponsorship ultimately became the basis for examinations in a large majority of the supervisory jurisdictions in the business.

A great advance had been made in standardization of practice, but in the final analysis the most far-reaching contribution of the Standard Accounting System was that managements now had a more adequate method of ascertaining the results of operation from week to week and month to month. Thus the standard system helped pave the way for the planning ahead which was so necessary to the management of a growing, revitalized savings and loan system in the years of recovery and expansion.

Society of Residential Appraisers

Another impressive step ahead in savings and loan operations at the grass roots came with the approach of residential appraising to professional status. The League had set up in 1930 a division concentrated on appraising. At that time the motivation for it was simply to provide an opportunity for those managers who were particularly interested in appraising to consider procedures to handle appraisals more effectively. The process of evaluating the basic security behind the loans which the association made was always a compelling interest to many, regardless of the financial situation of the institution with which they were concerned. In the depression, however, this interest in the process of evaluating the security moved much nearer to the center of the stage.

In 1932, the League's Appraising Division Report reminded the convention that the associations had loaned thousands of dollars on incomplete appraisals. It suggested that the situation was due partly to lack of means on the part of some associations and to the unwillingness of others to take the time to draft a proper form of loan application and appraisal. In the months that followed, as the division tried to develop a standard appraisal form, a much more ambitious project loomed before it. It became clear that the business was relying on thousands of appraisers not too well informed. Furthermore the savings and loan appraiser had no particular place to go to get informed. There was a flourishing Institute of Real Estate Appraisers under the sponsorship of the National Association of Real Estate Boards, but appraising of residential property had never received much of its emphasis.

Thus it came about that the Appraising Division became the nucleus in 1934 for an entirely new organization, called the Society of Residential Appraisers. As a precedent and something of a model, it had the Surveyors Institute in Great Britain. It was to be a nonprofit corporation to raise the standards of residential appraising for institutional lenders, but in so doing, it was to supply much needed information and educational services to its appraisers. Finally, it was to aim at proper recognition for residential appraisers. The new organization was to get its initial sponsorship from the League and to develop under that sheltering wing until it should be able to go on its own. To better the Society's prospects for maximum success the organizers decided in favor of open membership; qualified appraisers from all lending organizations were invited to join.

Within a year it had nearly 900 members, and while a majority of them were savings and loan appraisers, there was a substantial representation of savings bank and life insurance appraisers. Appraisal practices of savings and loan associations bore indelible marks of the Society of Residential Appraisers from that time forth. Local chapters were organized; the periodical, *Residential Appraisers Review,* went into publication; a clearing house for information was made available to all members; standard forms were prepared; and arrangements were made for formal instruction.

The Society has become a thriving organization with chapters throughout the United States and in many foreign countries, especially in neighbors of the United States. In 1960, it had some 13,000 members and 142 local chapters. Savings and loan appraisers no longer constitute a majority of its membership, but it has retained the direction of its initial movement. It is a professional society whose concern is not only with the recognition of those who have attained certain standards of knowledge and training; it is concerned also with the continual development of a greater storehouse of knowledge of residential appraising, and thus of greater opportunity for the practitioners to do a reliable job.

The trend of the real estate cycles has been almost continuously upward in all the years in which the Society of Residential Appraisers has been in existence. It might be argued with some validity that the real test of an appraiser in this field comes only when the downturn has started. But certainly no phase of the savings and loan business today receives more careful attention than its appraising practices. In a quarter of a century which has seen practically the doubling of the length of the average loan term and the increase of the typical loan ratio to property value from 70% to somewhere between 80% and 90%, the savings and loan business has been able to move with confidence as much because of the careful emphasis it gives to residential appraising as for any other single reason.

Education and research developments

In previous chapters the work of the American Savings and Loan Institute in miscellaneous undertakings has been referred to several times. But the role in which the Institute reached the greatest number of savings and loan personnel and did its most conspicuous service for the future of the business was its educational activity. Emphasis on that activity is appropriately a part of this chapter.

When the full-time headquarters of the United States League was opened in Chicago in 1930, the League took the Institute under its roof and wing. The organizations had been entirely separate up to that time, although the League had given the Institute some financial support ever since its start in 1922. Principal activity of the Institute when it became a League affiliate was educating the personnel of savings and loan associations in the techniques of their trade and to some extent in the broader economic activities of the business. With a program which had the benefit of the youthful enthusiasm of the younger generation in the savings and loan business, the Institute's educational efforts doubled and redoubled after it was sharing headquarters with the League. Fifty or 60 chapters were organized across the country; they ran their own night schools—very often in the office quarters of one of the associations.

Both the volunteer leadership of the Institute—its president was usually a top savings and loan manager in those days—and the staff made lengthy trips to organize new chapters. The difficulties with which the associations were meeting made attendance at Institute classes quite popular. Even managing officers could be persuaded to enroll in courses in accounting and appraising when these functions within the association were coming increasingly under scrutiny. Many Institute chapters organized forums so that managers could come and discuss current problems. In many instances the Institute chapters worked closely with local leagues, supplementing their efforts to provide avenues for exchange of ideas and succeeding in arranging for smaller, more intimate discussion channels than the larger League program could hope to provide.

Through this classroom practice in thinking and discussing, the Institute brought to the fore the natural leadership which existed but which might easily have been passed over. Not-to-be-overlooked training in leadership was often afforded by activities outside the classroom. The Institute had its own national Board of Trustees composed mainly of savings and loan executives in the younger half of their careers. They were looking ahead, anticipating what would be needed in the way of an educational curriculum three years or maybe five years hence. The across-the-table give-and-take which the younger generation experienced in Institute work helped train them as spokesmen for the business.

The alliance with the League paved the way for the elaboration of the Institute's research activities. The full-time executives of the League worked interchangeably for the two organizations, regardless of which organization issued the salary check. When a League committee or officer saw the need for some careful research on a problem or a project, the Institute rallied to its side and produced the necessary study. When the savings and loan business was experiencing for the first time in that generation the problem of real estate on the books, the Institute made a special study of the behavior of real estate cycles. This study emphasized the application of this cycle to home mortgage lending. It than published a research bulletin to incorporate its findings. Chapter 6 has described the Institute's early explorations of the possibility of insurance of savings and loan accounts.

The Institute also conducted the first survey of public opinion regarding savings and loan associations—certainly a nonprofessional job, if one compares it with the carefully weighted, technically complex surveys characteristic of the 1950s, but nevertheless it was a start in the right direction. Interviews in this survey were conducted by savings and loan personnel who did them in their spare time. The results helped the savings and loan business get a more objective look at its remaining strengths and at its flagrant weaknesses. The Institute carried the responsibility of savings and loan research until a more adequate League budget permitted, in 1938, the establishment of such a department in the League.

All in all the years of slow emergence from the shock and damage of the depression constituted a priceless experience for the men and women who worked in and for the savings and loan institutions. People in the business had then few, if any, ideas about maximum hours worked. They were peculiarly dependent in those years on the leadership which they got from their leagues, and later, too, from the Federal Home Loan Bank staffs, but they permitted themselves to be led along newly blazed trails which turned out to be broad highways to success. This course can only be viewed as a combination of good fortune and of some innate wisdom and basic belief in the savings and loan business.

The need of every nation in an hour of crisis for both men and leadership has been cited in classical lore. The savings and loan business happened to have both in the 1930s and the progress made at the grass roots certified to that.

Part two

The road to recovery

1937-1939

Chapter 8

The new

competition

By 1937 officers of savings and loan associations were ready to rebuild their 106-year-old system of financial institutions along the firmer lines that experience had shown to be needed. The somewhat ruthless purge of the business by the economic forces of the early 1930s—the crack-up of the banking system, business stagnation, unemployment and drastically falling prices—was for the most part over. As the last chapter indicated, some of the work of liquidating and reorganizing was still going on by the early 1940s. But the firm core of the business, consisting of enough associations with enough assets to determine the trend for the system as a whole, was ready for the outward look and the upward climb.

The men who tackled the recovery job were generally between 45 and 55 years old. In the main, they were those who had seen their associations through their times of trial. Fewer than half of them were holders of academic degrees but most had graduated

131

from that age's favorite businessman's alma mater, the "University of Hard Knocks." An impressive group had supplemented their studies with American Savings and Loan Institute training in class work and by correspondence. Even in that day, a few highly respected women sat in the officer group with the men.

For the management group in the aggregate, energies and enthusiasm were intact; and judgment had been sharpened as well as tempered by years of living with the unexpected always around the corner. There was, moreover, an *esprit de corps* among them which has always been typical to some extent of the savings and loan business. Some early hard feelings occasioned by the creation of the federal system spent their main force before the 1930s were over.

What did these people see in 1937 as they looked about them? They saw neighbors, friends and acquaintances who had recovered from the subconscious suspicion that the depression would last forever. Most people had jobs once more or at least some dependable source of income. More new clothes could be seen on the ladies; stores were dressing up their advertisements and their show windows. People were beginning to complain of the extravagances of Washington instead of occupying themselves solely with how they might get more of the largesse flowing out in the public effort to stem recession. The "Blue Eagle" of the National Recovery Administration had been quietly taken off the windows of business institutions after the United States Supreme Court outlawed it; merchants, manufacturers, dealers and all sorts of employers were beginning to see their accustomed world back in focus. The Japanese invasion of Manchuria joined the Italian occupation of Ethiopia as the principal public affairs topic of conversation. Such domestic concerns as "What is Roosevelt's social security program going to do to the thrift instincts of the people?" had taken the place of wondering if one would still be on a payroll next week.

By any standard of the years after World War II, there were still, in 1937, too many jobless, too much need for public relief, too low a level of business activity in nearly every community; but by contrast with 1932 or 1933, the American people as a whole liked their world very much. A striking evidence of this was their re-election of President Roosevelt in November 1936, by an overwhelming vote. Where 22,821,000 had voted for him four years before, 27,476,000 marked ballots for him in 1936. Since the President had so dramatically associated himself with the federal government's efforts to bring back prosperity, the 1936 vote could be taken as an indisputable indicator of how the people felt about their own economic status at that time.

Optimism prevalent

The 1937 convention of the United States League was held in October in Los Angeles, the first time that the national meeting had ever been held in southern California. Three "Golden West Special" trains carried an enthusiastic delegate body across the scenic wonderlands of America, and, as one speaker later said at the convention, the theme song on the trains was "Happy Days Are Here Again." A good evidence of the feeling of greater optimism in the business was the fact that some of the delegates took postconvention tours, going by routes as far away as the Canal Zone. This was the kind of expenditure which would have been out of the question in truly depression years.

The statistical evidence of savings and loan recovery was not startling when the League secretary made his annual report at that convention. When the figures were compiled by the end of that year, however, some notable upturns were evident. The associations as a whole reported a net gain of 100,000 customers for the year 1937. This was a sign that they had started their climb back into public favor. The cheer which this seemingly modest gain engendered can be best understood against the background of dwindling customer lists which had become a seven-year pattern, an average decrease of 800,000 to a million customers a year.

Furthermore a net gain of $100 million in total mortgage holdings took place in 1937. And this improvement showed on the balance sheets despite the trend toward the direct reduction loan, a changeover which automatically reduced the figure for total mortgage loan volume in any given association. By another year, the composite picture showed an increase of two percentage points in the ratio of total mortgage loans to assets, a yet more striking indication that the associations were back in the lending business in earnest.

The business had always looked at "assets" as the real measure of growth. This figure was certainly the simplest and most workable denominator of progress for associations which used such widely varying bookkeeping and accounting systems as had been customary before the depression. While many associations individually had the satisfaction of seeing their own assets on the rise before the end of the 1930s, the business as a whole had to cross the threshold of the 1940s before the composite assets started upward. It was, however, the feeling in the business, more than the figures themselves, which testified in 1937 to renewal of vitality in the thousands of savings and loan offices all around the country.

Real estate activity

Real estate activity was by far the most important business index which climbed in the late 1930s. The cycle had once more started upward, and vacancies in residential property were decreasing. Real estate activity had recovered more than 50% from depression lows in 13 out of 19 leading cities in one of the reliable surveys taken. The National Industrial Conference Board, a private organization whose index of rents carried authority, showed that by 1936 the low point in rents was two years past. Not until the "For Rent" and "For Sale" signs began to come down from apartment windows and front yards, however, did the real effect of rising rents make itself felt in increased demand for homes. Looking around them by 1937, association managers in city after city and in nearly every state saw these signs disappearing. As had been the story from all past history of the savings and loan business, significant growth by the associations began when home mortgage loans once again reached a normal level of demand on the basis of a normal public desire to stop renting and start owning a home. Trending steadily upward from 1936, the real estate market never faltered for the next quarter of a century.

Not so auspicious by 1937 were the political indicators. Washington's conscious part in affording the associations a new lease on life had now largely been played. The late 1930s brought little, if any, assistance to the renascent business of savings and loan from the federal government, aside from the working out of the devices already set in motion in the period 1932-1935. Year after year the leaders in the savings and loan business had carefully shaped programs for further improvement of these earlier statutes in the light of experience and of changing economic skies. The legislative strategy was as carefully weighed as it had been in the previous

134

years of high success. The business was better known, its friends on Capitol Hill were more numerous, and its representatives enjoyed perhaps more prestige than ever before. But the climate of Washington had changed with the passing of the more desperate years of depression. The principal legislative aims of savings and loan men were not embraced by the Congress and the President after 1935.

Instead, the victors in legislative conflicts in the later 1930s were more likely to be those who wanted to inaugurate radical innovations in the economic life of the United States. Some government leaders were not too concerned with making something which already existed work a little better. The great following which public housing attracted is a notable example, in the housing field, of the shift of legislative influence. But a curious, almost exact opposite of this reform-and-remake influence in government was the reviving power and influence of the commercial banking business in Washington.

During the depression the reputation of bankers had declined substantially. But the banks emerged into some of their old-time influence with congressional leaders and the executive agencies by the time recovery became an established fact. Commercial banking interests had never been happy about legislation favoring savings and loan institutions, and their dislike for the Federal Home Loan Bank Act has already been pointed out. Now they made their weight felt in strong and persistent opposition to the improvements in savings and loan statutes which the United States League was striving to achieve in the early recovery years.

The combination of inaction on the matters of most concern legislatively to savings and loan associations and the increasingly abundant legislation to entice commercial banks into the home lending field formed the nub of the problem of mortgage lending competition. Through it the savings and loan men had literally to fight their way to justify their place in the economy.

In fact, the world which the savings and loan institutions had known in the 1920s was gone forever. This was true of the market for their services as well as in the method of their own operations. The federal government had initiated a notable type of competition for the mortgage lending services of the associations in 1934 with the establishment of the Federal Housing Administration. This program moved consciously and purposefully to draw on new

135

sources of mortgage money and, what was more harassing to the associations, it held out to the mortgage borrowing public a Utopia of ease in borrowing terms. Looking back, however, one is inclined to question whether or not the savings and loan associations would have moved with such alacrity to avail themselves of their new opportunities in modernized ways of doing business had competition not pressured them to do so.

Survival of conventional lending

By and large, the managers of the savings and loan institutions had always thought of their role primarily in its home financing aspects rather than that as developers of savings and thrift institutions. To men in this frame of mind, the challenge of the strongly competitive mortgage lenders and of new mortgage lending ideas was indeed a call to arms. In analyzing how they met this challenge, one sees how it happened that the conventional home loan survived.

The importance of that survival can be measured by the integral part the conventional loan was to achieve in financing homes for the nation 20 years later. In 1959, 400,000 new homes were built with mortgage credit that savings and loan associations advanced primarily on the conventional loan plan, with no risk sharing whatsoever by the government. It would have seemed highly unlikely in the hotly controversial climate of 1938 or 1939 that this could ever happen. In fact the conventional loan dominated home mortgage financing by all lenders for all purposes so remarkably from 1940 on that the stubborn adherence to this loan instrument by the savings and loan institutions in the later 1930s and their revitalization of it must truly be seen as fortuitous.

Table 9 shows the significance of conventional lending in overall home mortgage lending operations for the 20 years, 1940-1960. At no time in this period did conventional loans constitute less than 64% of the total volume of new mortgage loans—and it was at that level in only two years, 1947 and 1955. In general the postwar years, even after the advent of the VA loan, with its up-and-down popularity, found conventional lending accounting for somewhere between 66% and 77% of the total.

The theory has been advanced by such eminent historians as Arnold Toynbee that a certain degree of difficulty to be met and

*Table 9. Home mortgage lending, by type of loan, 1940-1960
(percentage distribution based on dollar volume of
nonfarm mortgage recordings)*

| Year | All types of lenders | | | Total |
	Conventional	VA	FHA	
1940	81%		19%	100%
1941	81		19	100
1942	75		25	100
1943	80		20	100
1944	85		15	100
1945	89	3%	8	100
1946	74	22	4	100
1947	64	28	8	100
1948	66	16	18	100
1949	69	12	19	100
1950	66	19	15	100
1951	66	22	12	100
1952	74	15	11	100
1953	72	16	12	100
1954	73	19	8	100
1955	64	25	11	100
1956	68	22	10	100
1957	75	16	9	100
1958	76	7	17	100
1959	72	9	19	100
1960	77	7	16	100

*Note: FHA-insured mortgages were first made in 1934; VA-guaranteed
mortgages, in 1944*
*Sources: Federal Home Loan Bank Board, Veterans Administration and Federal
Housing Administration, annual reports*

overcome is essential to the health of nations. It is highly probable that, unwittingly, the federal government provided for the savings and loan associations this necessary counterforce.

Result of competition

Certainly the competition for loans to which the FHA program gave rise had one salutary effect on the entire mortgage lending and mortgage holding sector of the United States. It aroused mortgage lenders from a kind of shell shock from which they were suffering, an outlook of hopelessness about the future of mortgage financing and real estate investment. And for the savings and loan business with its yet vivid memories of foreclosures and losses on real estate, only such a drastic scheme as FHA's high percentage long-term mortgage could have caused the leaders to move on, in their own thinking, to high percentage conventional loans with longer maturities. Everything in their experience in the early 1930s made them dubious of more liberal terms. But the FHA was a reality on the horizon, and savings and loan men faced it with a flexibility and a singularly practical attitude.

The creation of the Federal Housing Administration to carry out the provisions of the National Housing Act was a government move which fathered a severe form of competition for the savings and loan association. It not only stimulated the mortgage lending activities of commercial banks, which was one of its original purposes, but also brought into being and fostered continually and energetically the mortgage banking business as it is known in mid-century.

The title of FHA has always been something of a misnomer. The general term, Federal Housing Administration, could mean many things more appropriately than the insurance operation it has settled down into being. But in 1934 the government was not yet in the housing operation more directly than by its insurance of mortgages. So the title of the new agency did not need to be more specific than to refer generally to its purpose, the stimulation of residential construction.

FHA Title II and Title III

Title II and Title III of the National Housing Act, providing for the insurance of mortgages, and the creation of national mortgage associations to buy the insured mortgages were part and parcel of the same general plan. It so happened that Title II eventually succeeded beyond the wildest dreams of its sponsors and that Title III lay idle on the statute books year after year with no fulfillment except the government-sponsored Federal National Mortgage Association. But together these plans sought to intertwine the home financing process of the nation with the large money markets. They were based on the prospect of siphoning short-term funds (at that time, especially, commercial bank deposits) into long-term real estate mortgages all over the country. Title II actually succeeded in accomplishing this, over the next 25 years, with some—but not spectacular—assistance from the one national mortgage association.

Most savings and loan leaders felt that the FHA approach to getting funds into home building was irreconcilable with traditional savings and loan principles. They were convinced that home mortgage funds should be created out of the savings of the thrifty; that they should be lent out, in the main, in the community where they were saved. United States League spokesmen had fought vigorously—and unsuccessfully—against the National Housing Act which the leaders in the business believed was designed to promote the new and opposite theory.

The scheme embodied in FHA had been suggested in part by the existence of billions of dollars of highly liquid commercial bank assets in 1934. Alongside this economic fact was the obvious lag in home building. Left to themselves, the commercial banks would probably have stayed away from any entanglement with home building at that time. They had done considerable lending on mortgages—on residential and all other kinds of building—in the 1920s; and a great many analysts of their subsequent troubles thought that such lending had been their largest single mistake. But the architects of the Federal Housing Administration had sought to devise a plan that would overcome the banks' reluctance to make home mortgage loans. At the same time they hoped to persuade the banks to make the loans on terms that would permit home buyers to make only small monthly payments, appropriate to incomes still shrivelled by years of depression.

Early FHA terms

The first FHA program relied on loans up to 80% of value for 20-year maturities with interest rates limited to 5% and a 1% premium chargeable on the full amount of the original mortgage loan balance payable as part of the monthly repayment schedule. The total cost of interest plus premiums was not notably beneath the going interest rate on conventional loans at the time. But early eagerness of FHA proponents to get borrowers to use their system developed a habitual negligence about including the insurance premium in references to the cost of the loan. The basic interest rate became the great subject of its advertising. Raiding of mortgage portfolios of the savings and loan associations by FHA-insured lenders was sufficiently frequent to be a real concern.

But during its first few years the Federal Housing Administration mortgage insurance plan was more successful in its publicity than in signing, sealing and delivering home mortgage loans. By the end of 1937—two and a half years after its launching—only 202,704 mortgages were listed as premium-paying FHAs, and the total volume was well below $1 billion. Moreover it was well into 1937 before as many as half of the mortgage loans which were being accepted by FHA for insurance were made for the purpose of new home building. Stimulating home building had been the avowed objective; yet in 1937 only 336,000 new units were started in the whole country—this figure was just a few thousand more than the total of new homes started in 1930.

As a force to stimulate home building, the FHA's first three years were thus negligible. The competition that the insured mortgage system gave to the savings and loan institutions in those years was more a harassment than a dollar volume reality. Meanwhile the United States League, having lost the battle against this new theory, set about the process of helping member institutions to live with it. Leaders urged all associations to get themselves qualified as "approved mortgagees" by FHA.

But there was no question that the majority of the savings and loan managers looked upon the FHA mutual mortgage insurance system as a competitive force of unpredictable strength and quite threatening possibilities. In their minds, government control of the entire mortgage lending apparatus of the country lurked in the shadows. In urging associations to be able to handle any particular loan on the FHA basis, if the applicant wanted it so, the leadership of the business was following the theory that "it is a good thing to have more than one type of merchandise on our shelves." But there was never any doubt about the fact that the shelves should be principally stocked with conventional mortgages.

Decision to compete

This decision to compete with the FHA's insured mortgage system was not arrived at without some dissent. In such a varied and widely experienced group as the savings and loan business it would be, of course, folly ever to expect a unanimous reaction. So it was that one group believed strongly that the savings and loan institutions should go into insured mortgage lending in such volume and with such tenacity as to make it "their" system. Their philosophy was that the times had changed, that mortgage lending had shown itself to be more risky than anyone had ever dreamed before, and that this new instrumentality of the government, regardless of what group of lenders it had been designed for, could be fitted in fairly easily with the old savings and loan mortgage plan. After all, it started with the monthly amortized mortgage, which its proponents had doubtless taken over mentally from the HOLC but which had been originally a savings and loan plan and no other. Interest rates were definitely falling anyway, and it would be only a matter of time before everyone was lending at rates well under the FHA ceiling. Those who counseled this course were also convinced that the savings and loan business, by dominating the lending done under the insured mortgage, could eventually dictate the policies of the FHA. The FHA's original overall insuring authority was only $1 billion. It was easy to see how the savings and loan institutions conceivably could dominate the program.

Although the business as a whole backed away from this course, its spokesmen were successful in getting many changes, suggested by a United States League committee, made in the FHA regulations. This committee was appointed to look into the relations of the savings and loan associations with both Title II and Title III programs. It reported by 1935 that nearly half its recommendations had been accepted by FHA. It was still urging, however, that the FHA be petitioned to stop its representatives from trying to organize national mortgage associations. Actually the futility of trying to start these new groups finally brought that harassing activity to a halt, without any petitions.

Some 1,311 savings and loan institutions had some FHA-insured mortgages on their books by the end of 1937; the figure included 252 which in 1937 made some insured loans for the first time. The FHA's report that year showed a fall-off in the percentage of insured loans made by commercial banks and an increase in the participation of insurance companies and mortgage companies. This subtle change in the attractions of FHA-insured mortgages to the various mortgage lenders was a harbinger of the future turn of events. Up to the end of 1937, associations found that the new factor on the horizon had neither dwarfed their lending opportunities nor become as large a bugaboo on any count as many had feared.

FHA amendments of 1938

The real competition of the FHA scheme to the savings and loan way of life came, however, in February 1938, in the form of significant amendments to the National Housing Act. After this enactment FHA could insure loans up to 90% on newly built houses costing up to $6,000; and even for larger and more costly newly built houses, the loan could be 90% of the value up to the first $6,000 and 80% on the value between $6,000 and $10,000. All borrowers on homes of this price bracket could have up to 25 years to pay off their loans. The effect of the change was quickly reflected in statistics: 42% of mortgages accepted for insurance in 1938 had loan-to-value ratios between 81% and 90%.

The premiums on FHA loans were substantially reduced as a result of this legislation. On the low-cost loans described in the above paragraph the premium was fixed at ¼ of 1%. Subsequent regulations of FHA, promulgated within provisions of the amendments, fixed the premium rates on all other FHA-insured mortgages at ½ of 1%.

The amendments postponed until July 1, 1939, the effective date when FHA should stop insuring mortgages on existing construction, a postponement which was repeated in subsequent years until insurance of mortgages on existing homes became normal. The 1938 amendments also backed with a permanent government guarantee the debentures which FHA contracted to give in exchange for a defaulted and foreclosed mortgage; the previous statute had provided for no such guarantee for mortgages executed after July 1, 1939. The maximum amount of insurance under Title II was raised to $3 billion. The administrator was given the right to lower the ceiling rate to 4½% (he waited until August 1, 1939, to put the new rate into effect but the other changes were significant enough to cut a wide swath immediately through the mortgage lending market).

Moreover, in 1938, FHA faced up to the investing public's total lack of interest in starting national mortgage associations. Consequently there was created with taxpayers' money (through the RFC) a Federal National Mortgage Association. The new agency stood by with the express purpose of buying FHA-insured mortgages whenever the maker did not wish to hold them in his portfolio. As the FHA administrator said in his annual report for 1938, "the fact that they were in the background, as a dependable secondary market, ready at all times to acquire mortgages, undoubtedly encouraged many local institutions to lend more actively. This was particularly the case in areas where some of the lending institutions had hesitated about making loans for more than 80% of the value or for terms above 20 years."

Participation in FHA-insured lending

Table 10 shows the participation in FHA lending by different types of mortgagees during the first five years of the insured mortgage program. The data for 1938 and 1939 show the trend toward mortgage company utilization of FHA. In another two decades mortgage companies were originating 42% of FHAs—a logical result of the encouragement which the system gave to their formation and progress. The table also shows a decline from 16.3% to 10% in the savings and loan ratio to the total during those first five years. Savings and loan institutions thus reached early the approximate ratio which characterized their participation for most of the years to follow.

Table 10. *Institutions active in originating FHA-insured mortgage loans and percentage of total originated, 1935-1939*

Type of lending institution	Percent distribution of gross amount				
	1935[1]	1936[1]	1937	1938	1939
National banks	38.1	28.5	28.4	29.5	25.7
State banks and trust companies	32.1	28.7	25.3	23.7	21.5
Total commercial banks	70.2	57.2	53.7	53.2	47.2
Savings and loan associations	16.3	16.4	14.4	10.3	10.0
Mortgage companies	4.0	10.6	14.3	20.9	23.4
Insurance companies	7.1	6.6	11.2	8.3	10.5
Savings banks[2]	2.3	4.2	2.6	2.3	3.8
All others[3]	.1	5.0	3.8	5.0	5.1
Total	100.0	100.0	100.0	100.0	100.0

[1] Mortgages originated in January 1936 are included in year 1935. The distributions for 1935 and 1936 are based on net totals
[2] Includes mutual and stock savings banks
[3] Investment companies, industrial banks, finance companies, and others
Source: Federal Housing Administration, annual report, Dec. 31, 1939, p. 41

By 1938 the competition for the ordinary home mortgage loan had begun to show its real force. The savings and loan business took a closer look at the situation. It decided that it must compete and make the conventional loan attractive enough to survive. Had the savings and loan institutions not been willing, or able, to take this stand when the real competition came in 1938, ultimate extinction for the conventional loan would easily have been possible. The highly important flexibility of the conventional loan in the variation of money rates would have been lost to the great postwar home building boom. While there was still a fairly low ceiling on the total amount of FHA mortgage insurance in 1938—$3 billion—the pattern had already developed that the Congress would keep authorizing more insuring authority as and when it was sought by the agency. The decision of the savings and loan institutions to regard it, in the main, as a competitor rather than a crutch was possible because they had revived sufficiently by 1938 to put up a fight for their share of the loan business. The will to do so, however, was grounded in the long traditions of the business.

Many years later at a congressional hearing (1958) a representative of the life insurance companies made the flat statement that he felt the responsibility was on the savings and loan associations to explain why they did not make more of their loans through the FHA system! The answer in 1958, as in 1938, was clear: The savings and loan associations did not believe that the home lending of the country should be done primarily with the federal government assuming the ultimate risks and with government personnel making the rules and regimenting the mortgage loan business. It is not an easy concept to defend in an age of expediency, but savings and loan thinking at the top and right down through the rank and file has always been based on a strong belief that a home loan should be an individual transaction between the borrower and the institution advancing the money. The savings and loan bias, if one chooses to call it that, is that there should be the greatest possible leeway in relationships from the time the applicant sits down and puts his case before the lender to the eventual repayment of the mortgage loan.

The savings and loan people of the day could not see how far-reaching their decision would be for the mortgage financing story of the 1950s and 1960s. They rather looked at the situation as it was. They moved cautiously but consistently. The story of how they made their product competitive with the FHA-insured loan was the principal drama in the life of a savings and loan man in that brief period of recovery between depression and war.

Subsidized interest rates

There were other less direct signs in the late '30s that mortgage lending institutions that chose to conduct their business strictly in line with market forces were in for difficulties. The 1938 amendments to the National Housing Act, which drastically liberalized the terms for insuring mortgage loans by a government agency, followed in the wake of a persistent agitation for the lowering of interest rates on the distressed loans which HOLC had taken over between 1933 and 1936. They came, too, at the time when the precedent was being set for forcing interest rates lower in the farm credit field, the next door neighbor of urban mortgage credit. Already by the late 1930s subsidized rates had driven nearly all private capital out of the farm loan market. Savings and loan observers feared it as a forerunner of the same thing in their own field.

Indicative of their concern was a resolution passed by the 1937 convention of the United States League commending President Roosevelt for having vetoed legislation to continue the artificially low interest rate of 3½% at the Federal Land Banks; the legislation was passed over the President's veto and the League resolution called this overriding "unfortunate." The basic tenet of the savings and loan resolution was that the emergency had passed and the time had come for "unqualified return to the interplay of supply and demand factors in the determination of mortgage money rates, farm and urban alike." The men who passed this resolution and many who succeeded them in posts of responsibility in savings and loan associations were not to see such a desired "unqualified return" to supply and demand factors in the determination of mortgage money rates at any time in the following quarter of a century. But the whole plan was young in 1937, and its deep entrenchment was not a foregone conclusion.

Public housing

Out of Washington, in these years when the savings and loan business was recovering, came a yet more disturbing development touching the provision of human shelter in the United States, although its threat to the savings and loan associations was somewhat larger in prospect than in retrospect. This was the United States Housing Authority, established in 1937 to empower the federal government for the first time to use taxpayers' funds to help citizens meet their rent bills. The Public Works Administration of depression days had previously built a few residential projects under public ownership, but these had been planned primarily as a measure to provide jobs for the building trades, and they had not been too successful either in meeting their objective or in their operations. The United States Housing Authority, on the other hand, while its enactment was urged through Congress on the grounds of the need to create employment in the construction trades, was essentially a nondepression measure; it was a precedent-shattering step into new paths of government responsibility.

Realists could only view it as a foot in the door of "nobody knew what" type of government intervention in the provision of shelter for private citizens. Certainly it helped stir savings and loan men to a mightier effort for their continued existence. They were inspired to do more to enable their local home lending institutions to foster home ownership among the less well-to-do as well as among the better-to-do parts of the population.

In a sense, the savings and loan struggle now became a matter of making the performance of the associations justify their existence. Men in the business saw in such successful performance the only way to obviate the threat that many persons of low income would become wards of the state. The savings and loan officer in 1938 saw on his horizon this strange cloud which might change its shape in this or that direction as circumstances came along, but might also destroy the traditional American home ownership system. The 1938 League convention adopted a vigorous resolution not only disapproving public housing but also recommending that the issue of whether or not a public housing project should be built in a particular area should be decided by local referendum. The resolution proposed that local approval be required before federal subsidies could be paid into a community.

The League had been successful in getting some of its suggestions adopted when the original legislation was being debated. These were intended to assure that the buildings erected for public ownership—with rent subsidies part of the plan for their financing

—were subject to fairly low ceilings on costs and thus appropriately devoid of luxury details. The business continued to oppose expansion of the public housing scheme and for many years had a special committee devoted to the subject. This group's aim was to increase the layman's understanding of the true nature of the very complicated scheme which had such plausible publicity. It also explored alternatives to meeting the needs of families with very low incomes but arrived at none which were politically acceptable in those years.

The House of Representatives in 1939 refused to sanction expansion of the public housing program. The fact that a major breakthrough was prevented at this juncture doubtless had a strong influence on keeping the program small until well after World War II. Yet even with this curtailment, the years 1939, 1940, 1941 and 1942 saw publicly financed housing starts amount to more than 10% of the overall total of all homes built in those years.

Chapter 9

Billions

for borrowers

I t was 1940 before the annual lending volume of the savings and loan institutions crossed the $1 billion line. As loan volume began to build back toward the level it had reached in the late 1920s, the business evolved a much-needed system of getting current figures on lending.

Those who rely upon statistics as a matter of course in the 1960s will find it difficult to realize that there was no real measure of the month-to-month performance of the business in those first years after the associations' return to the role of significant mortgage lenders. When the savings and loan business realized that the fight of its life was ahead of it, one of the first things which had to be evolved was some means of establishing how much lending the associations were doing. The annual loan figures published by the United States League secretary-treasurer were not current enough for public persuasion or for creating prestige with the federal government. Nor were these figures specific about the purposes for which the loans were made. Clearly, a current reporting system relying on frequent information from the associations was long overdue.

The United States League undertook this task beginning with December 1935, performing it until the time was ripe for the Federal Home Loan Bank Board to take it over, since it was clearly a proper function of the agency in Washington. The League asked its member institutions to return a fairly simple post card reporting their loans for the month, both dollar volume and number, and classifying them as to purpose in five categories: construction, repair and modernization, refinancing, home purchase and other purposes. Projections were then made for the entire industry on the basis of the figures from the reporting associations. More and more associations took the trouble to report as they began to see the overriding importance of having statistical information. In May 1936, the Federal Home Loan Bank Board's Division of Statistics assumed full responsibility for this monthly mortgage loan study; thus there began the first important statistical series dealing with the contribution of savings and loan associations to the home financing stream.

Rising loan activity

The Board's statistics showed for 1937 an optimistic $897 million of new mortgage lending. While this was scarcely more than one-half of the loan volume associations had achieved in 1929, it was nevertheless noteworthy. It must be recalled that the home lending of all mortgagees was far from spectacular in 1937. Moreover the savings and loan volume was nearly twice that of loans accepted for insurance by the FHA in 1937. A slight dip in loans came the next year, because 1938 was not only the big year of the FHA challenge with its new loan terms, but also a recession year from the standpoint of overall business activity. The Federal Home Loan Bank Board's 1939 statistics showed the associations lending nearly a billion dollars; and in 1940 mortgage lending reached $1.2 billion.

Table 11 shows the mortgage lending of savings and loan institutions from the last year of the previous prosperity period, 1929, through 1941, the last prewar year of unrestricted building activity.

150

Table 11. Mortgage lending of all savings and loan associations, 1929-1941 (in millions of dollars)

Year	Amount
1929	$1,791
1930	1,262
1931	892
1932	543
1933	414
1934	451
1935	564
1936	755
1937	897
1938	798
1939	986
1940	1,200
1941	1,378

Source: *United States League, secretary-treasurer's reports*

Table 12 shows the number of mortgage loans made year by year for the period 1929-1941 and provides a still more meaningful picture of the savings and loan activity during this period; the average loan at that time was considerably less than half the size

Table 12. Number of mortgage loans made by all savings and loan associations, 1929-1941

Year	Number of mortgage loans made
1929	500,000
1930	350,000
1931	300,000
1932	270,000
1933	230,000
1934	232,000
1935	300,000
1936	353,000
1937	397,000
1938	370,000
1939	429,000
1940	445,000
1941	522,000

Source: *United States League*

it assumed by mid-century when home prices had skyrocketed along with a generally higher price level.

At the turn of the decade the savings and loan institutions fought for the billion dollar loan figures. They did it by unprecedented expenditures for advertising and new methods of attracting loans. But primarily what they had to advertise was a savings and loan mortgage arrangement different in several particulars from the common arrangements before the Great Depression.

Management had moved fairly rapidly to eliminate a deep-rooted practice which had proved vulnerable to the depression and which the federal charters had discouraged. The old principle that borrower and saver were in the same boat and should share the institution's good or indifferent fortunes was obviously unacceptable to the new borrower. By 1937, less than 25% of the associations by number and a yet smaller part of the business in terms of assets retained the share accumulation loan.

Ascendancy of direct reduction loan

The simplicity of the direct reduction loan compared with the complicated older savings and loan arrangement was the most telling argument in its favor. A borrower could verify his balance at any time and aim for a definite repayment date. No longer was his time of debt-free home ownership linked in any way with the earnings of the association. The accounting system for the direct reduction loan was not only easier for the borrower to follow but also for the association to maintain. From the point of view of management this latter was a conclusive argument, once the changeover had been made. Savings and loan associations in 1937 were still by and large operating with quite limited payrolls. The long hours put in by management and by the faithful employee group naturally inclined the personnel to look forward to changes in method of operation that would reduce the work involved.

The development of procedures for the efficient installation and use of the direct reduction loan plan was one of the great contributions of the American Savings and Loan Institute. A special course of instruction in the direct reduction loan was devised for use in all the Institute chapters and likewise in the Home Study Division. An important part of the instruction was the new accounting procedure required by the changeover. Where the entire course was not offered in a locality, local leaders of the business, using Institute materials, arranged for two- or three-session forums attended by savings and loan personnel to set forth the practical "how-to" information on what procedures were necessary in a savings and loan office when the old loan plan was abandoned in favor of the new. Clerical help in the office attended the classes along with the managers to learn details of the process.

And here, as in other reforming and reconstructing programs in the savings and loan institutions already described, the Institute's printing and distribution of accounting forms for associations newly on the direct reduction loan paved the practical way for the adoption of the plan. Later, other printers followed the Institute lead and did a substantial business in selling these forms. But when the great wave of changeover to the plan began, only the Institute offered the ledger cards, ledger sheets, passbooks and other implements of direct reduction record keeping. Articles in *Savings and Loans* spread the information and did their bit in persuading thousands of associations to take the step.

The entire leadership of the business was solidly behind the move to make the direct reduction loan as nearly universal as possible. State league and United States League convention programs highlighted it. The considerable prestige of these organization leaders had strong influence toward its widespread adoption. The Federal Home Loan Bank personnel furnished still another persuasive voice in this direction.

Variable interest rates

In predepression savings and loan lending the fixed interest rate—one price for all—had been almost universal. The late 1930s brought into prominence, slowly at first but with increasing attractiveness, the variable interest rate. Under this arrangement the degree of risk on a particular loan was weighed in setting the rate charged for the loan. Thus an association made prime loans at a lower rate than those entailing a greater risk. This was an old and unchallenged practice of the commercial banking world; the only contrary practice is that in government lending. The variable interest rate plan was adopted by associations more and more as they were faced with a choice between it and another competitive "evil," making virtually all loans for a greater percentage of value.

The lower rate served especially as a talking point to the borrower who had a larger down payment to offer. The association could obviously cope with competition more effectively when its policy permitted a lower rate. By 1937 at least one association in four was offering such a variable scale of rates.

Longer maturities

The long resistance of the business to maturities beyond 12 years gradually yielded to the inevitable. Some loans were being made for terms as long as 12 and 14 years by 1937, although typical loans were still under 12 years. The HOLC, it will be remembered, had startled the mortgage lending world with its 15-year arrangement and the FHA had come along with a 20-year maturity to shake all precedent. A deep-seated skepticism about making loans for a term long enough to encompass possibly two dips of the business cycle lay back of the reluctance of managers and boards of directors to embrace such longer terms with unqualified enthusiasm. While recovery was undoubtedly at hand, every savings and loan manager in 1937 and 1938 was especially guarding his practices against a repetition of what he thought had brought on the problems of less than a decade before.

No one could foresee a period of rising real estate activity which never once halted in 25 years following the upturn after the depression. Consequently the decision to make longer term loans was arrived at by much soul-searching and nearly always with great reluctance. As pointed out in Chapter 8, the FHA competition exercised substantial push in this direction. On the other hand, savings and loan leaders acquainted with the counterpart institutions in England were well aware that one of the great successes of the English building societies in the 1930s lay in their embracing a longer term and a lower down-payment schedule than had ever before been admitted to conservative thrift and home financing institution circles in this country.

Service as a competitive weapon

As they looked at their "product," the conventional, nongovernment-assisted loan, in the late 1930s, the savings and loan managers saw one piece of ammunition that they could throw into the battle for home loans with assurance and with telling effect. They could offer an intangible called "service." A man coming to a savings and loan association to apply for a loan could find out within a very few days whether or not he was to get the loan. This kind of quick resolution of doubt was not possible for any applicant who dealt with a lending institution that depended upon a government agency for approval. By publicizing this ability to give the customer good service, friendly treatment and prompt replies, the associations made sure that the refinements in their loan plan did not fall on unattentive ears. If an applicant found he could get about as good a deal from a savings and loan association as he could get from the highly publicized FHA plan and at the same time get the arrangement completed more quickly, the chances were fair he would consider the savings and loan offer seriously.

Declining interest rates

The associations also were lowering gradually the interest charged for their loans in general. When lenders were making even non-FHA loans at 4½%, as some were doing by 1939, savings and loan institutions had to think about the whole problem all over again. Thus it was that 5% became more nearly the common charge for money as the decade rounded out. By 1939 the most typical rate reported at a management conference of the larger associations was 5½%. This decrease in the rate of return on savings and loan lending was revolutionary for that generation. It had been brought to a head through the pressures engendered by the government activities (the HOLC had reduced its interest rate to 4½% in 1939, and it has already been seen that FHA exercised its right to lower the rate to 4½% in the summer of that year).

But even the pressures of politically oriented lending schemes could not have succeeded had not the situation in the financial markets been amenable. The nation was in a period of declining interest rates generally. By the late 1930s the United States had a considerable volume of available capital. Money had begun to flow back into financial institutions. Business had not yet made the kind of comeback which would keep this capital busy. Savers and investors were rapidly forgetting their old fears; and there was enough employment to enable more and more persons to acquire once more a backlog of cash reserves. Monetary policy, as guided by the Federal Reserve

Board, was dedicated to the goal of an abundant supply of available credit to encourage expansion. These were some of the reasons why mortgage lending rates at that time reached new low points in the history of real estate financing in America.

The competition for mortgage loans was becoming keen; thus the late 1930s brought a practice of "pirating" of mortgage loans from one lender's portfolio into another. A provision was eventually put into the National Housing Act that no lending agency could refinance a loan for a borrower without the consent of the present mortgagee. A captive borrower is, however, a doubtful asset of any lending institution. Thus the strongest efforts of the associations had to be directed toward meeting the competition. They had to cope with the interest rate differential which facilitated the pirating of loans.

The period of declining interest rates brought up the whole question of whether or not an association should voluntarily reduce the rates for borrowers who had obtained their loans when a higher rate was prevalent and were still proceeding according to the old contract. Actually, the business never came to any consensus as to whether or not to adopt this policy. Ingenious schemes were put forward by some managers to try to do justice to the older borrowers who might feel they were being discriminated against because they were paying the old interest rate. None of these devices was commonly accepted; and association policy had more and more to be directed to giving new applicants for loans both the longer maturities and the interest rate arrangements which could be termed comparable with other lenders. Both these concessions enabled borrowers to make smaller monthly payments; and the smaller monthly payment along with the higher loan-to-value ratio emerged from the 1930s as the accepted mortgage loan pattern.

Motivations for construction loans

The years 1937, 1938 and 1939 provided new motivations for the savings and loan institutions to go into construction lending. In the 1920s many associations had made loans to builders of homes for sale and many more had made loans to individuals on custom-built homes. In the depression, however, the hazards and the headaches of lending to builders had come to the fore. Especially prominent were the problems arising from the unsold houses of builders financed by the associations. Significantly, Form 7, the application for membership in the Federal Home Loan Bank System (see Chapter 4), developed in 1932, required a specific tabulation of all instances where the applicant institution had five or more loans outstanding to any one individual. Thus long memories of a troublesome field of operation had to be tempered by newly emerging circumstances, if there was to be a widespread return to this activity.

One new circumstance which had to be taken into serious consideration was the public clamor for more home building; it came from both the economists and the government. The contention that the principal brake on home construction activity was a lack of mortgage money found a great following in the 1930s, and this theory has never lost its groups of dedicated adherents. Certainly in the late 1930s it had to be reckoned with as savings and loan institutions sought to re-establish their eminence as important contributors to the general welfare.

From its leaders the savings and loan business got a full measure of prodding to get back into the construction loan business. The United States League's official bodies repeatedly preached the doctrine that the government should not finance any new home building directly, and that there was no need for it to do so. The leadership emphasized that private enterprise was equipped to do

Chart 4. Mortgage lending by savings and loan associations, with percentage distribution by purpose of loan, 1936, 1939 and 1941

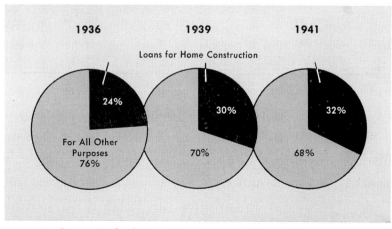

Source: *Federal Home Loan Bank Board, annual reports*

it, and that it would go ahead and disburse the needed money for home building, if it were not hampered by continual changing of the rules and threats of government funds coming into the field. Thus associations in many instances went into construction lending as a pledge of their good faith with the leaders of the business. Gradually, but increasingly, savings and loan dollars were responsible for the sound of hammer and saw and for the sight of skeletons of new houses pointing hopefully toward the sky.

As is indicated in Chart 4, construction loans in 1936 represented only 24% of total loans closed by savings and loan associations. In 1939 they moved up to 30%, and in 1941 to 32%. This category represented both loans made to builders as the construction progressed and those placed on new homes not previously financed. In either case the money advanced meant that a new home had been made possible by savings and loan financing. Table 13 shows the allocation of savings and loan funds by purpose during the recovery years.

Table 13. Mortgage loans made by savings and loan associations, by purpose of loan, 1936-1941 (in millions of dollars)

Year	Home con- struction	Home purchase	Refinanc- ing	Repair and mod- ernization	All other purposes	Total
1936	$178	$230	$178	$65	$103	$ 755
1937	234	327	181	62	93	897
1938	220	265	160	59	93	798
1939	301	340	182	59	104	986
1940	399	426	198	64	113	1,200
1941	437	581	191	61	109	1,379

Source: Federal Home Loan Bank Board, annual reports

Loans made for new construction are the politically popular type of credit. The success of the associations in their effort to maintain their role in the economy was considerably helped by their ability to point to a third of their dollars going directly to the start of new houses and the employment created by such endeavor. Even as late as 1940 the need for jobs in the United States was sufficiently great to influence public policy. Business endeavors were regarded as most significant when they were putting men back to work.

Business reasons for construction loans

Good reasons to regard home construction loans more favorably existed also on the operational side. The most important was the realization that a loan on sound new construction represented the smallest risk which could be undertaken at that time. The trend of real estate prices was a matter for considerable argument within the business, as well as in real estate circles generally and in the appraising profession especially. By 1940 the Federal Home Loan Bank Board was warning all lenders that real estate prices were exceedingly high and that extreme caution should be taken in lending on the basis of current prices. Even in the two years preceding there was a goodly amount of opinion that the peak was at hand. But even those lenders who agreed that construction costs were too high to be sustained were good enough businessmen to know that a brand new house has a better chance of retaining value in the eyes of the public than a house 10 or 15 years old. A strong witness to the superior marketability of a new house was the depression experience.

Moreover savings and loan associations in the late 1930s were still making construction loans on 20% to 25% down payments as a minimum. Only a few were making them with 10% down, with FHA insurance according to the terms of the 1938 FHA amendments. In case a swift downturn in construction costs did come, with its inevitable reflections in the market price of new homes, the association lending on substantial equity did not have to worry too much.

Care in construction lending

In these years the associations picked their builders with extreme care, doling out the money for a house or two at a time as the builder sold those and then went on to build two or three more. More and more associations, as they proceeded in this cautious manner, found that their construction loan plan and prompt service were more attractive to builders than the more highly advertised insured FHA arrangement. In the construction lending field more than in any other phase of the mortgage business, the associations found prompt service to be a superior competitive weapon.

But construction financing required specialized procedures.

Building techniques were in many ways different from those of 10 years before. Furthermore the builders for the most part were new in the field. Thus lending to a builder meant more trouble than a loan on an existing home; it had to be more carefully shepherded by the savings and loan institution. The Society of Residential Appraisers moved to take some of the worry out of this activity with the publication in 1938 of its research project on construction loan procedure. This was a manual providing step-by-step instructions, complete with forms and replete with suggestions about the various stages where inspections should be made. It inevitably led more associations into construction lending with more assurance, for it showed those that had never done construction lending (including brand new associations which never had a chance to make such loans) how to do it.

Moreover the construction loan appealed to the sense of public service which was never far below the surface of a savings and loan man's thinking, even when he had to be most hardboiled in his tactics to keep his institution sound. Most managers felt strongly that their job went beyond the making of loans; they ought to stay with the customer until he had been assured of sound construction and his money's worth in general when he acquired a new house. The extra detail involved in such supervision, they realized would be more than compensated for by the resulting good will. More and more institutions began to follow this line of reasoning. A few began to provide special home planning facilities within the association office so that impartial advice might be given about financing and building costs. Not to be overlooked was the virtually complete innocence of the public at the time about some of the smallest details of home financing which have since become rather commonplace through publications. A whole era of "how-to" literature for the consumer was yet to be written and published.

Finally the construction loan offered itself as an outlet for funds which were beginning to pile up in the associations, at least in some localities, as savings flowed back in the very late 1930s.

When the savings and loan institutions were able to point to more than $1 billion loaned in the year 1940, the leaders in the business could think of that year as the final shaking off of the depression hangover. They could look with satisfaction on their associations as once more a formidable factor in the financing of home ownership. Twenty years later $1 billion was to become a commonplace for loans disbursed in one month. But probably they could not have reached this goal in the postwar period had they not climbed back to something like their former position before the great changes occasioned by World War II engulfed the nation.

Middlemen advertising

Savings and loan men had learned, in this period of neo-prosperity in the 1937-1940 era, how to compete for the available home mortgage lending in their localities. They had learned to do it in a way that had not characterized the business at any time in the past. They advertised for loans in the newspapers. They indulged in considerable solicitation with real estate brokers. They urged existing savings and borrowing customers to tell their friends that savings and loan institutions were good places to get a loan. And for the first time in all of history, a nationwide campaign in publications undertook to promote not the service of one individual association, but savings and loan financing in general. A United States League committee took subscriptions from the associations on a voluntary basis to create a fund for advertising the loan services in professional publications of realtors, architects, building supply people and other middlemen of the home financing business. Over 100,000 of these individuals and firms were in operation. It was estimated that some 85% of all home buyers came in contact with one or more of them before they made the decision about where they were going to finance their homes. The campaign was directed, therefore, toward acquainting these middlemen with what savings and loan associations were already doing and the services they had to offer.

The backbone of the campaign was a series of nine advertisements that appeared in 75 leading building trade magazines and in the United States Chamber of Commerce publication. The project received broad editorial coverage in the business press, and many of the 1,000 subscribing associations conducted local programs to link up with the national drive. The League underwrote the campaign's administrative and promotional expenses so that a maximum of subscribed funds could be used to pay for advertising space. The business was highly gratified with the results of the campaign and attributed much of the growing appreciation of the associations and their services to the educational character of these appeals.

Let local savings finance local building and
NAIL DOWN HOME DOLLARS AT HOME!

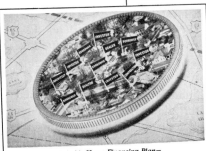

With this Home Financing Plan—
DOLLARS STAY AT HOME
to help local business!

Your Local SAVINGS OR
BUILDING AND LOAN ASSOCIATION

***When you support** Your Local Savings or Building
and Loan Association—**You help local business!***

10,500,000 HOMES AGO
Began the Home Loan that is *Paid-back-by-the-Month!*

Your Local SAVINGS OR
BUILDING AND LOAN ASSOCIATION

***When you support** Your Local Savings or Building
and Loan Association—**You help local business!***

*During 1937-1940 to acquaint
middlemen with the savings and
loan services that associations had
to offer, a United States League
committee undertook for the first
time in history an aggressive
nationwide advertising campaign. Advertisements were placed regularly in
newspapers and in publications of realtors, architects, building supply people
and other middlemen of the home financing business. The advertisements shown
on this page are typical of those used in the middlemen campaign.*

162

Larger mortgage loan portfolios

Encouraged by month-to-month statistics on new mortgage loans, the association managers had similarly gratifying reactions when they looked at the balance sheets of the associations. Mortgage loan portfolios were expanding. By December 31, 1940, the aggregate mortgage loan portfolio of all associations reached approximately $4.5 billion; thus a net gain of something like $1 billion in the combined loan portfolios had been achieved in the five years of struggling back to normal operations. This increase was a prophecy of the bright future which could be confidently expected, if the same vigor and determined effort to get a larger share of the home mortgage lending business continued to dominate the savings and loan thinking.

Table 14 shows the expansion of mortgage loan portfolios in the recovery years.

Table 14. Mortgage loan portfolio of savings and loan associations, 1936-1941 (in millions of dollars)

Year	Loans outstanding at year end
1936	$3,744
1937	3,848
1938	3,919
1939	4,111
1940	4,422
1941	4,796

Source: *United States League, secretary-treasurer's annual report*

Meanwhile changes in the structure of larger American cities were loosening the boundaries of the lending areas which had once been taken for granted as the province of particular associations. The United States League Committee on Trends had highlighted some of those changes as early as 1937; it had commented that the lending operations of some of the smaller associations might be vitally affected. Within a few years a trend toward the voluntary liquidation of some of the part-time associations unable to adjust to the new lending challenges and the merger of some small associations with larger ones bore out this observation.

Realizing the complexities of the times for many of the larger associations as well as the smaller ones, the United States League began in 1938 to issue what became one of its annual services, namely, a group of suggestions on appropriate operating and financial policies to be followed by associations. The suggestions came from the governing body of the League (consisting of savings and loan executives actively operating associations) and were addressed to the boards of directors of the associations.

Policies 1938 was particularly notable for its analysis of the new mortgage lending problems, such as the lower interest rates and more liberal terms probably necessary and the keener competition. *Policies* that year advised directors to meet competition with favorable interest rates and better service; and it also tentatively put forth the thought that associations might liberalize their policies in order to finance the small rental projects being called for by government leaders. Furthermore associations were told they should support the operative builder in order to maintain their position as "financier of the bulk of the country's small homes." While stating that uninsured mortgage loans should remain the principal business of savings and loan associations, *Policies* recognized the existence of applications for loans with very low down payments and for very long terms; therefore, it suggested that loans in excess of 75% of valuation and 15-year maturities should be "rejected or insured."

As new loans and a consistently expanding total volume of home loans in the portfolio became normal in the savings and loan world, the problem of real estate owned receded from its one-time prominence in the manager's concerns. Of course the liquidation of the real estate held depended upon the restoration of a normal real estate market. Real estate activity in the turnover of properties was back at a satisfactory level by 1939, and by that year real estate held by the associations was only 9% of total assets, whereas in 1936 it had constituted 19.9% of all assets (see Chapter 2). To those associations with a substantial amount of real estate yet on their books, the League's Committee on Economic Policies had significant things to say in 1940. It pointed out that no one could tell how long the "present real estate prosperity will last"; therefore, it said, in effect, "get rid of the houses."

Getting rid of the old real estate on the books played its psychological part in prodding the associations' managements into new lending operations. With this reminder of the past era gone or reduced to insignificance, the association executive could think more definitely in terms of the postdepression mortgage market. The ways in which it differed from the 1920s could be studied. For instance, the amortized mortgage had become the norm for all lenders. And the potential demand was glimpsed by a few of the most astute as soon as the figures were released from the 1940 housing census.

Drop in home ownership percentage

In the last days of the congressional session of 1939, a national census of housing had been authorized in connection with the 1940 population census. Questions were asked about the age of the house, the state of repair, whether mortgaged or not, the interest rate on the mortgage, monthly carrying charges on the debt and how long the occupants had lived there. The results showed that the home ownership percentage in the United States was only 43.6%; it had thus taken a downward tumble from the 47.8% achievement reported in the 1930 census. Worse still, the percentage of urban home ownership was down to 37.5%.

The report of the housing census of 1940 did not have the full and immediate impact expected by a very statistics-conscious nation. Before it became public, the United States was well on its way to being entangled with the unpredictable forces of world conflict that were to dominate the decade.

But the savings and loan executives saw in these figures a formidable challenge. When the time was ripe the business was able to offer unprecedented strength and tested facilities for reversing the trend away from home ownership. Savings and loan institutions had already arrived at a place of importance to the community and nation, sufficient to give them a continuing vital role during all the experiments of the government in the war years and all the social adjustments that war brought to every community.

This chapter has attempted to show the major lines of the development of savings and loan associations as postdepression, conventional-lending institutions. The other side of the coin is their emergence during the 1937-1940 period as a formidable contender for the savings of the public. Chapter 10 will review the principal changes in direction which assured this result.

Chapter 10

The comeback
as savings institutions

In regaining a position in the financial world as savings institutions in the later 1930s, the associations were working with the most intangible of all elements in a society of human beings. They had to convince a broad sector of the public that they were a desirable place to entrust money.

The great majority of the people did not know anything about this business, either in its pre- or postdepression phase. They did not know it had any depression experience, much less whether that experience had been good or bad. As Chapter 1 has already indicated, the predepression savings and loan system was never well known nationally, although it had been well publicized in those relatively few areas where it was large and successful. Moreover between 1929 and 1936 comparatively little savings and loan promotion had taken place; certainly nothing of an educational job on a broad scale had been undertaken. (Later on this chapter will take a hasty look at the premature effort of the United States League in 1934 to sponsor an educational campaign.) Meanwhile 12 million men and women had come of age by 1936 who before 1930 had been teen-agers with no thought about saving money. This segment of a new public had now to be added to the large group of those who never had known before 1930 that the savings and loan business existed.

But the savings and loan manager formulating a program for selling savings had to cope also with other characteristics of public opinion. There was of course some real distrust of the savings medium which had gone through the vicissitudes described in Chapters 2 and 7. A rough estimate is that a million or so persons were—at the outside—in this category. Those—and their relatives—who had had funds in savings and loan institutions and had lost a sizable portion of those savings or had had them tied up long and frustratingly might understandably want nothing more to do with these institutions, now or ever. There had been about 10 million savings and loan savers before the depression, and a large majority of them, as has been seen, emerged with a major portion of their money back, even if they had to wait for it, and they received fair earnings on those savings. But the small core of hard-hit savers, disgruntled and skeptical, had to be reckoned with. They added to the intangibles of the situation.

Furthermore in these years there was a wider discrepancy than at any other time—before or since—between the situation of the institutions in good condition and that of the associations in the worst plight. And it was a discrepancy which was quite apparent. There were still 10,000 institutions at the beginning of 1936; most of the work of rehabilitation, consolidation and voluntary liquidation was yet to be completed. In many cases the going association had to make its bid for confidence when its neighbor up the street or around the corner was still wrestling with the worst problems the depression had inflicted on it. So the effort to attract savings in those instances had to recognize that there was skepticism about the desirability of putting money in an association.

Apathy about saving

And there was still another intangible commingled with these other considerations. No one could—or had—really tried to measure the apathy of the people of the U.S.A. in the mid-1930s about saving money generally. Certainly the statistics of the financial institutions as a whole did not indicate that people had returned to the practice of saving money on anything like the predepression scale. By 1937 the dollar amount of savings in savings institutions had increased only 9% above its low point in 1933. About all a surveyor of the scene could be sure of was that the thrift instinct had not been absolutely killed by the depression calamities. Many had thought that the thrift instinct would be virtually obliterated by the disillusionment of bank failures and the pronouncements of many public officials that the accumulation of savings served no useful economic purpose.

Even the mutual savings banks which had maintained a relatively high level of confidence showed an actual decrease in the number of depositors in the year 1936. The life insurance companies had maintained a hold on public confidence all through the economic siege, thanks to the almost negligible attention to those which had gone into liquidation. They were heavy bidders for the savings of the 1930s, de-emphasizing their character as protectors against the risk of death and emphasizing their annuity and other savings arrangements. Life insurance companies were growing steadily, but their performance as financial institutions was not sufficient to assure that people on the whole were willing to save large amounts of money.

The prompt cleaning up of the situation in the commercial banking field with the advent of the permanent Federal Deposit Insurance Corporation program had halted the downtrend of savings depositors in the commercial banking system. But annual increases in savings depositors were well under a million for each of the years 1935, 1936 and 1937.

The United States government was pushing its savings bonds vigorously. Sometimes it indulged in advertising practices which gave the savings institutions the impression that their government was too strong a competitor. The credit unions, recently authorized with federal charters for the first time, were also being strongly advocated by the government agency that was supervising them. Postal savings continued at well over a billion-dollar level, which was due primarily to the depression-bred skepticism of large groups especially in such cities as Chicago and Detroit. But postal savings totals were not showing notable increases.

Challenge of building up savings

Thus the building up of the savings phase of the savings and loan business was a graver challenge in some respects to the combined managements and to their leadership than the re-establishment of the associations as a vital part of the mortgage lending operation. When a businessman fights competition, he can see his problem clearly and pick his weapons accordingly. When he fights an inextricably commingled public opinion of diverse elements, his battle lines are necessarily hazy and undefined.

But the savings and loan man knew this fight had to be made. The decision to stay in the mortgage lending business on the conventional basis, to struggle for savings and loan's place in the mortgage sun, could be justified only if the funds could be attracted to make the loans. And it was crucial to the business that the breakthrough in attracting a substantial flow of funds should come in the four-year period, 1936-1939.

There was a more subtle reason why this was a period of decision than just the obvious need for mortgage lending funds. It lay in the decisions which many men of ability had to make as to whether to pursue their careers in savings and loan or elsewhere. The compelling nature of this decision was due to the modest size of the majority of savings and loan institutions in the 1930s.

Vision of new management careers

The typical institution in 1936 was down to half a million dollars in assets. Fewer than 150 associations had assets over $5 million and these were located in fewer than half of the states. The majority of the units in a large number of localities were those which could not offer a means of livelihood to the manager, much less a promising career—at their present size. But a vision came to several hundred officers of small institutions who were handling the association affairs as a side line. It was this: If they built up their institutions to attractive and profitable size, if they steered them into the main stream of savings accumulation of the country, they could gain personal prestige and enjoy the satisfaction of helping mankind.

Thus it came about that secretaries of many associations of less than a half a million of assets took the plunge, got the institutions federalized and/or insured by the Federal Savings and Loan Insurance Corporation, and started in earnest to build up the savings requisite for a home financing institution which could command respect and make an impression on the public. Had these men decided against a savings and loan career, chosen to do something else with their business talents and energies, those institutions which they represented would probably have been among those consolidated or liquidated in the great programs of reconstruction. When one looks at the present list of very large associations—with assets of upwards of $75 million—and realizes how many of them can be traced to such a decision in the late 1930s, one gets some inkling of the substantial impact of these decisions on the expansion of the business as a whole.

New savings arrangement

The bid of the savings and loan institutions for the savings of the people in this period was in some ways a debut rather than a re-entry, for the savings service that was offered was something new under the sun. With this new service the association had an attractive new outside wrapping, featuring the word "federal" in its own name or in the insurance insignia it carried on its windows. This arrangement also was different enough in character from the pre-1930 savings and loan savings program to prevent most people from seeing any connection.

The new savings account on which the associations based their strongest bid for public confidence was, in the main, an "optional" account. Its availability to the saver who wanted his money back was inherent in the entire planning of the association from that time on. There were new bonus arrangements, fitting the systematic savings account into the new psychology of rewards for perseverance instead of penalties for falling behind. But in the atmosphere of the earliest postdepression years, systematic savings never got much of a foothold. The truly long-term point of view on savings accumulation was not prevalent, nor had it ever really regained any substantial popularity 25 years later.

New advertising techniques

With this new savings service to talk about, the associations started to use advertising techniques such as had never been the pattern in the business before and to spend money for advertising on a revolutionary scale. The United States League *Bulletin* carried this significant message in January 1937: "Institutions which have advertised, which have become liquid, and which are on a reasonable earning basis received money." The obvious hint to the rest of the associations was that they should go and do likewise. And on the whole the associations did. There was a surprisingly ready acceptance by 1939 that advertising cost a great deal and that it had to be bought in sufficient quantities if it was to be effective.

Figures on advertising expenditures obtained from the 1939 management conference held in Chicago show one $10-million association spending $9,000 a year, one $12-million association spending $18,000 a year and one $13-million association spending as much as $31,000 a year. At this conference the manager of one of the new federals protested against measuring the advertising appropriation in terms of size of the institution, pointing out that the amount spent should be geared to the requirements set by competition and to the results achieved. The manager of one association, which had been large before the depression and continued to be large as the '30s came to an end, said that it spent 3% of gross income for advertising for both savings and lending. This was obviously an era when the savings and loan business was looking in every direction for clues to the appropriate amounts to be spent for business promotion, and when there were almost as many ideas as there were managers.

The story of the advertising acumen of the savings and loan associations is not the tale of an overnight growth from naiveté to maturity in advertising thinking. It is the story of an evolution that was still in evidence a quarter of a century later. But its most significant early fruit came in the form of a lengthening line of savers in the late 1930s. Thus a resumé of the early evolutionary stages is appropriate here.

As is the case with treating many other phases of savings and loan operations, it must be noted at the start that some associations had advertised with considerable effectiveness before 1930. Some of them had even used advertising agencies and had their own staff advertising men in the 1920s. Their size and steady growth in those days reflected their employment of professional skills to promote the association, especially its savings services. But in the great majority of associations in the 1920s, even the smallest details of advertising decisions were left to the manager or even to some member of the board of directors, with assistance from the advertising staff of the local newspaper—the medium used most often. Practically everywhere the funds allocated to advertising were a very minor part of business expenses.

Early League advertising aids

The United States League's earliest efforts to encourage more advertising expenditures and advertising programs appropriate to the savings and loan business had begun in 1930, after the League went on a full-time staff basis.

Every annual convention featured an advertising contest in which associations competed by size groups, submitting panels portraying the different advertising devices of the competing associations. These panels were set up in exhibit halls so that interested delegates could look at them. The theory was quite simple—advertising ideas which worked for one association should be passed along to others. Moreover pictures of the winning associations' displays were published in the *Annals* each year so that the ideas could be circulated beyond those who went to the convention and, in theory at least, reach every reader of the *Annals*.

A special committee within the United States League tried to promote the accumulation of a half million dollars for a national advertising campaign in 1934 and 1935. The subscriptions reached some $400,000 but could not be budged above that figure. The National Advertising Committee deducted its expenses for trying and returned the money to the associations. The men in the business who believed the need was so great were bitterly disappointed. From hindsight it would appear that their mistake was in timing. Not enough associations by 1935 were in a financial situation which permitted them to grasp the vision.

Advertising Division

But out of that unsuccessful attempt came the birth of the professionally staffed Advertising Division in the United States League headquarters office. This division officially started operations in April 1935. In the very beginning it made itself useful in the creation of individually tailored programs for savings and loan associations and for cooperative advertising by groups or local leagues in cities and counties. The work was done at cost. First, one young college man who had majored in advertising was the only staff man the division then had. Soon an assistant was attached to his staff, with a similar background of training in advertising. Stock advertising pieces all the way from counter folders to calendars and window displays began to be offered to associations. Several institutions celebrated 50th anniversaries in the mid-1930s, and the earliest jobs of the Advertising Division were centered around the exploitation of the public relations possibilities of those occasions.

There was a concrete witness—by 1936—that people were beginning to look with interest upon the debut of the new savings and loan savings medium. An officer of the American Bankers Association had spoken that year at the ABA annual convention on the outlook for savings. He had seen the need, even then, to combat the competition created by the reviving savings and loan business. His remarks were excerpted and taken out of context and put into an advertising piece emphasizing that "savings and loan associations are not banks."

Several commercial banks distributed this piece which could appropriately be characterized as a "violation of competitive good manners." It made a point of an unfavorable comparison of the FDIC insurance with that of the FSLIC. It was the beginning of a long line of contentious and misleading representations of savings accounts in savings and loan associations on the part of commercial bank competitors. The prediction of a United States League officer, in January 1937, that "our banker friends will forget this sort of foolishness when they have had time to think it over," has, unfortunately, never quite come true.

The advent of the Advertising Department was one of the exciting developments in United States League headquarters because its results were so evident. One could watch the blossoming of more and more savings and loan advertising into sophisticated series of newspaper or radio appeals with punch and salesmanship. This activity gave a lift to all who worked with the business. The Advertising Division designed new stationery for the association clients; it influenced them to use better-quality paper and design; and helped them write letters to be sent out announcing dividends or enclosing year-end statements. The image of the savings and loan association, while not yet a strong competitor in the larger financial world, became an attractive, appealing factor to be reckoned with by all competitors for the savings of the American people. By 1938, there was enough experience and skill in the Advertising Division's staff to make savers sit up and take notice of the thrift services provided by the local organizations.

Newspaper advertising had always been the backbone of the savings and loan appeal for the saver's funds. But the progressive new advertising practices coincided fortuitously with the growth of radio advertising. (At least one association had done radio advertising as early as 1925!) It was estimated in 1935 that 75% of the people whom the savings and loan business wanted to reach had "receiving sets," as radio was called in the more formal discussions. By 1937, the winner of a prize in the advertising contest at the United States League convention was "on the air" for a half hour a week for 39 weeks. By 1939, enough associations were radio advertisers to merit having a special award for that category in the national advertising contest. That year, too, saw radio advertising listed as one of the three recommended media for a small association by the Advertising and Business Development Division of the League.

Savings statistics

There was an urgent need for information about the actual inflow of money into savings and loan associations in these recovery years. Both the Federal Home Loan Bank Board and the United States League had concentrated their first statistical efforts upon mortgage lending figures, for the simple reason that they needed such data most in order to establish the picture of a large contribution to home financing. By 1938, however, the business needed to know how its efforts to rebuild confidence were succeeding—regardless of whether there was any major public good will to be gained from some actual figures.

As a beginning, a simple post card requesting the association to fill in figures on new money received during the quarter was sent out by the League in 1938 to a representative group of associations. In its *Bulletin* in June, the League reported that 998 associations had answered and that their net increase in savings for the first quarter of 1938 was 41.5% larger than for the same period in

1937. The group that returned the questionnaires had total assets of about $1.5 billion (this was nearly 25% of the total assets, and thus the figures represented an adequate cross section).

It took time to get this reporting system on its feet; fewer associations sent in the data for the second quarter, but those that did reported a net increase in savings 39.2% greater than for the second quarter of 1937. By the close of the year this embryonic reporting system and the financial statements that came into League headquarters combined to convince the leaders of the business that a large number of savings and loan institutions had made a notable showing in attracting new money during 1938. Furthermore that year, as pointed out in Chapter 3, associations retired some of the depression-years government investments in their shares ahead of schedule and thus gave *prima facie* evidence that they were getting a more than sufficient flow of funds from the public to maintain their place in the mortgage lending field.

Data on the inflow of savings month-by-month was not to be available for all savings and loan institutions for some years to come. Some official figures on certain sectors of the business are examples, however, of what was happening.

Table 15 presents indexes covering the years 1935-1940 of the savings invested in a group of federal savings and loan associations.

Table 15. *Indexes of private savings in a fixed group of federal savings and loan associations (average month 1936 = 100)*

Date	Index of amount of private savings	Percent increase over preceding year
June 30, 1935	91	%
June 30, 1936	100	10
June 30, 1937	114	14
June 30, 1938	133	17
June 30, 1939	165	24
June 30, 1940	205	24

Source: Federal Home Loan Bank Board, annual reports

It is a measure of the relative flow of funds into federal associations during these five years.

Not even this skeleton measure of new savings is available from those years for other than federal associations. The Federal Savings and Loan Insurance Corporation did make a special study, however, to get an accurate account of the growth of associations insured by the Corporation during its early years. The study covered the two years from December 31, 1936, to December 31, 1938. It developed the fact that the savings in 1,383 identical associations rose by 29% in that period. The overall statistics as published at the annual convention of the United States League in Atlantic City in 1939 substantiate the story. In 37 of the states and the District of Columbia, assets of savings and loan associations had increased in 1938.

By 1939, the Federal Savings and Loan Insurance Corporation was gathering monthly figures on savings inflow for all insured associations. Table 16 shows the substantial flow which such associations experienced in 1939 and 1940.

Table 16. *Flow of savings in FSLIC-insured savings
and loan associations, 1939-1940
(in thousands of dollars)*

Year and month	New savings	With-drawals	Net inflow
1939	$557,200	$311,382	$245,818
January	79,100	43,000	36,100
February	37,800	21,000	16,800
March	39,500	21,600	17,900
April	37,800	21,600	16,200
May	36,700	18,800	17,900
June	40,700	15,800	24,900
July	74,300	52,200	22,100
August	44,900	27,200	17,700
September	36,800	29,000	7,800
October	41,200	24,200	17,000
November	40,000	19,537	20,463
December	48,400	17,445	30,955
1940	$708,650	$406,552	$302,100
January	102,571	57,096	45,475
February	55,332	28,042	27,290
March	51,377	27,195	24,182
April	55,809	28,123	27,686
May	46,655	27,150	19,505
June	43,626	20,418	23,208
July	86,496	73,111	13,385
August	51,025	36,060	14,965
September	46,203	30,928	15,275
October	53,982	30,286	23,696
November	49,990	25,278	24,712
December	65,586	22,865	42,721

Source: Federal Home Loan Bank Board, annual reports

The flow of savings to associations had brought their total savings by the end of 1940 to more than $4.5 billion (see Chart 5 and Table 17).

Chart 5. *Total savings of savings and loan associations, December 31, 1935-1940*

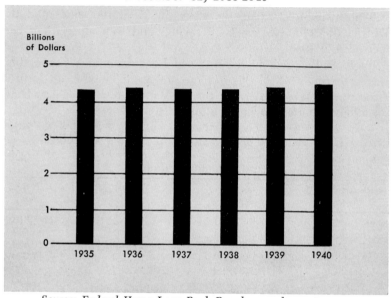

Source: Federal Home Loan Bank Board, annual reports

Table 17. *Total savings of savings and loan associations, December 31, 1920-1940 (in millions of dollars)*

Year	Total savings	Year	Total savings
1920	$1,890	1930	$6,296
1921	2,168	1931	5,916
1922	2,507	1932	5,326
1923	2,957	1933	4,750
1924	3,575	1934	4,468
1925	4,132	1935	4,310
1926	4,751	1936	4,356
1927	5,456	1937	4,339
1928	6,172	1938	4,338
1929	6,782	1939	4,369
		1940	4,542

Sources: 1920-1929, United States League; 1930-1940, Federal Home Loan Bank Board

Changing advertising appeals

The advertising of the savings and loan associations was beginning to place more and more emphasis on the soundness of the institution, its record and the quality of management. The government connection of the institution was no longer the main thread of the advertising story. Increasing numbers of associations were arriving at that point where they could stand on their own merits rather than on the shoulders of government. This development was a milestone in the postdepression history of the savings and loan business; and it was evident before World War II came.

The savings and loan institutions had entered the postdepression era with a savings plan that had one new emphasis above all others. As one member of the Executive Council of the United States League wrote in *Savings and Loans* of February 1940, "It seems to me that the public demand for liquidity is so definite and certain that any association that expects to go forward must bow to the inevitable and provide availability." He recalled that in pre-1930 promotion of savings and loan availability had ranked a poor third in the order of appeals, with safety and earnings the main props of the solicitations for savings in those years.

This new characteristic of the savings and loan account had to be sold to the public in subtle, often quite modest, statements. For there was within management a still widely prevalent apprehension that another period such as the early 1930s might make performance fall far short of promises. However since associations paid on demand millions of people had the practical experience of getting their money out without any delay or difficulty. This was more telling testimony than any carefully worded advertisement could have provided. In this respect, it was perhaps fortuitous that the unsettled international affairs at the turn of the decade created an opportunity for some heavy withdrawals. That associations were able to meet withdrawals enhanced their reputation as savings institutions.

Once the business had accepted the need that a savings and loan account be readily available to a withdrawing accountholder, it was indeed offering a new product. What had to be done concomitantly was to provide the necessary liquidity by carefully planned operational policies. How this was accomplished will be part of the theme of Chapter 11.

Chapter 11

New

directions in management

$\mathbf{A}$s early as 1937 the men who kept an eye on the broad trends were pointing out the remarkable difference between the associations emerging into normal operations at that time and the typical association only six or seven years before. In the years of struggle for the very existence of the business, the roles of boards of directors and of the full-time operating staff had also evolved along lines which were significantly different from what they had been for a hundred years.

With this change in the nature of savings association operations, the need for wage and salary standards that would attract well-qualified men to operate the associations became apparent. The late 1930s also saw the beginning of the movement toward appropriate titles for the men at the top in day-to-day operations. Thus the "secretary" became the "executive vice president" in an increasing number of institutions. (At this time the term "president" was still largely reserved for the presiding officer of the board of directors rather than for a man devoting full time to the association.) It took another decade to bring the title "president" into more general acceptance for the head of the savings and loan association, as had already been the customary designation in commercial banks for a long time.

Along with the upsurge of interest in management came a re-examination of the function of the board of directors. It would be useless to argue that there had ever been a clear-cut line of demarcation between the board's functions and those of the secretary in a savings and loan association. A workable division of authority in chartered financial institutions is a product of time and experience, and savings and loan associations had not thought of the secretary as the executive officer during their first century of existence.

One of the gradual but pivotal changes which the late 1930s brought to an increasing number of associations was the adoption of the philosophy that the responsibility of directors was to "lay down broad policy and to hire capable executives to carry it out." Out of this developing point of view was born the concept of a savings and loan manager, a man responsible for all operations. This distinction could be made between policy and operations in the 1930s because for the first time the directors had some real policy matters to decide. Up until the 1930s there had been little more for the agenda of directors than the minutiae of everyday operations.

Decision to grow

The fundamental policy decision to promote the growth of the individual association day in and day out had been made when the associations decided to battle to keep their institutions in the mortgage loan business with the conventional loan as their chief stock in trade. This battle could not be waged on a hit-and-miss basis, making loans available only as the funds happened to be on hand. As Chapter 10 has noted, the decision to improve the loan terms and to seek out loan business meant that the association would also be seeking savings all the time. The association was obliged to do this in order to take care of the loan demand. This point of view amounted to a commitment to promote steady expansion.

It is important to realize that such a commitment had been less than prevalent in the savings and loan sentiments of predepression years. While many acquired the taste for steady growth in the 1920s, a large body of thought within the business still persisted by 1930 that there was a limit to the size which a savings and loan association could attain and still keep its close personal touch. The story is told of the first president of the United States League who declared in the 1890s that he would be alarmed if at any time his association got over $1 million. There were many as late as the 1920s who thought the same way about getting into the multi-million dollar class.

Intimately intertwined with the move for growth were far-reaching judgments about financial policies. The directors had to arrive at practical conclusions about the liquidity ratio to be maintained. the rate of return to be paid to savers and the reserves to be built. And these determinations, although in a sense separate, were closely interrelated. Certainly in these choices the savings and loan business from the mid-1930s on proceeded in a different direction from its former course.

Liquidity policy

The association had to have a liquidity policy that would permit it to offer its savers the prompt availability of their funds. Relatively few had faced such a necessity up to then. True, there had already been questions in the minds of some of the most forward-looking executives of savings and loan associations as early as 1930 about whether or not the associations were pursuing a wise policy by having so little liquidity. The conventions of predepression years featured discussions of the so-called "problem of secondary liquidity" in which some savings and loan leaders recommended the holding of a certain type of investment which could be liquidated quickly but would still bring the association some nominal return. Thus with liquidity, as with many of the other changes in savings and loan policy in the late 1930s, the policy change was not entirely a revolutionary result of the Great Depression. The depression and its woes had dramatized the need and pointed up decisions in a definite direction where hitherto there had been hesitation between different points of view.

The emergence of the optional savings account as the main instrument for building up an association's savings was, of course, a strong influence in reshaping liquidity policy. The optional savings plan called for "reasonable" liquidity regardless of economic conditions. It implied the need for continuing ability to pay out relatively large sums of money to savers withdrawing all or part of their accounts at any time and on dates not particularly related to periods when earnings were being distributed or accounts were maturing.

A minimum of 10% to 15% of assets in cash or highly liquid investments, such as government bonds and Federal Home Loan Bank deposits, became the norm for the association which wanted to be on the safe side. It was a policy that often brought lively discussions in board meetings, since it was new and costly. Besides this major allocation to liquid assets, the consensus was that an association should retain for emergencies between one-third and one-half of its credit line at the Federal Home Loan Bank. Within the broad policy framework laid down by his board, the full-time operating officer was more and more given a free hand to decide how to maintain these normal ratios.

Part of the reason for the increasing membership in the Federal Savings and Loan Insurance Corporation at this time, even by those state-chartered institutions which did not particularly need the FSLIC to restore confidence, was the wish to minimize "scare" withdrawals at any future time. The FSLIC insignia quickly became accepted as a witness to the soundness of the institution, and it thus turned the savers' thoughts away from withdrawals.

Rate of return to savers

But liquidity of this magnitude meant that there would be a sizable portion of the association assets that were not adding very much to income. Thus the policy decision by the board of directors to place availability first led to another necessary choice: What would be the appropriate rate of return to accountholders? In fact, throughout the quarter of a century succeeding the depression, association directors had to make their most frequent decisions on this one matter of the rate at which earnings were distributed.

Accountholders were receiving an average of 3.5% in 1937, the year when the recovery signs were clearly evident for the first time. This rate was lower than the association directors would have

184

chosen to pay, given the same net income to distribute in, say, 1930 or 1931. The decision to keep the rate at that low level was a difficult one to make because association boards were made up of a majority of the men who had been on them before the depression. They were trained in the tradition that savings and loan attracted savings by paying as high a rate as possible. The person (whether the manager himself or some leader in state or United States League) who advised the members of the board of directors at a time of slow savings receipts to offer only 3½% seemed less than a Solomon.

But the battle was gradually won by the realists. The door was opened to the direction in which the savings and loan business must inevitably march to realize its destiny in the next two decades. The old cleavage between the two schools of thought in the business—the in-and-out savings account concept of operation as against the long-term investment concept of the savings and loan association—was resolved by practical considerations from 1936 to 1938. The great opportunity and necessity of the times was for associations to become primarily thrift institutions reaching out to the great mass of savers rather than for them to resume the status many of them had formerly had as more select investment institutions. The shift was away from attracting money primarily from those who expected a higher than common return on savings.

The downward trend of the rates from the 5%, or higher, pre-depression level had already set in during the early recovery days. Many of the newly organized federals distributed their first earnings at 4% per annum, a startlingly low figure to those accustomed to the older days. But the succeeding years of the mid-decade, characterized by lower money rates generally, emphasized the need for a still more drastic realignment of rates savings and loan associations paid to their members. The president of the United States League, speaking to the 1938 convention, described it as the year when both the associations and "the other people" in the country changed their ideas about the return they should get on the money they saved. By 1939 the most frequent rate was 3% and reductions were being planned to 2½% by many associations. One of the public relations problems commonly discussed in 1939 was whether or not the shareholders at savings and loan associations should be notified six months in advance if the institution was planning a reduction of the rate of return.

The impetus toward reserves

Almost as much of a new direction as the change in liquidity emphasis and in rate of return was the impetus to build up reserves. Again this policy change had to be made by the directors. The verdict was often arrived at after healthy disagreements, with the pros and cons frequently tied to the rate at which earnings would be distributed. The seasoned board of directors, whose service dated back to the 1920s, had been steeped in a background of "pay out earnings as much as possible."

Reserve accumulations showed the results of that policy. At the end of 1930, the surplus and undivided profits—as they were then listed in the composite balance sheet—amounted to only 3.11% of the total assets of the business. Research into the performance of a representative cross section of associations showed one reason why: In 1930, 91.3% of earnings had been paid out to accountholders. It has already been seen that the business quickly became reserve conscious during the depression and that state legislatures, prodded by the savings and loan supervisors and the more forward-looking leagues in the business, began to push a policy of building up reserves. By 1937, accountholders were getting only 77.3% of the earnings in the annual distributions of the same associations studied for 1930.

The relationship of the rate distribution of earnings to progress in reserve building was given careful study by the Federal Section Committee of the United States League in 1941. The group studied what had happened to reserves in a representative group of associations that had reduced their rate of return to savers between June 30, 1936, and June 30, 1937. They found that in 16 of the 18 states from which sample associations were surveyed, reserves increased more rapidly where the rate of return to savers was revised downward.

The normal bench mark for reserves came to be regarded in the early years of the depression as somewhere between 5% and 10% of total liabilities. In later years, when the losses from real estate could be more definitely assessed, it was realized that between 12% and 15% was a much more realistic figure.

After the Federal Savings and Loan Insurance Corporation got underway and attained substantial membership, its requirements for allocations to reserves became a handy criterion for associations whose boards of directors recognized the need for greater reserve strength. The Corporation's regulations provided that an insured association must allocate an amount equivalent to 3/10 of 1% of insured accounts annually to reserves in order to build toward the required 5% loss reserve by the end of the 20th year of insurance. The percentage of reserves which had to be attained year by year, between the fifth and 20th year, specified in later regulations was not then in effect, but the 3/10 of 1% formula for allocations dates from 1935. It was, of course, always a minimum allocation—never a maximum. And it helped the directors— of even uninsured associations—wrestling newly with the problem of allocations to reserves to get some idea of the appropriate amount.

While many of the reserve policies which came into being in the mid-'30s were shaped by indirection and circumstance rather than by theorizing, one widely accepted reserve building formula was born in theory. It related reserve allocations to lending volume and was fathered by the United States League staff. The staff found it helpful as an answer to the association executives voicing the simple question from their board rooms, "How do we determine how much to put in reserves?" The proposal was simply to add to reserves for any accounting period a discretional amount, say 1% of every new loan.

This formula was attractive because it had a tendency to build an adequate fund more rapidly than the FSLIC formula related to a percentage of total savings accounts. There was at that time a substantial concern that the next depression in real estate would occur before an adequate reserve had been accumulated. This was a prudent worry for men operating financial institutions with other people's money. There has been no real estate depression from that day to this, but the entire focus of savings and loan thinking had shifted definitely to the need for a strongly reserve-girded institution. And the fears which prompted men in the mid-'30s to start building higher reserves played a most significant part in strengthening the business.

New concerns for boards of directors

With stands to be taken on such far-reaching and fundamental policies as those described above, the board of directors of a savings and loan association had indeed a new direction for its activities. The question of whether to hold a weekly or a monthly board meeting was often debated, with the monthly meeting emerging as the most logical. An executive committee of the board to work more directly with the managing executive in the interim was a frequent solution. But monthly board meetings meant above all that the manager, whatever his title, made the day-to-day decisions in the "shop." The secretary in the old days had far from complete authority for hiring and firing. In the years of recovery and new directions more and more managers acquired complete freedom in dealing with personnel.

One of the larger functions of the board in the earlier days had been to look at loan applications in detail and decide which loans to make. A conspicuous step ahead in the division of functions between the manager and the board came when the management and staff were given the responsibility for making the loans. As the recovery period developed the board began to set loan policies, creating a broad framework within which the full-time people in the association could work. The executive committee had various degrees of responsibility in passing on loans. It generally ended by becoming a referee on any doubtful loans but seldom had the full control over all loans which had once been the board's function. In an era when service and quick "yes" and "no" decisions on loans were among the impressive savings and loan appeals to the borrower, it would have been unthinkable to continue so cumbersome a system as holding up approvals on all loans until directors or an executive committee met.

Even then there were beginning discussions of a retirement plan for the staff, although it would be another eight or nine years, with a world war intervening, before almost universal interest in this program developed. But the debut of the retirement plan into board of directors' discussions meant that management of an association was beginning to be regarded as a career. The membership of the secretary on the board of directors had not been too frequent a circumstance in the savings and loan business, but increasingly in these late 1930s the manager was elected a director and thus became a component part of the board.

The same period saw an urge toward stronger association directorates. Those institutions which were out in front in their efforts to mold a new image for community acceptance sought out more prominent and successful men from the general business community to serve on their boards, alongside the more familiar type of director from fields closely related to savings and loan—real estate, construction and insurance. The addition to the board of men of responsibility and status from other fields made it all the more imperative that the board's concerns be matters of policy such as those described in this chapter rather than the irksome operational details which had been the major concern in earlier times.

Other fundamental changes in direction were toward smaller boards (unwieldy boards of 20 or more were not uncommon before the depression); toward more appropriate attendance fees at board meetings (traditionally these were nominal); and prestige-bearing directors rooms. As association after association changed its physical environment to include a more attractive and adequate building, special emphasis was placed on directors rooms planned with interior decorating skill and equipped with the type of furniture which was appropriate to a policy-making body of men of substance in the community.

New office quarters

The new physical appearance which savings and loan associations took on in these years of their renaissance was invaluable in the establishment of their prestige. It, too, was part and parcel of a new concept of management and of that management's new vision for the institution itself. Certainly nothing had more to do with the public's recognition that a savings and home financing institution was functioning in its midst and expanding for greater service than the very simple device of modernizing the appearance of the office quarters. One of the things for which 1938 was especially remembered was a "wholesale rehousing" of the business. But this rehousing took place mainly because of the new direction in which management moved—the carrying out of the concept of savings and loan management as a career.

A comparatively few associations had owned their own buildings in the 1920s. Now many larger associations practiced the home ownership which they preached and acquired their own buildings —not often very pretentious ones, but normally two- or three-story structures with perhaps some space to rent out to another company on the third floor. Smaller associations modernized the quarters they already had or moved into new space; being on the street-floor instead of upstairs gained a new recognition for many of the associations. A few were able to get bargains in new office quarters because of the number of vacant former bank buildings which were still to be found in many communities. In summary, approximately a thousand associations moved into different quarters between 1938 and 1941.

The move was motivated by factors other than those inspiring public confidence. One was the very widespread tendency for associations for the first time to have offices of their own instead of sharing those of a real estate company, insurance office or even of a commercial bank. The Federal Savings and Loan Insurance Corporation had made it a requirement for insurance of accounts that the association divorce itself from an office tie-in with another type of business.

There was also a need for more space than the older type of savings and loan institutions had used. The many new federal instrumentalities with which most of the associations had some connection brought requirements for more record keeping in the association. The new concept of management had its effect upon the need for space, since an executive vice president with the new vision of the late 1930s needed either a private office, or at least a larger private nook of the general office, for the work he had to do apart from talking to customers.

New directions in supervision

Savings and loan management in the recovery era had to adjust to a somewhat new direction in supervision. These first recovery years underscored, at some times more than others, the divergent points of view of supervision and management. The president of the United States League in his address to the 1935 convention had stated: "When disagreeing with some of the proposals of the Federal Home Loan Bank Board and when insisting upon certain proposals of our organization, to which opposition is voiced by the Board, conflict of opinion between the League and the Board was at all times the *logical and sincere result of a viewpoint* on the one hand, of the industry being supervised and regulated and on the other hand, of a body charged with the public responsibility of administering supervisory and regulatory laws which they deemed in the public interest."

What this able speaker and thinker did not spell out was the even more basic philosophical difference between the supervisor and the supervised. The particular purpose of the supervisor is always first and foremost to protect the public interest. His primary concern is to avoid difficulties in the supervised institution, and such a concern may be a damper on experimentation and on the search for new avenues of service. On the other hand, management of any business whether supervised or unsupervised, if it is enlightened management, keeps always in the foreground the building up of the business, the increase of customers and the expansion of services to meet new opportunities. Supervisors are guardians and managers are builders; and the cleavage between the two points of view is fundamental.

The recovery period emphasized this divergence. The relationships of management with the relatively infant federal instrumentalities in the savings and loan business, which were manned by literally hundreds of new personalities, were subjected to much trial and error. Judgment was required as to the lines of distinction between supervisory functions and management functions. State supervision having been considered lax in many jurisdictions before the depression, the personnel of the federal agencies were often motivated toward the assumption of prerogatives once sacrosanct to management. Undoubtedly they hoped to avoid the pitfalls which had plagued the supervisory agencies only a few years before.

Association managers, for their part, often felt that the government supervisory agencies were operating on the assumption that each and every savings and loan practice was subject to improvement and ought to be changed. A controversy over the right of the Federal Savings and Loan Insurance Corporation, for instance, to circumscribe the advertising of all insured associations took a long time to be resolved in order that associations might be able to retain some of the advertising advantages of being insured. The United States League wrote its members in 1939 that the insurance of accounts was finally becoming an "insuring rather than a reforming activity." This outcome was important because many associations thought the main reason for their having insurance was to be able to feature it to some extent in their promotion. Some important persons in the Insurance Corporation had contended on the contrary that associations would make insurance a perpetual prop in their business development procedures and turn their backs on all other financial policies required to build their strength.

One way in which a clearer and more workable relationship was evolved was the Federal Home Loan Bank Board's policy of bringing experienced savings and loan managers to Washington for half-year tours of duty as acting governors of the Federal Home Loan Bank System and in other assisting capacities to the Board. Some of the Federal Home Loan Bank presidents, always considered more understanding of the point of view of management of the association than Washington personnel, held these temporary posts as well as a few active managers of associations. Conferences of the Federal Home Loan Bank presidents, held in Washington at the offices of the Federal Home Loan Bank Board, played their part in acquainting the Board and its personnel with some of the facts of life at the association level, a knowledge which led gradually but surely to a relationship of greater mutual respect between supervisor and supervised. The Bank presidents, chosen by the regional Banks' boards of directors, most of whom were savings and loan men, enjoyed, on the whole, significant confidence of the business. Many former association managers were brought into the examining staffs and they did much effective work in smoothing out the differences between supervisors and managers. The give and take, the mutual eye opening, of such programs served the business well.

The process of regulation making

An accommodation of the relationships of the savings and loan managers with the federal instrumentalities was increasingly possible because of an improvement in the late 1930s in the way in which regulations emerged from the Federal Home Loan Bank Board and the Federal Savings and Loan Insurance Corporation. When one sees the original statement in the Federal Savings and Loan Regulations—"the Board expressly reserves the right to alter, amend or repeal these Rules and Regulations in whole or in part" (October 1934 edition)—one can realize how far the agencies had to travel to reach the acceptable arrangements for putting regulations into effect which existed when a quarter of a century had passed. The more reliable and practical procedures for the adoption and amendment of regulations did not just happen; they were the result of a long series of consultations between savings and loan leaders and the Federal Home Loan Bank Board. Both the United States League through several of its committees and the Federal Savings and Loan Advisory Council were significant contributors to a happier situation.

It should be remembered, too, that the last half of the 1930s was a period fraught with some concern throughout the entire business community over the whole matter of administrative law. A long struggle was carried on through two Congresses to get definite laws adopted to give business concerns, subject to the increasing body of administrative law, the right to court protection against the usurpation of power. While the legislative moves were not successful, they had a salutary effect upon attitudes and procedures in the agencies.

Name changing

The business which was evolving such definitely new directions in the functions of the board of directors and in the concept of the manager's job went through a substantial period of name changing from the late 1930s up through the 1940s. Simplification of association names was recognized in the recovery period as a prime need. The name should, above all, give the impression of the type of institution which the new directions were creating, a thrift institution with a forward vision. Furthermore public acceptance of the individual institutions in a system with growing national prestige was obviously going to depend on the various institutions bearing a more nearly common identification. In the late 1930s "savings and loan association" was becoming increasingly the typical designation. In 1939 the United States League gave impetus to this trend by changing its title from United States *Building* and Loan League to United States *Savings* and Loan League.

In general, titles of associations were shortened for simplification. In the case of state-chartered associations, even greater simplification was possible than in the case of federals. Many associations dropped personal or church names that had been part of their titles in favor of terminology more appropriate to financial institutions. The many mergers of the 1930s afforded opportunity to modernize nomenclature. Where there had been a reorganization, a new name was definitely part of the program to restore confidence.

New League services

Just as there were new directions in management of the individual association, so the trade organizations in the business adjusted their aims to a new day and found themselves quite busy with new undertakings. This was true in the state leagues to some extent but more especially with the United States League. Its professional staff had been augmented both in size and effectiveness. By 1938 the League and its affiliates, the Institute, Advertising Division and Society of Residential Appraisers, had acquired a full-time staff of around 50 persons. In 1941 approximately a quarter of a million miles of travel by the staff was chalked up, 600 individual calls were made on associations, 137 state and regional meetings were covered, and mass mailings from the League averaged one every business day. Such was the active liaison between the personnel of the national trade organization and the savings and loan associations, as growth of the business and its newly attained vigor gave impetus to an ever-expanding network of new refinements in operations.

The savings and loan business as a whole, as it continued to study internal operations with an eye for improvement, was relying more heavily on research. The United States League responded in 1939 by establishing a separate, full-time research department. Through its facilities League committees could undertake more comprehensive projects. In its first year, for instance, the research department made studies for the Committee on Trends covering "Liquidity Policies and Problems," "Size and Plan of Operation" and "Public Attitudes Toward Savings and Loan Associations." It collected data preparatory to the development of a general savings and loan index, and made the first analysis ever attempted of the place of savings and loan associations in the savings structure of the country. Meanwhile its operations enabled the League to add materially to its usefulness as a source of savings and loan statistical information.

The League had been gradually building its library into a reliable collection of savings and loan reference material. It included state league and federal agency reports along with books, periodicals and other published material relating to all phases of the business and to the general fields of economics, housing and finance. In 1939, for the first time, a professional librarian was

194

engaged to help develop the service to its full potential to members and to the general public.

A growing list of publications attested the League's extended capacity for service. *Savings and Loan Principles,* a 700-page, hardcover book was published in 1938, giving detailed information on the policies, procedures and problems of managing a savings and loan association, and also covering the historical development of the business. It went into use immediately as a textbook for Institute classes, replacing a text written in 1925. Outside the classroom it also won solid acceptance as a fundamental interpretation of the business, having been co-authored by the League's executive vice president and the director of education and research of the Institute.

In 1937 the *Legal Bulletin* of the League which had been initiated in 1935 on a subscription basis began to be circulated, as part of the League's membership service, to lawyers of associations, as well as to managers. It included significant developments in savings and loan legislation, litigation, regulations and legal opinion—in an era when there were beginning to be many more such developments than there had been before. The same year saw the inauguration by the League of an entirely different type of publishing venture, *Home Life* magazine, a syndicated house organ produced by the Advertising Division and bought by associations for circulation to their customers. Because of large-scale production which reduced unit costs, it was brought within the financial reach of even the smaller institutions. Professionally edited in the style of leading consumer publications, it caught on quickly as part of the permanent promotional program of the business.

In the spring of 1941 the United States League moved to the entire 23rd floor of the skyscraping LaSalle-Wacker Building in Chicago, the site of its present headquarters. In the previous 10 years the League had had three different locations, finding it necessary every three or four years to move in order to expand its space. With the recovery years the leaders of the business foresaw that the League must be prepared to expand periodically, as the business itself grew. Thus they abandoned the policy of "just enough space to get by" and followed the lead of many of the associations themselves which were beginning to plan at least five years ahead in their space arrangements. Because the country was at war in less than a year and office space proved scarce along with almost all physical things in that era of limping production on the domestic front, the move of the League in May 1941 proved especially fortuitous.

The American Savings and Loan Institute was likewise moving in new directions, having a special hand in the late 1930s in assisting associations in the modernization of office procedure. By the end of 1940 it had a chapter in every city of 300,000 or more and over 2,500 students in its 20 courses. It was now publishing new textbooks especially written for Institute classes.

Graduate School of Savings and Loan

But the most far-reaching of all the forward-looking steps taken by the American Savings and Loan Institute was the establishment in the summer of 1939 of the Graduate School of Savings and Loan. This was a postgraduate course in the operation of savings and loan associations and began as a two-weeks session on the Chicago campus of Northwestern University. Eighty-seven students, with an average age of 38, most of them association executives and a few of them supervisors from the various jurisdictions, enrolled. They had advanced classroom work in such subjects as savings and loan management and law, economics, business forecasting and construction loan procedures. The plan was that three summer sessions of two weeks each would complete a person's studies in the Graduate School. The first class of three-year men was graduated in 1941, the summer before the United States entered World War II. There was no graduate school during the war years; when it was resumed after the war it was transferred to Indiana University.

By the end of 1960, 554 men and women had graduated from the three-year course at this school and the ranks of active management in savings and loan associations were heavily permeated by graduate school experience. A by-product of the Graduate School of Savings and Loan and its close collaboration with a leading academic institution over the years had been to deepen academicians' knowledge of the nature and role of savings and loan associations. The result was a helpful cross pollination of the thinking of leaders in fields of business and finance, as well as in savings and loan's top management.

By 1939 savings and loan managers with their new concept of their own obligation to shape the destiny of growing institutions had come to see the need for "talking shop" with other managers.

They wanted a much more detailed and concentrated type of exchange of ideas than the annual conventions provided. Therefore, management conferences were inaugurated for the associations whose assets were $5 million or over, the "larger" institutions of the period. (Only 125 of the League's nearly 4,000 member institutions were over $5 million in 1939.)

First management conferences

These first sessions of managers were devoid of all frills. The strictly business type of meeting was always held in Chicago, the headquarters of the League; any attendance by other than the managers was not only discouraged but was practically unheard of; families did not come because there was no attraction for them. There was, however, great attraction for the men who were searching for broader vision and for those who were seeking solutions to difficult business problems. At such conferences managers of associations in smaller cities held separate sessions from those managers representing larger cities in order to promote more fruitful round-table discussions.

Among the relatively new subjects for discussion was that of departmentalization. In 1938 the question was still being considered whether the setting up of separate departments would make for greater operating efficiency, and if so, at what juncture? This whole question took on special import at the time, because the proper delegation of authority was beginning to be vital to the continuance of the growth associations were experiencing. And this was among the first of the internal management problems which United States League committees helped members to solve. It represented one of the providential investments of time and energy on the part of the leadership, when the pressure for answers became so insistent during the growth period of the 1950s.

The men at the helm in savings and loan institutions by 1940 had about as many irons in the fire as could be imagined. But these were pleasant days for them, all in all. It could well be said of them what President Roosevelt had more than once said of the whole nation—"This generation has a rendezvous with destiny." And indeed many savings and loan executives of the time kept that rendezvous, to the lasting benefit of the postwar United States.

Part three

World War II
and its consequences

1940-1946

Chapter 12

Savings and loan
operations in wartime

The war years swept the savings and loan business much more surely into the business community as a whole than ever before. At the federal level savings and loan institutions found themselves classed with all financial institutions by wartime officials in Washington, as the federal government moved into a role of much more contact with the entire financial sector than it ever had before. Thus the savings and loan business attained greater stature than its size at the time might have merited. In the local community, savings and loan managers undertook leadership on a much broader scale. The executives of the associations found their places quite naturally on war bond drives, but they also assumed posts of responsibility on draft boards, rationing boards, fair rent committees and even in some larger cities in civil defense programs.

The making of the savings and loan executive as an original thinker owes much to the war years. All businessmen faced many new challenges to their ingenuity during this 1941-1945 period. They had to find solutions to shortages of many things. A savings and loan executive, for instance, had his appraisal activities particularly handicapped by the need to curtail the use of automobiles, because of car and gasoline shortages. Office equipment that was outmoded and buildings that were beginning to be dowdy and crowded were among "make do" situations the executive had to accept. Throughout the war the challenge of adequate personnel was continually before the savings and loan manager; not only did he have to cope with the threat of military service for all of the younger staff members, but also with the wage controls which the government had instituted so that men might be moved into war essential activities.

During the war years the leadership exercised by the United States League became much more important in phases other than legislation. All financial institutions had more contacts than formerly with some of the executive departments in Washington and in the new temporary agencies for mobilization of the economy. The Office of Rent Control and the War Production Board were among the agencies which the League had to include in its regular contacts for the business. There were more national stands to be taken than ever before because more issues than ever before confronted a business trying to do its job for the country.

Government bond investments

During the war savings and loan management in general learned for the first time about the government bond market. Mortgage lending opportunities became increasingly more scarce as construction was curtailed and almost halted by the need for conservation of materials. Savings opportunities, on the other hand, were enhanced by wartime aspects of the economy. Associations found themselves with more money than they knew what to do with—a quick about-face from their situation of only five or six years before. The need of the United States government to sell its bonds to institutional investors fitted well with the associations' new necessity for investment outlets. Thus thousands of savings and loan managements, both the full-time executive and the boards of directors, had to study the government bond market; and they acquired a knowledge which was invaluable to them in postwar years.

202

Between September 1939, when the Nazis invaded Poland, and the proclamation of an unlimited National Emergency by the President of the United States in May 1941, the savings and loan institutions were little affected by the country's defense preparations. The Selective Training and Service Act, adopted September 4, 1940, required several thousand savings and loan employees and executives to register for possible military service, but it was some time before the draft was actually in operation.

By the autumn of 1941, however, restrictions on the use of materials, especially metals, had begun to come in rapid succession and the associations faced a damper on their newly aroused interest in construction lending. Rumors began to fly about—months ahead of the actual issuance of the limiting order—that home building was about to come under the austerity program. Fears of shortages played their usual part in aggravating the situation, but the country had declared war by the time the restricting order was promulgated. There had been so much talk about defense housing and so much emphasis upon the need for sufficient and adequate shelter in the communities which were swollen by defense activities from the very beginning of defense preparedness that home building was among the last phases of the construction industry to encounter the "shut everything down" attitude.

Aftermath of Pearl Harbor

Several hundred savings and loan executives and their families were on trains returning to their homes from the United States League's 1941 convention in Coral Gables, Fla., when the Japanese struck their surprise blow on the U. S. Naval Base at Pearl Harbor, Hawaii, on December 7. A few of the convention delegates took the first airplane rides of their lives to get home from a post-convention sojourn in Cuba, as news of the outbreak of actual hostilities between the United States and Japan came excitedly over the wires.

Some of the grimmest months of the nation's experience in the world conflict came during that first winter. The savings and loan business, for the first time since it lifted its head from its depression woes, faced some months "in the red" on savings. Heavy withdrawals conjured up grim visions of another time of troubles. The unsettled situation continued throughout the spring, but by June a definite upturn came in net savings. From that time forth savings volume trended upward throughout the war. The rash of withdrawals had come with the bad news of the first months of the war, the sinking of ships and the losses of ground and strategic positions by the Allies on many fronts.

Some savings were withdrawn from all types of savings institutions also in order to buy war bonds, since a new fervor of patriotism pervaded the land. There was also a return of some hoarding and a spurt in the buying of things inspired by rumors of the imminence of widespread rationing of consumer goods. The Federal Home Loan Banks, by making cash available to meet the heavy demands of those first war months, performed a service for which the business was most grateful. It must be borne in mind that a heavy turnover in money in the associations had not become routine by any means in 1942. The morale of the business during the early war period could have been badly damaged if associations had been required to cope with a prolonged period of heavy withdrawals.

In the spring of 1942, the United States League appointed a War Policies Committee whose job was to recommend operating policies for the business during the war. The committee saw two major areas in which savings and loan institutions could make a contribution. One had to do with the financing of the war; the associations could step up their sales of savings bonds and also make a substantial investment themselves in government securities. The other was to help finance war housing. The committee reminded the savings and loan institutions that they should participate in war housing "even if it involves taking a lower rate on mortgage investments and taking more than ordinary risks." The implication was plain that the more permanent new housing in war areas the government built, the more private enterprise would be held responsible for its failure to measure up to its opportunities.

Mobilizing for war financing

In July 1942, the president and officers of the United States League asked the savings and loan institutions to buy a minimum of $100 million in government bonds for their own portfolios during the last half of that year. This was the first organized effort to mobilize the funds in these institutions for war financing. The

League appointed a chairman for each state to arrange for personal contact with every association, assigning a quota to each on the basis of the savings and loan assets and the population of the state. A review of the list of the original group of state chairmen shows five who were later to become presidents of the United States League and others who were to become members of the Executive Committee and Board of Directors. Leadership opportunities blossomed during the war years to the great advantage, not only of the individual, but of the business itself.

The Secretary of the Treasury sent a message to the next annual meeting of the League emphasizing the valuable service the associations were performing in the war financing program. Back of the patriotic motive was also an economic consideration which orthodox, financial-minded men could not overlook. The purchase of a large volume of government securities by the associations helped prevent a runaway inflation in the financing of the war. Then, as in all the periods of inflationary scares before or since, any resort to complete dependence upon commercial banks for the financing of new government debt presented the threat of an unfortunate swelling of the volume of money in the country. The efforts of the Treasury in World War II were always directed partly to getting the large bond issues absorbed by savings institutions which did not "create" money in the process of buying the bonds.

As the years went along, the large-scale bond purchase program became a fixed part of savings and loan's contribution to the

Table 18. Government securities owned by savings and loan associations and ratio to total assets, December 31, 1938-1946 (in millions of dollars)

Year	U.S. Government securities	Total assets	Ratio
1938	$ 75	$ 5,632	1.3%
1939	73	5,597	1.3
1940	71	5,733	1.2
1941	107	6,049	1.8
1942	318	6,150	5.2
1943	853	6,604	12.9
1944	1,671	7,458	22.4
1945	2,420	8,747	27.7
1946	2,009	10,202	19.7

Source: *Federal Home Loan Bank Board, "Savings and Home Financing Source Book, 1961," p. 8*

financing of the war. After the successful attainment of the first goal of $100 million in six months, they went on to provide well over $3.5 billion by the end of the war.

The impact of bond purchases by associations on their own balance sheets is revealed by comparative figures: In 1940, government securities amounted to 1.2% of total association assets; by 1945, they represented nearly 28% of assets. Table 18 shows the rapid acquisition of U. S. government securities.

Selling war bonds

Even before the unlimited National Emergency was declared by the United States, the Treasury had launched a campaign to sell defense bonds. In the winter of 1940-1941, while the program was being shaped, United States League's representatives held conferences with the Treasury Department to assure that savings and loan associations would be permitted to qualify as issuing agents. In 1942 the program changed to selling war bonds instead of defense bonds and the savings and loan institutions stepped up their efforts substantially. The cumulative effort of the savings and loan business during the war period accounted for approximately $1.6 billion of bond sales to others.

The story of these bond sales by the associations is full of human interest; many associations sold a larger volume of war bonds than they had assets. One reason was the successful effort of many savings and loan groups of foreign extraction whose leaders did a spectacular job of enrolling their fellow first-and-second-generation Americans among the supporters of Uncle Sam's war effort.

Colorful and highly imaginative bond selling devices were part of the associations' wartime operations. Rallies focused attention on the bond program, with entertainers of top rank to attract crowds and with speeches by Treasury officials and members of the armed forces. The associations often established booths on sidewalks and in hotels for the convenience of people who would be more likely to buy bonds without having to go to the association's quarters, a bank or a post office (there were practically no branches of associations in those days).

Window displays were commonly devoted to advertising savings bonds sales. Many associations developed payroll allotment plans in connection with industries in the community, taking charge of

TREASURY DEPARTMENT
WASHINGTON, D. C.

November 14, 1944

United States Savings and Loan League
Chicago, Illinois

Gentlemen:

I am delighted to learn of your excellent plans for cooperation with the Sixth War Loan. Savings and loan associations have ably assisted the Treasury in past drives and I am confident their aid in the forthcoming campaign will be even more outstanding than before. The Treasury appreciated the generous services of your personnel, your advertising support, the bond purchases by your members and your sale of hundreds of millions of dollars of government securities to the public. I know you will go forth to meet the Sixth War Loan with determination and unflagging zeal. Our country is still at war and so are we on the War Bond front. Let us hasten the day of victory.

(Signed) HENRY MORGENTHAU, JR., *Secretary*

One of several Treasury Department citations awarded to the United States League for participation of savings and loan associations in support of the war bond effort

the handling of the funds and placing them in war bonds. In their own offices the associations used friendly persuasion to channel 10% of employees' pay into the regular purchase of war savings bonds. A woman staff member of one of the associations speaking at an American Savings and Loan Institute Conference referred to the associations as "Savings, War Bond and Loan Associations," thereby underlining the fact that their participation in the sales had become a major factor in their operations in the early 1940s. The Treasury cited the United States League for its part in war bond sales in 1944 and also gave citations individually to the regional chairmen of the separate war loan drives and United States League participants.

The publicity value of the war bond sales by savings and loan institutions can never be measured. Certainly the associations made a lasting impression on the public in those years not only by the spectacular devices they used for selling bonds, but also by the very fact that they issued the bonds at all. The associations were also active in later war years in the reverse side of the war bond program: They qualified as agents for the redemption of bonds. Cashing bonds was simple enough for those educated in financial transactions, but it was sometimes quite mystifying to the uninitiated bondholder. Thus again the associations achieved a marked advance in public relations by offering this service.

The emphasis which associations placed on lending money to Uncle Sam to win a war did not even slow down the continued heavy flow of money into their own institutions. The abundance of savings accumulated by the American people during the war years was so great that both savings bonds and private savings enterprises could be well provided with funds.

While thousands of savings and loan associations accepted all the money offered them by the public and bought government bonds to take the place of mortgage loans which were their normal outlet for funds, many restricted savings inflows. They did so by setting limits on the amount which they would receive from any one accountholder; often for temporary periods they would open no new accounts. Some took this alternative to the obvious path of reducing the rate at which earnings were distributed to the members. But even with that rate declining from 3% in 1942 to 2.9% in 1943, 2.8% in 1944 and 2.5% in 1945, the flow of savings remained strong. Throughout the war, leaders in the business urged all associations to accept all funds so that they would be prepared to meet the great demand for home loans which was sure to come with the cessation of hostilities.

Mortgage lending demand

The outlet for funds in home mortgage lending was not, however, completely shut off. Expansion of the demand for loans on existing homes did its part in sustaining a fairly high level of home mortgage demand, even if it was below normal levels. By the last full year of the war, 1944, the associations lent well over $1 billion for the purchase of existing properties. That year the ratio of home purchase loans to total lending reached 70.3%. Home purchase lending was now highly competitive, since it was the one major channel for mortgage investment, and savings and loan's success in the field came as a result of an aggressive program. This program emphasized contacts with realtors and other middlemen, a continuation of the appeals which had been used years before in the cooperative advertising campaign in middlemen publications.

The demand for money to finance home purchase came, too, as somewhat of a surprise. Most observers had expected a slow real estate market as long as the war lasted, since nine million young men entered the armed forces. But the higher wages and full employment produced by the war brought the undoubling of the hundreds of thousands of families whose precarious finances in former years had compelled them to share homes with relatives. The undoubling absorbed quickly the 1 million dwelling units which had been vacant at the start of the war and left none to spare among the 1.2 million units built in 1941 and 1942. A push was thus given to the rising price of residential real estate, which began to be evident as early as 1943. The rise came not only in the defense centers, where population was crowding in to work on war material, but also in the country at large. Besides the heavy demand, additional factors influential in driving up price tags on homes were the speculation that it would cost even more to buy a home when the war was over, and the general cheapening of the purchasing power of the dollar which came with the war years.

War housing

The savings and loan associations contribution to war housing, the second great area in which the War Policies Committee had envisioned their opportunity to serve the nation, can be measured only in terms of their overall contribution to the financing of new home construction. The difficult circumstances under which the entire housing industry had to function during World War II are described in greater detail in the following chapter devoted to wartime legislation and its significance for the savings and loan business. Suffice it to say here that the savings and loan institutions disbursed over a half a billion dollars for the financing of home construction during the entire war period. Practically all the new homes built, after the restrictions went into force, were war housing; no other kind could qualify. The half-billion dollar savings and loan part in this achievement was a sizable contribution.

In retrospect one must conclude that the associations gained substantial experience from their war housing emphasis in 1942-1945. They learned much from their work in financing the wartime building operations. Here for the first time they mastered some of the techniques of financing "housing projects." Here, too, many of the practical problems of working with a new generation of home builders were tackled and solved. Furthermore a genuine respect for the savings and loan institution—its personnel and its mortgage lending acumen—grew up on the part of the new operative builders in the field, as they worked with savings and loan mortgage departments on war housing.

Personnel developments

On the associations' premises, operations had a definite war look from 1942 on. Wartime shortages and unaccustomed restrictions created disrupted personnel schedules and, as has already been pointed out, taxed the ingenuity of management in coping with them. The appearance of the staffs changed materially as the war progressed. Most conspicuously there was a preponderance of feminine faces at tellers' windows and at many more of the desks where the association personnel met the public. The Selective Service program, as the draft was officially called, eventually took the majority of the younger men out of the savings and loan offices. As early as mid-1943 a United States League survey showed that the associations had already lost, mostly to the armed forces—although to some degree to defense industry—1,800 of their 18,000 employees. The numbers moving away from their savings and loan desks increased steadily as the nation mobilized. Management was faced with the realization that it must devise a system to provide for the temporary absence of staff. It will be recalled that the draft law placed upon the employer the obligation of restoring a serviceman to his former position without loss of seniority when he returned.

Thoughtful managers in the savings and loan business had done some serious thinking about the new problems the draft law would bring and the United States League's Personnel Committee offered helpful suggestions. A majority of associations instituted the practice of continuing to pay part (about 10% was normal) of the salaries of staff members who had entered the service, since very often their military pay was less than they had received from the association.

Obviously such arrangements were an extra load on the salary account, since they represented an outlay which offered in exchange no hands and brains for the day-to-day operations. Associations on the whole reconciled themselves to doing the normal or greater volume of business without enlarging the staff, in order to keep the salary budget in line.

As in other businesses, women got the great opportunity of their lifetime to handle the vacated jobs. By the end of 1943, approximately 42% of all savings and loan employees were women, including 13% of the senior executives and 44% of junior executives. A sign of the psychology of the times was the fact that a number of associations had their women employees attired in military type uniforms.

The abnormal turnover of staff and clerical help created a heavy demand for accelerated training. (Of course even the hiring of women was no full solution, since the rapidly stepped-up rate of marriages during World War II sometimes took the most promising of the new feminine staff members out of the city to be with a husband stationed in a far-off camp.) The American Savings and Loan Institute adopted special methods for teaching its indoctrination courses in the shortest possible time and also developed some short courses to train temporary employees.

In the early years of the Fair Labor Standards Act, associations had not judged themselves subject to its maximum hours and minimum wage provisions. But early in 1941 legal authorities at the Department of Labor notified the United States League that, in their opinion, associations in general were subject to wage and hour restrictions. This decision came at a time when the maximum work week had been reduced to 40 hours and when all employees covered by the wage and hour regulations had to be paid "time and a half" for overtime hours worked.

Another upward adjustment of salary accounts was only just

beginning to be digested by the savings and loan business when the war came; this was the Social Security payroll tax. In January 1940, all associations, state and federal, had been brought under Social Security, after a period of several years in which the relationship of this business to the Social Security program had not been clearly defined. The rate paid in those beginning years, however, was only 1%.

Spread between income and expense

Despite the multiplication of factors leading to higher salary budgets in the associations, the savings and loan business had a greater spread between income and expenses during the war years than it had ever had before. This development arose from the drastically lowered cost of money to the associations. Meanwhile the bulk of the loan portfolios continued at the relatively high yields of prewar lending, although earnings were being distributed at the lower rates. Only those loans made during the war years yielded a relatively low rate of return.

These conditions created a new look in the advertising budgets of the associations. With this extra leverage in expendable income the associations could pay for business promotion on a scale not before possible. Although some managements were reluctant to seek savings aggressively in the unfavorable investment atmosphere of the war years, the general tendency in the savings and loan ranks was to make the most of the fact that many people had hitherto undreamed of opportunities "to get some money ahead" and to see to it that some of this money was put into their institutions. Certainly one of the fruits of the war for the savings and loan business was some valuable experience in attracting savings. The experience was gained both from spending more money for business development and from trying new methods. From the success of these tryouts managers acquired a taste for rolling up unprecedented dollar volume of savings month by month—a taste which they have never lost.

Effect on conventions

The war also brought a new appearance to the get-togethers of savings and loan people. Opportunities to mingle with fellow

212

savings and loan practitioners and exchange ideas were curtailed in number. A special kind of celebration had been planned for the 50th birthday of the United States League in 1942, with a golden anniversary convention as the highlight. Because of wartime restrictions and voluntary cooperation in lightening the transportation load, the meeting was changed to a program more in keeping with the times—a War Conference on Housing and Savings. This gathering, which set the pattern for the war years (and like the two succeeding ones, took place in centrally located Chicago), was confined to business sessions dealing mainly with major considerations of the economy. Attendance was less than 1,000. In one year, 1945, after the war had ended, travel facilities and hotel accommodations were so overtaxed that the League held no national meeting.

The League extended its publication services still further in this period. The magazine *Savings and Loan News* was transferred from the American Savings and Loan Institute to the League in 1942 and, under a full-time editor, was broadened to meet the needs of the full membership. At the suggestion of one member, the League inaugurated a new type of publication in January 1942; it was the *Directors Digest* and was intended as a major information piece for the directors of the savings and loan associations who had neither the time nor inclination to master all the written materials which came across the managers' desks. It played its part in the adaptation of savings and loan association policies to wartime necessities.

Growth in size and contacts

The war years also saw a drawing together of businessmen from many different types of endeavor into a more closely knit community, and the savings and loan business was benefitting from its relations with the United States Chamber of Commerce. In 1938 for the first time a representative of the savings and loan business had been elected to the directorate of the chamber and he was re-elected for several terms. This savings and loan contact with the inner circle of 44 men on the Chamber of Commerce directorate had led to committee appointments for savings and loan men and to a more general recognition of the part played by these institutions in the business life of the nation.

Altogether the years 1942-1945 represented an extremely vital period for the savings and loan business. Most prophetically the Executive Committee of the United States League had expressed in *Policies, 1942* and sent to all member institutions this cheering thought: "The same forces which create great problems bring with them commensurate opportunities if the problems are successfully solved. Savings and loan associations can and will solve their problems and take advantage of their opportunities."

Nearly all the associations grew, in terms of assets, during the war because of the stimulus that the existence of wartime scarcity conditions gave to saving money. Some observers have thought that it might have taken in peacetime another 10 years to build

Chart 6. Trend in assets and liabilities of savings and loan associations, December 31, 1938-1946

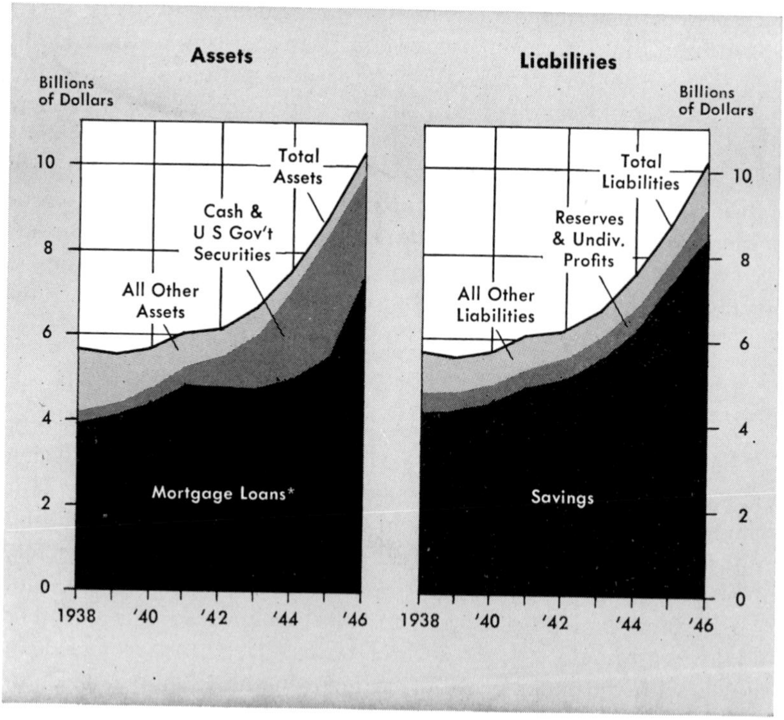

*Less Pledged Shares
Source: Federal Home Loan Bank Board,
"Savings and Home Financing Source Book, 1961," p. 8*

up as large a volume of savings as that garnered during those four years by savings and loan institutions. And it was the billions of savings available which immediately put the associations in a position to become the dominant home lenders of the postwar period. Chart 6 reveals the component parts of assets and liabilities of associations for the years 1938-1946. These years undoubtedly made their great intellectual contribution also in that they enlarged the vision of both managers and directors as to what their savings and loan associations could and should do to continue to contribute further to the betterment of the economic life of the nation.

Chapter 13

Wartime legislation and its
significance for savings associations

The Congress of the United States fell into certain legislative habits during World War II which it has never gotten over. Just as those years of turmoil changed the social face of the country, they led both the legislative and executive branches of the federal government along new paths from which they have never consciously turned back. The enactment of wartime measures began the first year after Hitler invaded Poland, at a time when the United States made itself believe it would stay out of the conflict. The accumulation became very great indeed before the war was over and, psychologically speaking, legislation fed upon itself in those years.

Before the United States actually entered the war there was some increase in expenditures on defense. The period was also marked by the creation of a rash of emergency government agencies. Both the defense expenditures and the creation of agencies were multiplied many times over in the following years.

Several types of legislation got their impetus from the war, and savings and loan associations were affected to some extent by all of them. The federal government's accent on reorganization had the most immediate impact upon the business.

On February 24, 1942, the National Housing Agency was created, the Federal Home Loan Bank Board was abolished, and the programs under the Board were consolidated under the housing agency. When this new alignment of government housing agencies was proclaimed, the official announcement said, "The plan of consolidation resulted from uncommonly widespread agreement among the government agencies actively engaged in the day-to-day administration of housing activities." Actually, the new agency was widely conceded to be the brain child of those quite interested in the government's regulation of larger and larger sectors of the housing industry and its ownership of an increasing portion of the nation's shelter.

The Federal Home Loan Bank Board was far from giving "widespread agreement" to the plan. In fact, the dismantling of the Board and the superimposing of the National Housing Agency upon all its operations resulted in genuine alarm at 101 Indiana Avenue, headquarters of the Board. Savings and loan leaders were shocked and apprehensive and they protested. It took years for the protest to be effective but the savings and loan business never ceased to make clear its stand that the new arrangement was ill-advised and unjust. The Federal Home Loan Bank Board, being inside the government, was in no position to clamor, since protest was not the order of the day in wartime Washington.

Effects of the National Housing Agency

A look at what was accomplished by the creation of the National Housing Agency will show the reasons for the apprehension. The agency, which was created by Executive Order of President Roosevelt, had the following effect on existing entities, most of which had come into being many years before: 1) the duties of the five-man Federal Home Loan Bank Board were turned over to a newly created commissioner of the Federal Home Loan Bank Administration; 2) the Federal Housing Administration was included, its administrator being changed to a commissioner and definitely reduced in prestige by the creation of the superagency; 3) the U. S. Housing Authority, the agency which administered public housing and was then fostering it with uncommon zeal, was put into the new agency with a new name, the Federal Public Housing Authority. This new FPHA unit was made responsible for defense housing built with public funds—a program which was destined to take billions. Thus the Federal Public Housing Authority became at once a much more important entity than the old U. S. Housing Authority had been.

Under the consolidation, a former assistant director of the Bureau of the Budget became administrator of the National Housing Agency. The chairman of the abolished Federal Home Loan Bank Board became commissioner of the Federal Home Loan Bank Administration; the heads of the other two agencies were continued as commissioners in their respective responsibilities. In the realignment, however, the administrator of the National Housing Agency was given authority over all the personnel of the agencies consolidated under him, so that he could make transfers and eliminate jobs as he saw fit. He was to do it whenever it was "in the public interest"—already by that time a much overworked phrase.

A quite serious implication to the prestige of the savings and loan business was at once apparent to its more forward-looking leaders as they regarded the new captivity of their Washington instrumentalities. The central banking system of the savings and loan business, the Federal Home Loan Bank System, was not yet 10 years old; but it had made great strides in its young life in enhancing the prestige of the business in legislative and administrative circles. It was, let it be remembered, a privately managed, privately owned system; member institutions of the Federal Home Loan Banks were doing one-third at least of all the home mortgage lending of the nation.

The Federal Home Loan Bank Board was reduced by this new consolidation to a role of minor importance in Washington and was made to march in harness with two other programs which were far from sympathetic to its objectives. One of its new teammates, the FHA, was still regarded principally as the sponsor of mortgage lending institutions in competition with savings and loans.

The other teammate, the public housing program, was aggressively working for greater use of public funds for increasing sectors of the residential building of the nation—an objective which could never be compatible with the basic reason for the existence of savings and loan associations. The savings and loan leaders saw, moreover, some of the immediate implications of the one-man (administrator) type of supervisory authority for their operations as contrasted to the five members (Board); obviously, the dangers of arbitrary determination of issues in the supervisory areas were much greater where one man stood at the peak of authority.

Savings and loan leaders feared furthermore that their own agencies supported by several hundred thousand dollars annually from the savings and loan institutions might be turned into unwilling instruments for the expansion of government housing. A Washington correspondent of the *New York Times* had commented in a similar vein a few days after the agency was launched, declaring, "The necessities of waging war have silenced or deferred criticism of federal paternalism in housing." He went on to say, "But if it shall appear that the new agency is being guided toward state socialization of realty after the war, or if . . . an attempt rises to use it for that purpose, then the battle of psychologies will be resumed with much greater intensity." As it happened, the principal way in which the National Housing Agency promoted more government housing was through its temporary control over all housing during the war.

Economic controls

The second large area of wartime legislation of concern to the savings and loan business was that of economic controls. The home building industry had to proceed during the war years under a staggering load of such controls.

In April 1942, Construction Conservation Order L-41 was issued. It established preferred ratings for builders seeking materials for housing to be built in designated defense areas; residential building outside such areas could go ahead only by special authorization. Remodeling, if it cost more than $500, was also subject to "construction conservation restrictions"; later an amendment to L-41 reduced to $200 the amount of remodeling which could be done on a one-to-four family residence without a special authorization. A builder got his priorities which came to be described as a "hunting license"—for he had to find the materials as best he might—once he had the official right to use them. The local FHA offices increased their power and prestige considerably during these years by the fact that the housing agency had delegated to them the responsibility for issuing the priorities.

Control of the building of new housing was exercised to a much broader extent through the fact that the National Housing Administrator was given the task of programing war housing. Theoretically he had to secure the critical materials necessary for building the necessary number of units (in competition with other users of materials) and make sure the funds were available for building them. He also had to plan to make the existing supply of housing go farther than it ordinarily would go in providing shelter. Upon re-examination of the war housing procedures, in the clear light of nearly two decades later, one finds how strongly the emergency of the war operated in favor of those who thought it highly desirable to manage the country's economy from a drafting board in Washington. A large number of newly assembled government officials had their great opportunity to try out their theories during the war. The citizens as a whole were not too well aware of what had happened. Had they been aware it is doubtful they could have done too much about it. Nowhere was this opportunity to make the planners' dream come true more eagerly snatched than in the housing program.

During the war years virtually all home building was done by the sufferance of the National Housing Administrator in Washington. Planning in Washington was carried to a fantastic level. The total number of units needed, what percentage of them should be for single people, what percentage for childless couples, what percentage for families—what portion of the need should be taken care of by remodeling existing units, and what portion by the building of temporary units—were among the specifics in the war housing plan. As to permanent dwellings needed to be constructed, the housing agency decided how many the government should build and how many should be allotted for private ownership.

The results were far from satisfactory. Some of the restrictions on the private enterprise system, including the restraints on war materials, were relaxed after the first year because the needed housing was not being built. But throughout the war years, the private home building industry in the United States stood ready to accomplish a great deal more of the job which needed to be done than it was ever permitted to try. Red tape and confusion in Washington were among the larger obstacles; but the desire of many of those in power in Washington to put up public rather than private housing was also a major drawback to the full utilization of the private home building system of the nation.

Lanham Act Housing

As early as October 1940, the expenditure of public money was authorized to build housing needed in areas which had mushroomed in population during the defense and war period. The original appropriation was for $150 million, and it came as a result of legislation sponsored by Representative Fritz Lanham of Texas. Lanham Act Housing was the name by which all government-built war housing was known thereafter. The average cost per unit was fixed at $3,000, with a maximum of $3,950, for any locality inside the continental United States. The wide discrepancy between housing costs in the 1960s and in those early war years is nowhere better highlighted than in this figure originally written into the Lanham Act; far from signifying the war housing was to be a mere shell, these cost specifications would then permit the erection of a house well up to the standard of the time, even if small in area.

Speaking at the United States League war conference in 1942, Mr. Lanham declared specifically that this program was far removed from both the objectives and the character of public housing. Local real estate taxes were to be paid upon it. The temporary construction was to be salvaged after the war and whatever was permanent construction was to be sold and the money, as Congressman Lanham put it, "placed in the Federal Treasury."

These safeguards in the Lanham Act were the result of the conservative-minded Congress. They must be partly credited also to the vigilance of the real estate and mortgage lending businesses which had observed the bias in favor of permanent government-built housing in the performance of government officials, despite the lip service always given to private enterprise. The National Association of Home Builders, later so effective an influence on Capitol Hill, was not organized as an independent group until September 1942. Therefore, its influence in combatting the Washington takeover of home building during the war was necessarily that of a young organization. It should be given some of the credit, however, for the fact that things did not get worse for private enterprise building as the war progressed.

222

Approximately $2.3 billion was spent for publicly built housing for the emergency needs of war workers and military personnel. Nearly 627,000 units were provided. Permanent units, suitable for long-term residential use, constituted 30% of the total; the rest were "temporaries," consisting of demountable housing units of a wide variety of types. Some of the latter could still be seen around the landscape in the mid-1950s, especially on college campuses because they were turned over for the use of veterans in the great housing shortage of the early postwar period.

Disposition of the government-built war housing on the whole was retarded by the postwar housing shortage. It was not until the Housing Act of 1950 that orderly programs for the disposition of the major part of the Lanham Act housing were authorized.

Rent ceilings

Price control legislation affected savings and loan operations principally through rent ceilings. Rent controls emerged upon the scene in early 1942, under provisions of the Economic Stabilization Act adopted January 29 of that year. They represented the only area of individual consumption in which World War II controls were placed upon prices without any effort to ration supply. In the major areas of short supply, such as meats, fats, sweets and shoes, the price control program recognized that prices are the normal distribution device in a free economy; once prices were controlled there was a need for an artificial distribution device. Thus rationing was instituted for these specific commodities. But rents were controlled in most of the urban areas of the United States with no control whatsoever being exercised over the demand. The result was a distortion of the entire demand and supply situation. The most victimized were those who had to find a place to live. In the main, those who already lived in rent-controlled apartments and houses continued to occupy these facilities, realizing that they had a very good thing indeed with rents rolled back to a prewar level.

Owners of property were also penalized substantially; the disadvantage to many of them was accentuated by the choice of the date to which rents were rolled back (this choice was made community by community). Although the prices of commodities and services were frozen in April 1942, at their March 1942 level, rents in 64 areas were rolled back that same month to levels of 1941. In 259 other areas they were frozen as of March 1, 1942, but even the latter date represented a discrimination against property owners, since rents had not risen to anything like their predepression levels anywhere. On the other hand, most of the items in the cost of living had gone up considerably from depression lows by March 1942. Thus the landlord faced a severe dilemma if he wanted to do anything to maintain his property; he had to pay the higher prices for services and materials out of an income which reflected still depressed rents.

Roughly three-fourths of all the areas in which savings and loan associations operated were under rent control before the end of spring 1942. Of course, many associations still owned real estate and suffered distinct disadvantages from the roll-back or freezing of rents. Upon those which had disposed of their real estate, rent controls with their attendant influences and disturbances had only an indirect effect. But these controls constituted a discouragement and an uncertainty in the entire real estate world. The very essence of property ownership, freedom to do with the building as one saw fit, had been negated.

Control of down payment

But something even more far-reaching was included as a by-product of the rent control dilemma. This was the right of the owner to sell his property when the sale meant putting the tenant out. The restriction on residential property sales which would result in evictions was a complicated order commonly known as the "control of down payment." Its ostensible purpose was to put a stop to landlords' maneuvers to evade rent ceilings. A method frequently used to circumvent rent ceiling controls was to require the tenant—if he remained in possession—to buy the property at contract payments substantially higher than the monthly rent; if the tenant balked at this arrangement, the landlord sold the place to another who would make the higher contract payments; he then asked the old tenant to vacate.

Late in 1942, the Office of Price Administration put into effect the regulation that a property owner could not start eviction proceedings against a sitting tenant until 90 days had elapsed after the sale of the property. Also, the regulation required a purchaser to make a 33⅓% down payment, exclusive of borrowed money (this down payment was later reduced to 20%). The regulation had no effect where owner-occupied houses were being sold, and sales of such properties became an increasingly large proportion of the mortgage lending business of savings and loan associations as the war continued. On the other hand, in the larger metropolitan areas where considerable turnover of one-to-four family homes occupied by renters could have been expected, the OPA down-payment control was credited with discouraging the transfer of such buildings. An officer of the United States League listed the OPA ruling as a contributing factor to a 30% to 40% drop in the sale of old houses in his locality.

On the other side of the picture, the exemption of real property from the overall freeze of prices was the brightest spot in the control program. Perhaps real estate prices managed to stay clear of the heavy hand of the price controller because of the obvious impossibility of doing an acceptable job in a field where there were no price tags printed and affixed to the article, and where sales were still made by the bargaining between a seller and a borrower. Whatever the reason for this fortuitous circumstance, the exemption of real estate from price control was the main reason why existing properties, especially single-family homes, continued to change hands and the associations continued to be able to make loans in volume.

Regulation W

All the controls so far described were applied to phases of the economy with which savings and loan dealt. They did not, however, affect the internal operations of the association to a substantial degree. It was a different story with Regulation W, promulgated by the Federal Reserve Board in August 1941. This regulation placed an 18-month repayment limit on small loans; it was aimed chiefly at easing off the supply of installment credit in an effort to fight inflation. Its main effect on associations was in two areas. It applied directly to their modernization loans, although these at that time accounted for only about 4% of total loan volume. It also applied to passbook loans which had always been a convenient device for savers who wanted to have an emergency source of funds without withdrawing the account.

The first order of the Federal Reserve Board applied to installment repayment loans, including real estate, of $1,000 or less. A later amendment subjected loans up to $1,500 to its 18-month repayment limit. The regulation was one of the first introductions of the savings and loan business to the extra paper work which the war entailed. It meant that every association had to be licensed by the Federal Reserve Bank of its district, if it were going to make any installment loans; the definition of "extension of installment loan credit" included real estate loans of $1,000 or less. The general lending operations of associations were excluded from regulation, but the registration for licensing purposes was necessary.

Effective November 1, 1941, an amendment to Regulation W complicated the problem still further. It related the "extension of installment credit" to borrowers who wished to repay obligations held elsewhere; an association had to discuss with every loan applicant whether or not a part of the proceeds of a loan on his property were to be used for the repayment of other obligations. If so, the association had to get a written statement from him to that effect and had to require that this part of the loan be repaid in 18 months or less.

This first experiment with the regulation of installment credit set a precedent in Washington which has remained attractive from time to time to members of Congress as a means of putting brakes on consumer expenditures. It was reinvoked during the Korean War and emerges periodically in proposals of how to fight inflation.

A wartime control which posed strictly internal problems was the "freezing" in October 1942 of all salaries and wages. Pay increases could not be granted without special approval, except where they came as a result of pre-established plans for promotion, reclassification or other form of advancement. Only fairly large business organizations, as a rule, had such codified systems in 1942. Savings and loan adherence to the regulations was a special problem to the manager because relatively few associations had any regular system of promotions and raises to rely upon.

New tax burdens

The revenue structure of the United States creaked and groaned under the burden of wartime expenditures; unprecedented taxation was imposed during the years 1942 and 1943.

The Public Debt Act of March 28, 1942, withdrew thereafter all federal income tax exemptions from earnings on stock and share accounts of federal instrumentalities. In the Home Owners' Loan Act of 1933, the federal savings and loan associations had been exempted from taxation in the degree to which state associations were exempt. While subjecting the dividends from such associations to the federal income surtax, the Act inadvertently exempted them from the normal income tax, a precedent set by the treatment of numerous federal corporations. This arrangement created a slight discrimination in favor of federals and against state associations (the exempted normal income tax was a nominal 4%, which was raised to 6% late in 1942, but the dividends were always subject to the surtax which was at a higher rate).

Efforts had been made for many years to correct the situation but the correction was not made until 1942. This is the reason why some associations, owning Federal Home Loan Bank stock issued prior to March 1942, receive dividends thereon which are exempt from all federal income tax, and why a very few of the federal association accounts, containing funds dating back before March 1942, are still exempt from the normal tax while subject of course to the surtax.

This minor impress of the early 1942 legislation upon the savings and loan institutions was far from the only impact of wartime revenue laws. While the business retained during these years its specific status under the Revenue Code in regard to corporate income tax, it did face significant additions to the burdens of office work arising from new revenue laws.

The Revenue Act of 1942 (enacted October 20) added to the work in every business office: A new "Victory" tax of 5% was levied on the income of everyone earning more than $12 a week, and it was collectible at the source. It was the forerunner of the 1943 Revenue Law which required withholding on the major income tax liability of all employees. This latter departure from previous collection practices, placing an even greater burden on employers than the Victory tax, became a permanent part of the Revenue Code, and its repeal has never been sought by any serious efforts.

Both savings and loan institutions and their savers escaped, however, a very seriously discussed provision for a withholding tax on all dividends and bond interest which the House of Representatives had included in its version of the Revenue Act of 1942. The measure would have required the withholding of 5% in 1943 and 10% in 1944 on all the earnings distributed by savings and loan associations and co-operative banks. When hearings were held by the Senate Finance Committee, witnesses from the United States League testified that the dividend withholding proposal would work an unnecessary hardship and would discriminate against savings and loan institutions, inasmuch as commercial and mutual savings bank depositors were exempt.

A special subcommittee was appointed by the Senate Finance Committee to look into the withholding section, as a result of the hearings. The good news came to United States League officials on August 31, 1942, that the "subcommittee reported in favor of cutting out those little building and loan payments, and the full committee has adopted that recommendation." The savings in executive and clerical time, postage and supplies to each savings and loan institution were quite significant; these were especially important in a day when manpower was at a premium.

FHA defense housing

Defense and wartime legislation substantially changed the Federal Housing Administration program. The anticipated need for rapid production of new housing units in localities which would mushroom during a period of new emphasis on munitions and military training opened the way. Even before the Pearl Harbor debacle Congress was working on a defense housing program within the FHA; it was enacted in the winter of 1941 and became Title VI of the FHA statute. The bill was signed by President Roosevelt aboard a cruiser in the Caribbean where it had been rushed to him by plane on March 28. This was a highly sensational occurrence in those days, and the dramatics of it emphasized in the minds of the public the importance of putting the FHA insurance behind the production of defense housing.

Title VI extended 90% financing to rental property for one-to-four families, whereas the 90% insurance had been available heretofore only for sales-type houses. Basically the reason for Title VI was the recognition that more risk was involved in insuring mortgages on residential buildings in defense areas whose economic future was at best uncertain. Thus FHA set up an entirely separate mutual insurance fund for Title VI.

The League's Board of Directors endorsed the new Title VI proposal before it actually became law and viewed this application of government insurance for credit as more clearly justified than any previous FHA operation. A sidelight on the politics of the times is the divergence between the positions taken on the proposal by the then separate labor organizations, the AFL and CIO. While the AFL's Housing Committee's chairman was contending that this was an unprecedented attempt by the federal government to foster and stimulate speculation "at the expense of the worker and ultimately at the expense of the taxpayer," the CIO said that the proposal was directly in line with its recommendations for the last two or three previous years.

The President designated 146 localities as eligible for the use of Title VI; 38 states and four territories were included in the list. The original defense housing title of the FHA Act was later amended to include larger rental projects. In the main, it was the financing of these larger buildings which created problems after the war and bore out to some extent the AFL's warning about the stimulation of speculation. All in all some $167 million worth of newly built defense and war housing was covered by mortgages insured under Title VI FHA; 37,924 units were added to the housing supply by this device. Various amendments to the law were adopted in the course of the war.

The centering of a special insurance operation on housing in defense areas through Title VI was to lead to a whole network of special purpose provisions in FHA over the next 20 years. This— much more than the volume of mortgages insured for war and defense housing—was the real significance of this step taken during the war.

Veterans home loan program

The war years brought another breakthrough into new ground of government assistance to home finance in the home loan program for veterans. It was the result of a determined effort by the American Legion to safeguard World War II veterans from some of the most harassing problems which World War I veterans had faced, the shortage of homes and a scarcity of jobs. The Legion's Rehabilitation Committee drew up a program for college scholarships and for elimination or reduction of the required down payment in the case of veterans borrowing to buy homes, farms or businesses. It found ready sponsorship in Congress and was introduced in both houses in January 1944. Money for the loans was to come from federal and state governments at 1% and 5% interest, respectively. The measure went through several changes, with the Legion supporting significant amendments in the nature of the financing. Some of the changes reflected conferences between representatives of the United States League's Legislative Committee and the Legion's Rehabilitation Committee, out of which came the eventual provision for a government guarantee of a portion of the loan.

The Senate version, adopted in April 1944, provided for the United States Treasury to make second mortgages up to $1,000 at 3% to take care of the down-payment problem, but left the way open for private lenders to do the primary financing. The House of Representatives adopted a substantially amended bill in May 1944, providing for a government guarantee of 50% of the loan, or $2,500, whichever was smaller. On the method of financing, the House version prevailed in conference, except that the maximum guarantee was reduced to $2,000. In days when $4,000 would procure an acceptable home, this was not regarded as niggardly.

The Servicemen's Readjustment Act of 1944, as its official title ran, thus relied on a government guarantee of part of each loan to persuade mortgage lenders to go beyond precedent in high percentage loans. The guarantee was, in a sense, an equalization program. The country had been very prosperous during the war, and those who had stayed out of uniform had had great opportunities to accumulate money for down payments, an opportunity denied to servicemen.

In return for the government guarantee of a part of the loan, the mortgage lender was to charge an interest rate no higher than 4%. This rate was only about one-half of one percentage point below the going mortgage loan rate at that time and, therefore, represented a concession but not an unacceptable one.

The National Housing Agency worked zealously to bring the veterans guaranteed loan program under the agency's jurisdiction. But Congress placed the administration of the entire project in the hands of the Veterans Administration. This old-line agency had long experience in handling pensions, hospital benefits and other government assistances to those who had fought in the country's wars. It never regarded the guaranteed home loan program as an opportunity to remodel the country's mortgage lending operations but conceived it always as just what it was, a means of helping the veteran.

The home ownership program for veterans was immediately tagged with the familiar appellation "G.I. Bill of Rights," which the American Legion had first used with regard to it. For those who wonder two decades later what the title really means, the explanation is that "G.I. Joe" was the generic name for a private in the ranks of the armed forces during World War II. The abbreviation, "G.I.," meant "general issue" and referred to equipment which was provided a private.

VA loan regulations

The VA loan was a natural medium for savings and loan institutions, which were local in character and possessed a long experience in financing small- and medium-sized homes. Leaders in the business recognized immediately some of its possibilities for good—both to the veteran and for the overall cause of home ownership vs. renting. The statute, however, required elaborate and far-reaching regulations to implement it. The subsequent wide participation of savings and loan associations was made possible by significant conferences between representatives of the United States League and the Veterans Administration and other Washington agencies charged with responsibility for the regulations.

Within a short time after the enactment of the law in June 1944, the United States League and the state and local leagues were holding meetings to give association executives a chance to study actual operations. By November 1944, the final regulations had been printed and the League hastened to name its annual meeting that year—The National Conference on Veterans Loans and Home Ownership. A letter addressed at that time to the Board of Directors of the United States League by President Roosevelt declared "one of the basic obligations of our country is to help our returning veterans to share as soon as possible in the full benefits of the democratic community life which they are fighting to preserve."

The League's president in 1944 prophesied that the Servicemen's

THE WHITE HOUSE
WASHINGTON

October 12, 1944

Gentlemen:

One of the basic obligations of our country is to help our returning veterans to share as soon as possible in the full benefits of the democratic community life which they are fighting to preserve. Certainly the right to decent homes is a part of this obligation and I am glad to know that the United States Savings and Loan League is pledged to help veterans achieve it.

The Servicemen's Readjustment Act of 1944 provides that the veteran shall be given assurance that any loan he obtains through the aid of a government guarantee will be for a home soundly built, well located and economically financed. That promise can only be carried out through the full cooperation of private housing enterprise, communities and the Federal Government. This cooperation is of particular importance because the limitations on construction during the war have resulted in a demand for housing which lends itself to inflationary prices. Returning veterans must not be victims of an abnormal market.

Your responsibility will not be confined to returning veterans, of course. When the war ends, millions of other Americans and their families will need new and better homes. They must be provided in a manner to help build better cities and towns than this country ever has known in the past.

This is our future task. We have another to finish first—and nothing must be allowed to interfere with it until complete victory in this war is won. But a part of our job today is to guard against inflation in real estate, as well as other parts of our economy, if our postwar goals are to be met.

I am sure you will continue your contribution to the war-time housing program and to the War Bond drives in which you have served so well in the past.

Please extend my greetings to all those attending your conference.

Very sincerely yours,

(Signed) FRANKLIN D. ROOSEVELT

Board of Directors and War Conference,
United States Savings and Loan League,
221 North LaSalle Street,
Chicago 1, Illinois

Letter from President Franklin Delano Roosevelt stressing the postwar need for the cooperation of savings and loan associations in providing loans for adequate housing to returning veterans

Readjustment Act was the one piece of legislation adopted by the 69th Congress which would have the greatest bearing on the future of the savings and loan business and the economic future of the nation. Certainly the contribution of the veterans loan program to the readjustment of returning servicemen was one of the outstanding successes in all the planned efforts of the nation to cope with after-the-war problems. And as far as savings and loan institutions were concerned, the League president's prophesy was certainly borne out.

The savings and loan business not only led the way among private lenders in making the VA loan work, but it also thereby placed itself high in public understanding and favor. Certainly the inspiration which had led leaders of the savings and loan business to study carefully the various legislative drafts of the G.I. Bill of Rights and "to stay with" the legislative developments until they emerged in an acceptable statute was vindicated to a degree not previously approached, except in the efforts to establish the Federal Home Loan Bank System. The following chapter will give more detail of the veterans home loan plan in operation and its relationship to the postwar economy.

The influence of the government guarantee of veterans home loans upon subsequent government relations with mortgage lending became ultimately entangled with the whole problem of legislative or administrative controls of interest rates charged in private credit transactions. Much more than in the FHA program, the VA loan arrangements tended to keep alive a belief that it is possible to fix the price of money at a level which disregards the variations of demand in relation to supply. In contrast to the obvious benefits of the VA loan program to the savings and loan business, and to the veterans, must be balanced the disadvantage of the preoccupation with controlling interest rates which lingered into the 1960s.

Chapter 14

The transition
from war to peace

The United States spent three and a half years in a state of hostilities, with the people and their business and social institutions turned aside from normal objectives to focus on winning a war in Europe and Africa and in the waters of the Pacific. The nation was thus engaged in an overall effort entirely new to most of the men and women then living and working. It was, however, an effort to which they grew accustomed. Thus it took time for people and their economic processes to be refocused on that "domestic tranquility" mentioned in the preamble to the Constitution.

Moreover the creaking and groaning of the economic and social ship of state, as it sailed into the unprecedented waters of "reconversion," was almost as notable as that which accompanied its violent precipitation into war. Roughly, the transition required approximately a year and a half. The European phase of the war ended on May 8, 1945, and the Pacific conflict came formally to an end on

August 14, 1945. Thus the time span from mid-1945 to the end of 1946 can appropriately be characterized as the period primarily concerned with retooling (a favorite word of the time) for peace-time pursuits. The retooling had to be applied to the minds and ways of many human beings as well as to factories that could now resume making automobiles instead of bombers and fighter planes. The savings and loan business did not so much have to retool itself as to adapt to a retooling world.

Most people had tried to get a head start on the process. In fact, the United States had been in combat status scarcely a year when some thinking in business and government began to be directed toward what should be done about a number of problems, once the war would be over. A story illustrative of the public fervor about solving the problems of the postwar period was that of the man who asked his 12-year-old daughter in the seventh grade what the class was taking up this year and got the answer, "We are taking up postwar planning."

It was as if the nation, having mastered the technique of financing the war, turning out armaments and mobilizing the manpower for both military and civilian needs, was ready by 1943 to think about the challenge beyond the routines of the war. It could leave to the military (including of course the Commander-in-Chief, the President of the United States) the grand strategy of war. Meanwhile it could think ahead to a day and situation with which the ingenuity of individuals would be more compatible—a peacetime world.

Characteristics of postwar planning

The postwar planning of 1943 and 1944 was dominated by a perfectly normal drive to avoid the pitfalls which the nation had faced in 1918 and 1919, when the last Great War had stopped. Practically all such thinking, therefore, anticipated a recession in business such as that in 1919. This was, of course, a mistaken premise and many problems of the transition years arose from this conspicuous error in judgment.

But the postwar planning activity also labored under a bequest from the planning, devising and legislating which had dominated the 1930s in Washington. Apart from the forward thinking which looked principally to avoiding expected and temporary troubles, many plans were sweepingly Utopian. They bore the certain fingerprints of those who wished to solve most major human, as well as economic, problems by way of government. They often caused delays, confusion and even resentment—and thus they hampered what would have been a more natural process of transition through the interplay of supply and demand.

Private industry spokesmen as well as government personnel were articulate as they looked ahead at the postwar scene. For instance, Henry J. Kaiser, whose name carried magic for all who had seen his performance in the production of Liberty Ships, came out with what he called a "plan to end all plans," and he had much to say about housing. Following the pattern of most of the thinkers of that period, he suggested the need for organization of companies to build modern housing "for rent as well as for sale."

The discussion of the incentives of the Servicemen's Readjustment Act in the previous chapter referred to memories of veterans of World War I and their trouble in finding a place to live. Two motivations converged in the postwar planning about housing which began in 1943. One was the determination that the veterans would not again have to put up with grave hardships about shelter when they came back to civilian life; the other was the large hangover of theory and experiment and successful innovation in the methods of financing homes which had come out of the depression of the 1930s.

This duality of approach was characteristic of all shades of economic and philosophical thought about postwar needs and problems, even though the major emphasis differed according to the source of the plan. Indeed the formulators of blueprints for postwar housing production included all shades of ideological convictions. The Chamber of Commerce of the United States, always the great bastion of conservative thinking, was, for instance, just as avid about planning as were the best-known public housing advocates.

Savings and loan planning

The savings and loan business had the kind of leadership that could not have turned a deaf ear to the rumblings of postwar planning. This was the idea of the hour, and all had to delve into it to some extent. But the motivation of the savings and loan people, looking squarely at the postwar prospects of the business, was much more concrete than merely mounting the band wagon of the national fascination with planning for postwar. Savings and loan leaders were well aware that some influences in the government in Washington were in dead earnest about changing the entire pattern of housing production and finance. As practical men and women, they thought that the best way to counteract this influence was to see how the traditional methods of financing home ownership could be adapted to new needs and unprecedented opportunities and to pave the way for that adaptation.

In the spring of 1943 the president of the United States League appointed a Committee on the Postwar Program of the business, and its 32 members went to work that summer. For them the League staff had collected a stack of papers containing every postwar plan that had been published with any reference to mortgage financing and home ownership; some sane ideas and several fantastic ones were included. The committee thus had the materials at hand to appraise the atmosphere in which its own proposals might have to establish their validity.

The appointed group looked at where the likely competition for both savings accounts and mortgage loans would emerge after the war. They took the measure of the thrift incentive and appraised its sturdiness in the face of social security and a possible government compulsory savings plan, such as had already been suggested. Most challenging was the question they asked each other, "Can we conceive a better mortgage plan?"

The committee proceeded by way of several subcommittees and each made its progress report in 1944, presenting the major substance of its findings to the business as a whole, before it shaped the final report. Many savings and loan executives thus took part in developing the postwar plans. From the vantage point of nearly 20 years later, the major surprise is the realization that some commonplace occurrences in savings and loan operations in the 1960s were rarities in association practice as late as 1944.

Forward-looking loan plan

The really new ground which was ploughed by the postwar committee was its work in devising a modern style, conventional loan characterized by flexibility and liberality. A significant advance for savings and loan thinking emerged. The major proposals were

238

intended to counteract some of the disadvantages which detractors of home ownership had been repeating for years; for instance, the recommendation was made that the borrower be entitled to a lapse of a certain number of payments as long as he was paying ahead of his contract. Another liberal interpretation of the borrower-lender contract was suggested in the six-months leeway in monthly payments to be granted after the first advance for new construction, with interest charged only from the date of each advance. And the borrower would have a right to a grace period of six months, if need was indicated, once he had paid according to schedule for three full years; this grace period was to be his right and not by sufferance of the lender.

All these particular recommendations reflected the depression concern of people who had lost their homes because they could not meet the payments. These recommendations as well as others offered by the Postwar Committee were designed to get away from that rigidity in mortgage lending practice which had made the home owner's problems more difficult when he got into trouble in the 1930s.

As a background for the insistence of the committee on such provisions, one must remember that as late as 1944 no one was sure that the traditional belief in owning a home would return in full force on the American scene. No one was sure that there would ever again be wide-scale acceptance of the idea of going into debt for a home. This skepticism seems incredible in view of the spectacular leaps ahead in percentage of owner occupancy of homes in the United States in the decade of 1950-1960. But the makers of postwar plans had to operate out of their experience, having no clear crystal balls.

Because there was a hue and cry about low interest rates on home mortgage money—then as now, and *ad infinitum* one suspects—the Committee on the Postwar Program recommended that associations adopt a step-down interest rate plan for their mortgages. It suggested an attractive interest rate with a minimum of three contractual reductions, each of one-half a percentage point during the lifetime of the loan. The average rate to be paid over the full period of the loan was suggested to be no more than 5%. Other features recommended for an extremely forward-looking association included loan maturities up to 16 to 20 years; the right to prepay the mortgage without penalty; required budgeting of taxes and insurance on a monthly basis (it was only optional in most cases in 1944); an open-end clause in the mortgage permitting additional advances for repair, modernization, equipment or other purposes; and promptness in making a loan commitment as well as in closing the loan and disbursing the funds. It also was recommended that associations provide for assistance to operative builders by offering blanket mortgages under which money would be advanced for labor and materials, the individual houses being released for permanent mortgage arrangements as each was sold.

The planners of the postwar program must be credited with prophetic vision in realizing that financing operative builders was going to be a dominant activity in the future. And again, reflecting the widely propounded theory that there would have to be more rental housing, the League committee talked about associations making multiunit loans as part of their forward mortgage lending plan. And to meet still another home ownership objection often repeated by the liberals of the day, the committee suggested a provision in the mortgage for assistance to the borrower in disposing of his house when he had to move. (The contention was frequently made in those days that a seller would lose money on his house if he had to move.)

With so many suggestions for breaking with overall precedent in the business, it is not surprising that the committee prefaced the release of its loan plan with the comment that it was "submitting its most bold, most interesting and most controversial study." Ten years later the United States League Committee on Loan Procedures updated the plan, giving it the specific name of the "Savings and Loan Mortgage Plan," thereby witnessing to the fact that the basic features had become commonplace.

But the plan was launched with fanfare in 1944 and got wide newspaper and periodical coverage. Of course some of the features were either limited in their appeal, because problems of the postwar period turned out to be different from those expected, or were designed to meet home ownership objections which no longer made any sense in an era when home ownership swept forward with a great surge. Certainly the main outlines of the postwar committee's suggestions in 1944 went far to preserve the competitive impact of the conventional loan program. Not least among these was that associations make loans with maturities up to 16 and 20 years.

Aside from doing its own postwar planning in order to get savings and loan thinking recast into the mold of the future, the business had to keep on studying and trying to help shape the other postwar planning in which the nation was indulging.

Utopian housing plans

More Utopian postwar planning in and out of government was focused on housing than on any other phase of the economy. The National Resources Planning Board—an agency of the federal government—drew up a blueprint in 1943. It claimed that the American building industry had never been organized on the scale suitable to undertake rebuilding America's cities; therefore, it wanted the terms and conditions of federal intervention after the war to be spelled out clearly. Here one finds the first official advocacy of a Federal Urban Affairs Department in the executive establishment, an idea which later became part of the program of the administration of President John F. Kennedy.

The House of Representatives was alert to the obvious hostility to the private enterprise system in some of the proposals of the National Resources Planning Board and cut off the appropriation of this agency for the fiscal year 1944, ending its activities. To fill the gap, the Senate created its own Special Committee on Postwar Economic Policy and Planning. Since this committee was a congressional group, its activities were much more in the open than those of the planning board had been, and its policies were formulated only after lengthy hearings at which many segments of American life were heard. This group printed volumes of comprehensive statements made by those asked to contribute; it was 1945 and well near the end of the war before this committee's report was rendered.

Taft subcommittee on housing

Dividing its work into several subcommittees, the Senate group committed to the Honorable Robert A. Taft of Ohio, who was later to become one of the most influential voices of the Republican Party, the chairmanship of a Subcommittee on Housing and Urban Redevelopment. The Taft subcommittee held extensive hearings. Among the matters on which it asked views was the proper organization for the savings and loan agencies then under the Federal Home Loan Bank Administration. The United States League Executive Committee drew up a comprehensive and detailed statement of savings and loan convictions about the role of the government in housing and in meeting foreseeable future needs.

The influence of the Taft committee's report upon future legislation and upon the direction of government action in the housing field can scarcely be overestimated. Out of it came the large volume of new housing provisions which reached the statute books as the Housing Act of 1949. And out of it, too, came the push for a top-level housing agency of permanent character, with the Federal Home Loan Bank Board, and the instrumentalities under its aegis, as only downgraded constituent units of the agency.

Its influence came from much more than the voluminous collection of views and proposals made by the Taft committee. The Ohio Senator had long since made an exception to his basic conservatism in the case of his views about housing. He conceded that the hand of the federal government in removing the "impossible" housing conditions in cities was a necessity. He hoped that it would not have to be *too great*. But forever after, his declared stand on this issue was the subject of reference and commendation by every exponent of big government housing programs. It provided a thin, but faithfully cherished, top soil for the growth of the sentiment that government housing was a nonpartisan issue.

Influence of VA loan

But the most successful and significant postwar planning from Washington was the enactment of the Servicemen's Readjustment Act. Most importantly in 1945 and 1946, it represented the most conservative approach of any that was being developed in Washington to solve the housing shortage after the war. Proponents of this plan were working for home ownership when hundreds of planning experts were talking about rental housing, multifamily dwellings and use of the centralized facilities of government to plan the whole housing production for 150 million people.

Table 19 shows the importance of the financing furnished under the VA loan plan in relation to total home mortgage lending during the first five years after the legislation was enacted. The figures speak for themselves as to the effectiveness of the Servicemen's Readjustment Act as a piece of postwar planning.

Table 19. *Home loans guaranteed by Veterans Administration and total nonfarm mortgage recordings, 1945-1949*

Year	VA loans	Total nonfarm mortgage recordings
1945	$ 192,240,000	$ 5,649,819,000
1946	2,303,307,000	10,589,168,000
1947	3,286,166,000	11,728,677,000
1948	1,880,967,000	11,882,114,000
1949	1,423,591,000	11,828,001,000

Sources: *Federal Home Loan Bank Board and Veterans Administration, annual reports*

As a result of the Servicemen's Readjustment Act over 14 million men and women were entitled to a guarantee, by the Veterans Administration, of a significant portion of their debts incurred to own a home. The law was enacted in a period of high-hearted idealism about those in uniform. In the summer of 1944 a large number of these men were finishing their most heralded undertaking, the invasion of the Normandy Coast. Making life more desirable for these people when they returned home was thus a natural sentimental response of a nation which realized that so much was being dared and suffered by those in the armed forces.

Making the VA-guaranteed home loan program work, however, required something more than a sentimental response. As was noted in the preceding chapter, savings and loan institutions had recognized the appropriateness of their type of financing as a channel through which the veteran might get his loan. Representatives of the business working with the Veterans Administration technicians evolved, over long and tedious sessions, a set of regulations with which the private financial institutions could do the job.

Making the VA plan work

The League had publicly, and privately in its discussions with officials, pledged all-out support to the Veterans Administration; when lending got under way the savings and loan associations demonstrated their sincerity in this pledge. They made the first loans in the majority of communities. They did the bulk of the VA loan advertising. They explained the program to practically everybody, from members of draft boards to the personnel of commercial banks. They were on the receiving end of the great bulk of in-

243

quiries and applications for loans. In many cases the Veterans Administration was directly referring the applications for loans to savings and loan institutions.

This kind of comprehensive effort to put the program across had not come by accident or by just moving with the tide and extemporizing as the situation demanded. Here was an activity which fitted the United States League's well-organized machinery and personnel perfectly. It had public appeal; it had savings and loan appeal. The government and the Congress were intent upon seeing it succeed; therefore, the League's efforts were across the board. It produced pamphlets explaining the VA loan from the point of view of the veteran so that these could be printed in quantity and the associations could have them handy at their counters. It devised a procedures manual for the use of all savings and loans in making VA loans.

It made contacts with veterans organizations to offer the services of savings and loan associations to returning servicemen. It organized clinics on regional and local bases so that questions and answers unsolved by reading pamphlets could be thrashed out. A special course of the American Savings and Loan Institute was written and taught on the subject of VA lending. The Advertising Division of the League created advertising copy specially designed for associations to attract VA loans.

Back of all other considerations on the part of the savings and loan leaders was the realization that this plan of depending on existing lenders to finance veterans homes was definitely on trial. No one had any illusion about the permanence of this plan, if it did not make a good showing. The original draft of the legislation, which had in it the form of direct government loans at unparalleled low interest rates, could always be resurrected to displace the guaranteed loan plan, if the lenders did not make loans to veterans. With its deep-seated conviction and tradition against government lending, the savings and loan business knew that it, too, was on trial in 1945 and 1946.

The venture of faith in regard to veterans home loans was indeed bread cast upon the waters by the savings and loan business. Through its initial work in making loans of both unprecedentedly high percentages and long terms, the savings and loan business got invaluable experience in this type of mortgage arrangement. Over the years during which the veterans proved to be remarkably good risks, the associations came to realize that they needed to re-examine many of their previous notions about loan percentages and maturities. Thus the VA loan program was the first step on the way to the conventional loan arrangements of the late 1950s, which permitted loans up to 90% without government guarantees of any kind. The dual parenthood of the conventional loan program of the postwar expansion period may be found in the VA loan program and Postwar Planning Committee of the United States League.

A managing officer of one association gave a testimonial at the United States League's annual meeting in 1946 out of his first year's experience in the VA loan business. He had analyzed all such loans put on the association's books in 1945. It was a performance which could well stir many of his fellow mortgage lenders to action, if they had not previously been seeking such loans. The average loan was $3,950, and 78% of all the VA loans made by the institution that year were for $5,000 or less. Over 75% of the loans carried monthly payments of less than $40; the average veteran borrower was 29 years of age and earned a salary of $182 a month; the average size house he bought was 17,600 cubic feet, and over half of the houses were between 15 and 35 years old.

The description of the association's mood in undertaking the program is characteristic of the period. "We admit that we entered into the program somewhat as an experiment," said the speaker. "At the outset we had in mind a volume limited perhaps to 10% of our assets. We have long since abandoned that limitation. . . . We believe that it is good business; we believe that every savings and loan association in the country must enter the program."

Table 19 shows only $192 million of veterans guaranteed loans made by all lenders in 1945, the first full year after the program was inaugurated. This is not surprising, since relatively few veterans were home from the wars until the fall of that year. But of that $192 million, savings and loan institutions supplied $175 million. Then in 1946, when the number of men once more wearing civilian clothes increased, savings and loan associations made $1.25 billion out of the overall total of $2.3 billion of VA loans (Chart 7). These loans accounted for nearly 35% of the mortgage lending done by savings and loan institutions that year. This high percentage attributable to the savings and loan interest in the program levelled off as other lenders watched the savings and loan performance. Others saw that the law was workable and that

Chart 7. Annual volume of home loans guaranteed by Veterans Administration by type of lender, 1945-1949

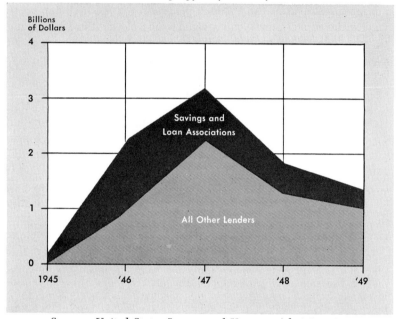

Sources: *United States League and Veterans Administration*

lenders could live with the risk of the new high percentage loans and the limited rate of 4% on the money lent to a veteran.

Savings and loan associations found the physical arrangements for making VA loans to their liking. Because the Veterans Administration already had its far-flung network of district and regional offices to handle various veterans benefits, it was able to assume the VA loan program with a minimum of extra payroll; thus the program did not suffer from having to assimilate a vast group of new personnel prone to create red tape. The VA's arrangement of qualifying a list of local appraisers acceptable to it, and leaving the choice of such an appraiser to the lending institution, was most acceptable to savings and loan executives.

VA influence on residential appraisers

The use of the fee appraiser system by the Veterans Administration was the keystone in the rapid postwar development of the

246

Society of Residential Appraisers, which the savings and loan business had sponsored in the mid-1930s. By its dependence on the professional appraisers practicing in the locality rather than on appraisers employed full-time on its own staff (the FHA system), the Veterans Administration created a prolific volume of new business for appraisers. They had to be the kind of appraisers who could do a creditable job and the Society of Residential Appraisers worked with the Veterans Administration in qualifying appraisers while accelerating its efforts to create a truly professional type of appraiser. Through these developments the entire level of residential appraising performance throughout the savings and loan business was improved.

Furthermore the development of the professional residential appraiser by the impact of the VA loan program encouraged more and more use of qualified appraisers in the savings and loan institutions at a time when new ventures in mortgage lending terms and maturities were becoming common. This development was one more way in which the VA loan played a noteworthy role in the evolution of the savings and loan institution as the foremost mortgage lender of the mid-century.

In the first two years most VA loans were made on existing rather than on newly built homes. The small stream of new home construction, which in 1946 was just beginning to trickle in, is an unforgettable part of the story of America's transition from war to peace.

Trials of the home building industry

The U.S.A.'s most prolonged period of trial and error in restoring the pace of peacetime production came in the building industry. This fact made the transition period a memorable one for savings and loan institutions, but the facts of the performance should be of interest to all the American people. An unprecedented housing shortage cried out to be solved as early as the fall of 1945. The federal government, many of whose officials had been talking about postwar plans for two and a half years, was unprepared to do its necessary part when the problem arose. But the housing shortage after World War II presented a veritable laboratory for trying out the dream of planning housing production from a central source, with the allocation of materials and manpower devised on a drafting board in Washington to achieve a prearranged and widely announced goal.

The whole attempt was calamitous in its execution. Over a year and a half was wasted in attempts to meet the housing shortage by plans diametrically opposed to the experience of the building industry. The authorities in Washington chose to retain an elaborate system of priorities in building materials, with price control on the materials, despite the early abandonment of controls over building wages. Coupled with this situation was a price ceiling of $6,000 on all new houses built (with the cost of labor uncontrolled, the whole price-fixing scheme seriously restricted all-out production).

Furthermore the various housing authorities (and there were several different ones trying to treat this phase of the problem) in Washington were working on the basis of three hypotheses. One was that rental housing should be the primary means by which the housing shortage was met. Another was that the home prefabrication industry was the destined instrument for a rapid wiping out of the shortage. The third was that the new housing must be concentrated in the area of low-cost, minimum types of shelter.

By the time Congress convened in 1946, the housing shortage created by the continuation of controls and the dominance of the questionable policies mentioned above had caused the public to be up in arms. It was to remain a burning question throughout the year; as the Housing Committee of the United States League summarized it, "Never before in history has housing so concerned the public, the press, the business and the government, and never before have savings and loan leaders and organizations had a greater responsibility for promoting clear thinking and intelligent action in home building." The scene now began to be cluttered with trailers and hundreds of thousands of temporary housing units, along with a few thousand "prefabs."

In May, when the war had been over almost a year and the shortage loomed so spectrally, Congress enacted legislation which compounded the problem. The new law offered $600 million in subsidies to the building materials dealers and to the housing prefabricators to persuade them to push production with zeal and determination. But the controls were not relaxed. As a spokesman for the building materials group told the United States League convention the following November they did not need the incen-

248

tive of the $600 million. What they did need was the opportunity to produce free from the restrictions of the Office of Price Administration.

Freedom to build

This freedom finally came in December 1946. About the only significant limitation retained in the liberalized legislation enacted during the Christmas period in regard to home builders and buyers of the United States was the 1,500-square-foot limitation for a single unit (a relic of the conviction that new housing must be built in the lower price ranges). It took another four or five months and some legislation by a more conservative Congress before the whole experiment could be written off. But with the relaxations permitted at the end of 1946 the building industry was able to tool up for the housing job ahead. Before 1947 was very far along it was working veritable miracles in production; a total of 845,000 new units was started in 1947.

In 1946 the word "starts" had had a particularly ironic flavor. One of the frustrations of home builders and home mortgage lenders was the repeated inability at that time to bring a house to completion because of the lack of some piece of wood, brick or pipe. Human nature proved, however, to be no less resourceful in this crisis than in any other. It became fairly common for a shell of a house to be built with the thought that it could be completed once materials were plentiful.

But one of the haunting fears of savings and loan institutions with regard to financing home construction had always been the risk of an uncompleted building. They had acquired this healthy conservatism in an era of fly-by-night builders in the 1920s. The obvious loss that a mortgagee would have to take, in such a situation, was written large in their consciousness. Thus the savings and loan associations' eagerness to concentrate on home construction suffered temporarily from the situation into which home building had fallen in the months immediately following the war.

The associations loaned only $616 million for new construction in 1946, while extending $2,357 million of credit for home purchases. But this comparative drop in the bucket to their future performance in construction lending does testify to the effort being made by hundreds of associations to assist the small home builders in their localities wherever the risk was at all compatible with the good sense of management. On the whole, managers worked hard to back up their leaders, who joined with other components of the construction industry to support the saner, traditional American approach to building homes.

First inflationary fears

Also by 1946 the mortgage lenders and the people as a whole had begun to have their fears of something which has had a menacingly long life, namely, inflation. The United States had financed World War II primarily by increasing the money supply; thus it built into the economy a base for a higher price level. By strict controls over prices while hostilities were on, the effect of this financing operation was hidden. Once the price controls were removed a major upward thrust of the cost of living was apparent. Rents were held down, because they were kept under control long after everything else was allowed to seek the level determined by supply and demand.

But by now building costs averaged about 50% higher than their prewar level. The inefficiency of the building operation hampered by controls was expected to be cured and to usher in a period of lower costs. Thus there was one widely held opinion that people were going to have to pay high prices for new houses in 1946 or 1947, and then see their values decline drastically in another year or two. Warnings came from all quarters against lending on the inflated values of the period. At the start, one of the salient features of the VA loan program was the provision that the veteran must be protected against overindulgence in a home he could not afford.

At the urging of the American Legion's Rehabilitation Committee an appraiser for a VA loan was charged with the responsibility, above all else, of seeing that the veteran got reasonable value in the house he was buying. By one of those quirks of fate, the lawmakers, administrators and appraisers, who were trying so hard to protect the veteran at that time, ended by discouraging thousands from buying properties whose values doubled or possibly tripled in another 10 years!

Today's readers will find it hard to realize that, in 1946, when a 1,500-square-foot house could be built for $7,500, anyone should have been worried about the borrower paying too much for the house. But people were indeed worried about it then—and even for a few more years afterward.

The cessation of hostilities brought an end to an era of transition and marked the beginning of an era of expansion. The new era, as it will be seen in Chapter 15, was characterized by massive changes that were beyond the ability of even the most careful observers to forecast. These changing forces shaped the savings and loan business as we know it today.

Part four

The great expansion

1947-1960

Chapter 15

National background
of the great expansion

The modern savings and loan institution was the result of consistent improvements during the 1947-1960 period in its forms and procedures. Because of these developments savers were assured safety, good earnings, liquidity and convenience. At the same time the cumulative improvement of the mortgage contract assured that the unprecedented reservoir of savings which the associations attracted was desired by, as well as available to, the people who wanted to own homes.

But these improvements alone do not explain the great expansion of the savings and loan business in this period. They must be viewed against the background of the economic and social changes which followed World War II, if the full story of what happened to the savings and loan business is to emerge. The economic changes were sweeping in terms of size of production, levels of prices and methods of doing business. The social changes, involving such widely varying things as where people lived and what they thought, were also notable.

The main outward circumstances of 1947-1960 which had a bearing on savings and loan development were: 1) the nation's unexampled prosperity accompanied by a permanently higher price level and a conspicuous enlargement of the middle class; 2) the urbanization (and suburbanization) of society bringing about a mobility unparalleled even in a country noted for its mobile population; 3) the gradual but firm establishment of housing as a continuing concern of the federal government; and 4) the dominance of national thought patterns by those who had left 1930-1947 behind and who characteristically accepted changed institutions with the same alacrity as they bought the new products that came into the market with every rising sun. These factors which had a profound influence on savings association growth are described in subsequent sections.

In 1947, in the first blush of release from all the restrictions of war, the ordinary citizens did what anyone would have expected: They spent some of their accumulated savings; they made fewer and fewer trips to the savings windows of financial institutions with any of their crisp new currency. Then, in 1948, they saved a little more of their incomes, having exhausted some of the force of the first temptation to spend. By the 1950s these people as a whole were conditioned to saving about 6% to 7½% of total income annually.

Observers who had predicted that the postwar bubble was going to burst very soon had a short-lived but genuine alarm over the slight dip of the business indexes in 1949. When, however, this turned out to be only a minor adjustment, the country was well on the way to a prosperity that people began to accept as a permanent thing. General deflation failed to materialize in 1949 and thus the postwar era was launched on a plateau of high prices. The adjusting populace developed a new addiction to the somewhat irrational behavior of saving money with one hand and going deeply into debt with the other in order to buy consumer goods and such permanent assets as a house and yard. In reconciling this behavior with common sense they were assisted, of course, by the income tax laws. Rates on individual and corporate incomes remained high, but full deductions were permitted for interest on borrowed money.

Spending pattern

The country's spending nearly doubled in the 1947-1957 decade. Unsatisfied wartime demand and highly liquid assets in individual bank accounts had apparently touched off a spending pattern that was lasting. And the government's fiscal behavior led the way. Although 1947 would generally be recognized as the year the American people forgot World War II, one should remember that as early as the spring of that year the first rumblings of the cold war between the East and West could be heard; the Marshall Plan was launched in 1947. And within 10 years federal government purchases of goods and services had risen 103% above the 1947 low point. State and local outlays were close behind.

The full extent of the price rise from pre-World War II days was obscured when a new base period of 1946-1947 was adopted for all the major government statistics on purchasing power. This decision also represented an admission that no one any longer thought prices would go very much below this level in the foreseeable future. Meanwhile the entire nation enjoyed a remarkably bracing business climate in which associations shared.

Rise in price level

The gradual nature of the increase in the price level enabled mortgage lenders to accept, without too many misgivings, the most spectacular price increase of all, that in homes. The chapters dealing with the war have already made frequent reference to minimum homes costing $3,000 and $4,000. There were no homes in this price level, new or old, by the 1950s. The cost of building had roughly tripled by the end of the decade from the prewar level. The cost of a home was ordinarily three times as great, not only because of the rise in the cost of construction but because the American people were demanding and getting much more and better material and equipment in their homes.

And the dilemma of how to keep costs in line was compounded by the rising cost of land on which to build. A considerable body of opinion has persisted that the continual liberalization of credit, fostered by the federal government in most of these postwar years, had its part in the price increases. At least, the stretching of credit terms made it possible for the booming building industry to get new customers by lowering the monthly costs to the buyers; and there was, conversely, little need to strive too laboriously to get the cost down to their pocketbooks.

For the savings and loan institutions the spectacular increase in the cost of residential properties spelled a need for a much larger dollar volume of loans. Even without the important increase in the number of home loans made in the postwar period, the demand for savings and loan dollars would have been magnified considerably by the larger individual mortgage the average home owner had to have in order to buy. Higher percentage loans were increasingly accepted; they also contributed to the year-by-year expansion of the mortgage volume of savings and loan institutions. Associations were serving a larger number of families, helping them to buy, build or remodel, than they had ever imagined possible.

Home building boom

The scope of the home building pattern of the 1950s defied all previous predictions. The wilder dreams of those who wanted the government to take over building to insure that enough units would be produced per year to keep housing going were far surpassed by the performance of private home building under the impact of market forces. Thirteen million new units were built between 1947 and 1960 (see Chart 8).

The earlier predictions about real needs for new homes fell short of actual needs principally because they had not anticipated the exceptional force of the move from the farms to the cities and from the cities to the suburbs. As a special phenomenon, the spreading out of the American metropolis over the countryside of yesteryear became not only the most talked about event of the 1950s, but also one of the most influential. The immediate impact was the creation of many times more one-family homes than had been envisioned in the rosiest postwar planning. It will be recalled that emphasis on rental housing was included in all the look-ahead pronouncements during the war years. As it happened, rental housing was the last phase of the home building boom of the 1950s.

Contrary to popular impressions that people would be reluctant about home ownership, every family that could scrape together a down payment and could stretch its income to meet a monthly payment on the house decided to buy one. In the earlier postwar

Chart 8. Nonfarm housing units started, privately owned, 1947-1960

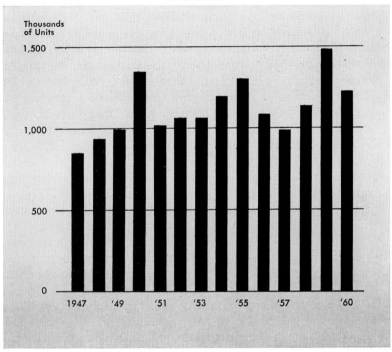

Note: 1947-1958, old series; 1959-1960, new series
Source: Housing and Home Finance Agency, annual report, 1960, p. 317

years a great many were forced to do so because there were no places to rent. The continued interest in the privately owned home indicated clearly, however, that the average American family really preferred this way of life, if it could have it. The one-to-four family home had, of course, been the mainstay of all lending activity of savings and loan institutions from the start. The almost exclusive concern of the home building industry in the 1950s with one-family homes gave the associations a much greater than expected entree to one of the major markets of the times.

Families on the move

The migration of families to entirely different sectors of the country lent great strength to the demand for new homes to be built. The breaks with tradition in living conditions which accompanied wartime marriages tended to make people willing to leave their home communities. Thus they found it easier to move to a climate where gentle breezes and more sunshine beckoned or where unusual opportunities for work and income abounded. Since homes cannot easily be transported, the predictions about the overall need for new housing were overthrown during this particular period by the fact that many couples had to have a new home in the town to which they were moving, even if they owned one in the old home town. They would, of course, also need to have the services of a mortgage lender all over again.

Some official statistics will shed a little light on the extent of this moving around. In 1940 the enumerators of the regular decennial census had found that about one-eighth of the entire population was living in counties where they had not resided five years before. By 1947 the Census Bureau estimated that about one-fifth of the population had changed its county of residence during the preceding seven years. For the postwar story the Census Bureau has more minute data. Every year from 1950 through 1958 roughly 1/14th of the people crossed county boundaries for new dwellings.

But there was the even more startling intracounty migration. In 1947 the Census showed that 44 million civilians were in the same county but not living in the same house as seven years before. And every year of the 1950s saw, for the country as a whole, a minimum of 20 million families moving to a different house in the same county where they had been living.

In 1949 the Congress enacted a housing act with a lengthy preamble. The gist of it was that the government had a duty to see to it that every American citizen had a decent home. The preamble became a platform on which shapers of housing legislation in the Congress stood sturdily year by year and from which they continually pleaded and declaimed.

Congress and home building

An emerging home building industry, whose units of operation were larger and whose sights were higher than had ever been characteristic before 1930, rose to meet the great demand for new homes, once the trammeling regulations of war and transition had been abandoned. The National Association of Home Builders, founded in 1942, had 44,000 members by 1960. And its research showed that in 1960 the average builder had been in business just about 11 years.

The sturdy new giant industry made fast friends with the leaders of the Congress; housing had early proved itself to be a politically popular issue. Housing subcommittees were appointed in Congress after Congress by the Banking Committees of both Senate and House of Representatives. Scarcely a year passed but major attention was given to new needs for legislation in order to make the rate of home construction a major factor of the nation's prosperity. A decade of amendments to the basic housing acts fixed permanently in the minds of the general public the concept that housing activity of the nation was a normal, natural and inevitable concern of the government of the United States. By these enactments, increasing portions of the nation's capital funds

Chart 9. Annual volume of nonfarm mortgage recordings by type of lender, 1947-1960

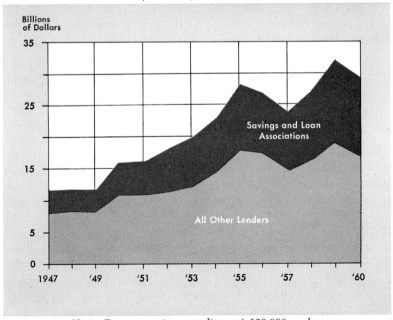

Note: Data comprise recordings of $20,000 or less
Source: Federal Home Loan Bank Board, annual reports

went into the financing of home construction.

A review of the governmental actions which influenced the mortgage market during this period will show the swings of the pendulum from credit expansion to contraction and vice versa. The swings toward expansion, however, went much farther and were more frequent than those toward contraction; and in the dominance of the expansion swing lies the clear witness to a government philosophy which was new. This philosophy was that housing is a segment of the economy demanding special treatment to assure a flow of credit which it would not ordinarily attract. This attitude in federal affairs from 1946 on was new and far-reaching. Chart 9 shows the trend in the volume of nonfarm mortgage recordings accounted for by savings and loan associations and by all other mortgagees combined.

Government impact on mortgage money

Roughly 30 major steps by government agencies and by Congress can be detected in this first era of conscious, continuing Washington policies toward home financing. The steps are worth reviewing, since home financing is the major function of the savings and loan business:

Expansion. In the spring of 1946 the Congress amended the FHA mortgage insurance provisions, reviving such liberal wartime Title VI practices as basing appraisals on the concept of "necessary current cost" rather than "value." Maximum insurable loan amounts were substantially increased on owner-occupied, as well as rental-type, properties.

Expansion. The Housing Act of 1948 authorized higher maximum loan-to-value ratios and longer maturities for the permanent FHA mortgage insurance program under Title II. The maximum maturity for mortgages on any new construction was extended to 25 years; and 30-year maturities were authorized on mortgages of $6,000 or less on new construction. The new law also provided for special new programs of mortgage insurance and gave the moribund Federal National Mortgage Association a new lease on life, with authority to purchase, with Treasury funds, VA-guaranteed as well as FHA loans. The FNMA was also given power to issue advance commitments to purchase such loans.

Expansion. In 1949 the mortgage lending situation was eased by an extension of the liberal terms of Section 608 FHA insurance (war, and later defense, housing) beyond their March 31 expiration date. (This was the first of several extensions which continued this Title in effect until March 1, 1950.) By this move a significant expansion program was kept alive.

Expansion. In the Housing Act of 1950 the attractiveness of VA and FHA mortgage programs to borrowers and, to some extent, to lenders was enhanced. The VA-guaranteed portion of mortgage loans was increased from 50% to 60% and the top limit of the guarantee, dollarwise, was raised from $4,000 to $7,500; the permissible maturity of a Veterans Administration guaranteed loan was raised from 25 to 30 years. For FHA the new Housing Act instituted a new program of mortgage insurance, on liberal terms, for small houses in rural communities and areas outside those usually regarded as economically sound for Section 203 mutual mortgage insurance.

Contraction. In a little over two months after the 1950 Housing Act was approved, the Korean War broke out; the direction of government influence on mortgage credit policy was abruptly shifted. For about three years thereafter Washington used its influence to restrain mortgage lending. Under terms of the Defense Production Act, adopted in September 1950, authority was given to the President of the United States to regulate, for the first time, conventional mortgage credit; the Board of Governors of the Federal Reserve System acting for the President adopted Regulation X in October 1950; the regulation applied only to conventional credit extended on new residential units. The maximum loan-to-value ratios ranged from 90% on homes with a transaction price up to $5,000, through a series of steps down to 50% when the transaction price was over $20,000.

Contraction. In October 1950 the FHA and VA, by authority granted under the Defense Production Act, tightened up the terms of their assistance to loans on *existing* real estate as well as on new construction. Length of maturities was reduced from 30 to 25 and 20 years. The FHA loan-to-value ratios on all types of properties were placed at the same levels as those on newly built homes prescribed for conventional lending under Regulation X. Loan-to-value ratios on VA loans were set from five to 10 percentage points higher than on other types of loans in order to maintain the veterans preference according to the provisions of the Defense Production Act.

The period during which Regulation X and the accompanying FHA and VA tightening-up of terms was in force also saw the functioning of a National Voluntary Credit Restraint Committee. Its main activity was in the area of credit transactions where no legal restraint was applicable; generally speaking, its moral suasion was used to discourage any lending on more liberal terms than Regulation X.

Contraction. While not appearing on the surface as a direct part of the mortgage contraction program of the government, the accord between the Treasury and the Federal Reserve Board, providing for the Federal Reserve Board to stop buying government bonds at par in February 1951, had the effect of restricting mortgage money more seriously than the changes in loan terms. Mortgage lenders with government bonds still left in their portfolios could no longer sell them without experiencing the stresses and losses of the market. The general effect was a firming of interest rates over the ensuing years. This action initiated the first considerable period of years during which the maximum interest rates allowed on FHA-insured and VA-guaranteed loans were below the going rate on mortgage funds.

Contraction. In the period generally referred to as one of mortgage restraint by government influences, 1950-1953, the Federal National Mortgage Association faced four contractions: 1) stiffened requirements for eligibility of FHA and VA loans; 2) more limitation on lenders as to the percentage of loans they could sell to FNMA; 3) allocation of some FNMA funds to special programs; and 4) the suspension of all FNMA purchases not covered by special programs (such as the Defense Housing program, rushed into enactment as Title IX of the National Housing Act in 1951).

Expansion. In the summer of 1952 amendments to the Defense Production Act initiated the process of easing out the credit

264

restrictions. This legislation permitted down-payment requirements to be gradually lowered.

Expansion. By April of 1953 all remaining credit restrictions
were revoked by administrative acts. Statutory terms of mortgage
lending were restored to what they had been on October 12, 1950.

Expansion. Early in May 1953 the maximum interest rates on
both FHA and VA loans were raised to 4½% by the respective
agencies in charge.

Expansion. The Housing Amendments of 1953, enacted into
law on June 30, created a definite atmosphere of mortgage expansion again. The new legislation repealed a previous provision which
had forbidden the absorption of VA discounts; thus discounts
could again be used when interest ceilings required adjustment to
the going interest rate. It opened up new avenues of expansion
of mortgage funds by way of the Federal National Mortgage
Association: 1) part of the $900 million which had earlier been
reserved for military, defense and disaster mortgages was released
for purchase of any FHA or VA mortgages; 2) the so-called one-
for-one program was established through which FNMA could
agree with a lender, who bought mortgages from it, to buy an
equal amount back from him within one year. The $500-million
authorization for this program was exhausted before the year was
up, having proved an attractive means for builders to obtain short-
term interim financing for construction projects.

Expansion. The Housing Act of 1954, enacted August 2, was
the most comprehensive housing legislation the Congress had enacted since 1950, representing the program of the Eisenhower
Administration, which had just come into power, and incorporating
many recommendations of the special advisory committee that
had reported to the President the previous December. It substantially liberalized the terms under which the FHA could insure
mortgages on both new and existing properties, raising the maximum amount of loans on one- and two-family dwellings from
$16,000 to $20,000; it increased the maximum loan-to-value ratios
on new properties, from 90% to 95%, and on existing properties
from 80% to 90%. This action lengthened FHA mortgage ma-

turities from a maximum of 25 years to 30 years on all new construction.

Expansion. The Housing Act of 1954 also made specific changes in the federal statutes affecting the savings and loan business. The maximum amount of loan which a federal savings and loan association could make was lifted from $20,000 to $35,000, and the Federal Home Loan Banks were authorized to accept as collateral mortgages with maturities up to 25 years (the limit had been 20 before that).

Expansion. The Voluntary Home Mortgage Credit Program, established under the Housing Act of 1954, set up within the Housing Agency a clearing house for FHA and VA loan applications, principally from rural and minority groups that could not get financing from local sources. By this device mortgage credit was expanded some half a billion dollars over a six-year period.

Expansion. A major portion of the 1954 bill completely reorganized the Federal National Mortgage Association. Through this change it became three things: 1) a secondary market operation partly government, partly private enterprise; 2) a management and liquidation operation, dealing with the old FNMA portfolio acquired up to November 1, 1954 (these mortgages would be disposed of as the market permitted; by being held off the market when money was not plentiful they would thus have an indirectly expansionary effect on the market); 3) a special assistance function carrying over in a limited fashion the type of direct financing from the Treasury which had characterized the whole FNMA operation up to 1954.

Contraction. In the spring of 1955 the Federal Reserve Board reversed its policy of "ease" in the money markets to take action against inflationary developments, to "lean against the wind" as the Federal Reserve chairman expressed it. The "Fed" increased the rediscount rate four times in 1955 to supplement its open market operations in limiting bank credit expansion. In support of this general anti-inflationary credit policy, the FHA and the VA announced on April 28 the first of a series of moves to dampen the demand for mortgage credit; they announced that all closing costs associated with homes purchased with their assistance would have to be paid in cash. On July 30, they further restrained credit terms by adding two percentage points to the required minimum down payment and by reducing maximum loan maturities to 25 years.

Contraction. In mid-July the Federal Home Loan Bank Board urged member savings and loan institutions of the Federal Home Loan Bank System to curb their forward commitments to make loans. By the end of the summer of 1955, Federal Home Loan Bank advances had risen for the first time in the history of the Bank System to $1.2 billion (they had been less than $700 million 12 months earlier) and all Federal Home Loan Banks had raised their interest rates on advances. On September 13, a Board communication to all Federal Home Loan Banks suggested that they advise all member institutions to meet loan demands entirely out of new savings and loan repayments. The whole program was a decisive curb on the lending of many savings and loan associations which were relying more heavily than hitherto on borrowing to finance their expanded loan programs.

Expansion. By the end of 1955, however, most of the federal government policies with regard to mortgage credit were reversed. From then on to the end of the decade they were directed toward stimulation of market activity in home lending. In December 1955 the Federal Home Loan Bank Board eased restrictions so that member institutions were permitted to borrow again for the purpose of mortgage lending. The Board ruled, however, that member institutions could do so only up to 10% of their total savings capital.

Expansion. In January 1956 the FHA and VA once again authorized 30-year maximum maturities. To round out the series of Washington actions in favor of mortgage expansion, the FNMA announced an optional mortgage repurchase plan on January 25, 1956; it offered to repurchase at the same price the mortgages it had sold, provided they were offered back to it within nine months. Thus lending institutions were to be permitted to obtain temporary funds for new lending without losing permanently the good mortgages they might wish to retain.

Expansion. The Housing Act of 1956 (adopted in August) made the FHA loan-to-value ratios on existing homes equivalent to those on new houses. This change represented the final conclusion by the Congress that FHA had a *raison d'etre* not only because of the need of money for new construction, but also as a factor in an improved overall home mortgage lending system. The 1956 Act also increased loan-to-value ratios and maximum loan amounts on multifamily housing. It lowered from 3% to 2% the amount of the stock purchase required of sellers of mortgages to FNMA and gave the FNMA president discretion to lower it to 1%.

Expansion. In 1956 an extension of the VA loan program for World War II veterans—previously set to terminate in July 1957 —was enacted so that it would not expire until July 1958.

Expansion. Administrative action liberalizing government policies followed in September of 1956. The White House dramatized the release of restrictions by an announcement of coordinated action. The FHA reduced down-payment requirements on low-priced houses of $9,000 or less in value; the Federal Home Loan Bank Board increased the ratio of credit lines which the savings and loan institutions could use at Federal Home Loan Banks to 12.5% of their savings capital; the Federal National Mortgage Association lowered the stock purchase requirement to 1% of the value of mortgages sold.

Expansion. In November 1956, in order to lend all possible support to the new housing market, the Federal National Mortgage Association announced it would limit purchases to mortgages insured or guaranteed four months or less prior to the date they were offered for sale.

Expansion. The FHA increased its interest rate maximum to 5% in December 1956, the first time in three-and-a-half years that the rate had been changed. The change came as a result of the market forces. The great demand for credit had forced yields on long-term corporate bonds to 3.68%; on municipals to 2.86%; and on government bonds to 3.3%, the highest since the early days of the Great Depression. The average conventional loan rate was estimated at 5.07% for this latter part of 1956.

Expansion. The reversion to a new expansionist philosophy in late 1956 was the last major change in federal housing policy in the decade. The Housing Act of 1957 carried on the march toward lower and lower minimum down payments. Through it the Congress moved to let the FHA down-payment schedule approach that of the VA loan, inasmuch as VA loans, stymied by the low 4½% rate, were no longer being made in any volume. This legislation included another attempt to control the discounts on FHA and VA loans; the step was intended to expand the housing market but actually restricted the mortgage flow to some extent.

Expansion. The 1957 Act also increased the Treasury authority to buy the stock of the Federal National Mortgage Association; thus the possible total of FNMA debentures which could be sold was pushed up to $2.25 billion. The maximum amount of debentures which the Treasury could buy was also increased.

Expansion. By 1958 the nation had had a taste of recession again. As a consequence the Congress in April, in almost record time, adopted an Emergency Housing bill. It moved part way toward freeing the rate to coincide with market forces by enacting a new 4¾% interest rate ceiling on VA loans. New and more liberal minimum down payments on FHA loans up to $13,500 were authorized, subject to the discretion of the FHA commissioner. The FHA could now insure a mortgage where the borrower put up only 3% of the first $13,500 of house value. The discount controls adopted in 1957, and found restrictive and unworkable, were repealed.

Expansion. The meat of the Emergency Housing bill of 1958 was the provision for the FNMA (special assistance function) to have $1.5 billion to buy, at par, FHA and VA loans for new construction (up to $13,500 per mortgage). The FHA immediately cut the minimum down-payment regulations to the lowest points prescribed in the new law and the Veterans Administration raised the rate at which VA loans could be written.

Expansion. Again, in 1959, the Congress provided for a still lower minimum down-payment schedule for FHA loans, but gave the FHA commissioner discretion to put them into effect. (He

269

ordered them into effect in May 1960.) New higher mortgage limits of $22,500 and $25,000, respectively, were permitted on FHA-insured one- and two-family units. A new maximum mortgage limit for purchase by FNMA was placed at $20,000.

This is a bare outline of the Washington relationship to the home mortgage market in the years from the end of World War II through 1960. It will be evident that by the early 1950s the annual housing bill was a perennial favorite on Capitol Hill.

Conflicts over housing legislation

In 1954 the Democratic Party returned to power in both Houses of the Congress and remained in control of Congress up through the end of the Eisenhower Administration. This change in the political complexion of the legislative branch of government inaugurated a veritable tug-of-war on housing between the Congress and the administration. This situation operated to minimize the extreme expansion of mortgage credit sought by some members of Congress. Many members of the Housing Subcommittees of the respective Banking Committees felt that the preamble to the Housing Act of 1949 was a call to arms to the Congress and that each year must see further progress in the government's all-out program to assist the American people to better and better homes. Restraint in the form of vetoes was frequently exercised by the administration.

An example of the kind of program which was proposed, year after year, without success during this period was a subsidized housing program for middle-income families. Many different approaches were offered in successive Congresses. Doubtless the failure of these proposals was the result of the conflict over housing measures between Capitol Hill and the White House. But the idea was very much alive as the new decade of the '60s emerged. And as the 1960s dawned, the question was already being seriously asked by housing experts in the Congress whether or not further devices were needed to assure more capital for home construction.

There were some unfortunate aspects of the expansion and contraction pattern which Washington imposed on the home mortgage lending operation during these years. From time to time the federal government chose to use home construction as a lever in the business situation; it tried to stimulate or retard business activity as a whole by regulating the flow and ebb of mortgage money. When mortgage funds were scarce, the housing industry suffered acute setbacks; producers of building materials and operative builders were subject to loss of markets and labor faced a fall-off in employment as a result of the flight of capital to other investments. This was true, despite the fact that savings and loan institutions, whose sole business was mortgage lending, filled part of the void. Savings and loan funds were insufficient to finance all the home construction operations which had been supplied from other sources.

But savings and loan institutions established themselves in such periods without any doubt as the primary source of home mortgage money which could be tapped month in and month out, year in and year out. Furthermore the higher prestige of housing in the nation's governmental policy was one of the environmental factors that took savings and loan institutions to new financial heights. In this atmosphere savings and loan associations were able to realize a great deal of the promise of their earlier days of turmoil, adjustment and virtual rebirth. It is merely academic to ask the question, how much farther they might have gone in a less government-impacted mortgage lending situation. Chapter 17, which treats more specifically the legislative programs and positions of the savings and loan business in Washington during the postwar prosperity period, will provide more insight into the actions and reactions of leaders of the business in the course of these events.

Eyes on the future

The final factor of the general situation in which savings and loan institutions expanded after the war was the result of the inevitable passing of time. Practically a whole generation of Americans had lived in a state of crisis; those who came to business maturity in 1930 faced depression, readjustment, war and conversion back to peace. Inevitably they based decisions on the experience of those years. But with the late 1940s men who no longer were concerned with the earlier problems moved increasingly into positions of influence and high policy making.

Far more than has generally been given credit for the swift

changes of the postwar years, the coming of these men whose eyes were on the future must be regarded as pivotal. Their eyes were on the future in the sense both that they did not know the old issues and that they chose to see from a new point of view. They accepted the heavier hand of government in the private affairs of citizens of the United States as a matter of course; they might deplore it, but they were not preoccupied with fighting it. They tried rather to understand how it might be turned to the advantage of business and thus increase the service of business institutions to the public.

Furthermore the new men had an inherent belief that the objectives of the Employment Act of 1946 could be met by government; the pervading sentiment that "the government will not let a serious depression occur" expresses the approach of the average businessman of the 1950s as distinctly as one could expect it to be phrased. The so-called built-in stabilizers of the economy were accepted and relied upon. Time alone will tell whether or not this trust was well founded.

In such a frame of mind, the building up of an impressive financial institution as a major interest in a man's life was seen not only as a possible but also as a highly desirable goal. The men who were mainly responsible for savings and loan expansion were those who still cherished the dream of becoming captains of industry. The next chapter will attempt to appraise the contribution which management in the person of these men of acumen, ambition and energy made to the great savings and loan expansion of the era.

Chapter 16

Management
grasps the opportunity

The growth of the savings and loan business after World War II was astounding, viewed from any angle one chooses. Combined assets of all savings and loan institutions expanded more than six-fold between the end of 1946 and the end of 1960; the rise was from $10 billion to $72 billion in those 14 years. And in the course of that growth the savings and loan system passed some notable milestones.

It outdistanced the mutual savings banks in amount of savings in 1954; it had more money entrusted to it than was invested in United States savings bonds by 1958; and by 1958 it also had savings volume 80% as great as that held by commercial banks, compared with only 25% in 1946. Virtually all savings and loan institutions, large and small, participated in this expansion.

The growth is dramatically portrayed by comparisons of the size of the largest associations at the beginning and end of the 1946-1960 span. At the end of 1946 the largest member institution of the United States League had assets of $83.5 million; the two giants among the institutions by the end of 1960 had $862 million and $603 million, respectively. The next two boasted more than $400 million each (the two largest had been built partially as a result of mergers but the third and fourth ranking institutions had grown to that stature by sheer expansion of the original institution). Only 38 members of the United States League had assets of as much as $20 million at the end of 1946; there was no $100-million institution until 1948; by the end of 1960, 89 associations had more than $100 million.

The same dramatic contrast shows when the size of the average association is viewed; at the end of 1946 the average was only $1.6 million and by 1960 it was well over $10 million. A glance back to prewar years will remind the reader that "an over $10 million" savings and loan association was one of the "big ones" well up into the 1940s.

Home lending expansion

Obviously, even the amazing economic circumstances and new directions of governmental policy of the period described in the previous chapter could not have been solely responsible for such development. Most notably, the prevailing economic wind which thrust home building to the fore made easy sailing for the savings and loan craft. The great opportunity to put an unprecedented amount of savings to work in mortgage lending was the major determinant of the upward course of the business. It was as home lenders that the expanding institutions rose to their heights in the 1950s. Savings and loan became a $72-billion business mainly because there was a home loan demand for many more billions than had ever before been needed.

Mortgage recordings by savings and loan institutions neared $2 billion in 1945 to match, for the first time, the top years of the record 1920s. They jumped to $3.5 billion in 1946, remained close to that figure for the next three years and then hit a new $5 billion mark by 1950.

Table 20 shows the year-by-year expansion of the loan volume of the savings and loan associations during the decade of the 1950s and also demonstrates in its percentage of total home mortgage lending how the business was pulling away from its competitors by the end of the decade.

Table 20. Mortgage lending volume of savings and loan associations and their proportion of the nation's total amount of mortgage recordings, 1950-1960 (in millions of dollars)

Year	Mortgage lending volume	Percentage of total mortgage recordings accounted for by associations
1950	$ 5,237	31.3%
1951	5,250	32.3
1952	6,617	35.8
1953	7,767	37.4
1954	8,969	36.2
1955	11,255	36.7
1956	10,325	35.2
1957	10,160	38.0
1958	12,182	38.4
1959	15,151	40.6
1960	14,304	41.4

Source: *Federal Home Loan Bank Board, "Savings and Home Financing Source Book 1961," pp. 26, 36*

In the last year before World War II, the savings and loan institutions had done only 31.6% of the total home mortgage lending; as early as 1945 they accounted for 35.8% of it. By 1953 they moved into new high ground with 37.4% of the total. After a slight decline in their share of the total in the next three years, they were building steadily up to new highs at the end of the decade. In 1960 their percentage was 41.4%.

For roughly a decade, 1945-1955, interest rates on mortgages moved within the very narrow range of 4½% to 5½%. In 1956 with demand for mortgage loans outstripping savings, a general shift to higher mortgage rates began. The tendency of the government-assisted mortgage loans, both FHA and VA, to fall behind the market rate in permitted interest charges gave the conventional loan a strategic position in such a period of rising rates. Relying chiefly on the conventional loan, savings and loan institutions moved effectively and intelligently into the home lending area during the 1950s and earned recognition as the lenders "who were in there making loans all the time." They became mortgage lenders of such popular acceptance that it was hard to believe their leaders had once feared that savings and loan could be crowded out of the home mortgage market.

But the managers of the associations in this period realized that they were operating something more than merely a lending business; they were building financial institutions. From this recognition stemmed many of the changes in policy and in operating techniques and many of the new emphases of the postwar period.

Two pressing operational problems had to be solved quickly to make possible the building of financial institutions of size and stature. The growing associations had to have adequate personnel and ample office quarters. These immediate concerns were in the foreground at the 1947 convention of the United States League in San Francisco. Just as a California convention had been the occasion for celebrating the uplift of the business' spirits in 1937, so this next California convention seemed to signal the turning point which left the war years behind in thought as well as in fact. The San Francisco meeting brought together delegates who had converged from a number of special trains taking alternate routes across the wonderlands of America. Thus many had a chance to spend whole days talking about activities in the "shop" and comparing notes about what the future probably held.

Personnel policies

There were no tape recorders around, but imagination supported by documents can recreate a typical conversation of a group of savings and loan conventioneers San Francisco bound. Certainly many talked about the report of the United States League's Committee on Personnel Policies, which had reached the desk of all 3,616 associations in the League's far-flung membership a few days before the Convention Special started to California. This report contained a study of possible incentives for savings and loan careers; pension plans and their likely benefits, for example, were carefully analyzed. The beginnings of such concerns in some associations' board of directors has already been seen as early as the late 1930s. Now this League committee focused much more significant attention on keeping the manpower which the savings and loan business sensed it would need in order to fulfill its destiny in the years ahead.

276

In 1947 savings associations had begun an aggressive program of hiring young men. Many of these men had exceptionally fine educational backgrounds, by comparison with typical employees of earlier years, and most had a war veteran's knowledge of how fellow citizens of their generation thought about life in general. The associations made many of them junior officers in the late 1940s. Associations were wisely aware that they should be sure—if possible—that these young men stayed in savings and loan employment. Places were even being found on the boards of directors for young men who had seen the fighting and thus taken part in the great cataclysmic adventure of their generation.

The individual association's new personnel policies in these years had a direct connection with the building of financial institutions. Good customer relations were recognized as an important factor in keeping people satisfied with their savings and home loan arrangements, and many of the new employees could now be assigned to specific phases of savings and loan operation. The small conveniences which rank high with customers were being watched with increasing attention because there were more people working in the association to make them possible.

New office buildings

The 1947 convention train to California made a special stop in the Pacific Northwest; the delegates paused to take a conducted tour through an imposing new building which one of the larger associations had just built. It was a glass-walled structure, such as was to become quite common in later years but at that time was a pioneering type of architecture. The stop was pertinent to the concerns of the hour, even though few savings and loan association executives at the moment had ambitions for so towering a structure. Office quarters constituted the most tangible area of discussion and excitement.

Practically everyone had inadequate office space; the need for physical expansion was now much more acute than it had been in the late 1930s. Furthermore there was no dissent from the idea that an attractive, impressive office was needed to emphasize financial stability. During the convention alert managers learned which architectural and business firms were beginning to specialize in designing, building and partially equipping savings and loan offices.

One-half of the member institutions of the United States League either built new offices or remodeled them in the first seven years after World War II. Remodeling and enlarging of offices continued at a rapid pace throughout the 1950s, and many associations had to plan a second new office by the end of the decade. These were usually entire buildings owned by the association, a pattern which became normal with the great growth of the postwar years. The new offices eventually represented a contemporary treatment in financial architecture. The savings and loan "style" utilized the most functional design; and its interior aimed especially at an impression of friendliness and informality through modern lightings, warm colors, unobstructed teller windows (replacing forbidding wire-grilled cages) and officers' desks in open areas accessible to customers.

As the postwar years went along managers had continuous assistance from the United States League on the ever-present problems of a steadily expanding institution—personnel and office quarters. The League's assistance included several studies on such subjects as recruitment, selection and training of savings and loan personnel and planning of a new office. In the latter 1950s a comprehensive study of location factors was made by the School of Business of Indiana University, permitting a much more scientific approach to the important choice of office location.

Advertising policies

The most significant decision management made to create financial institutions of a new magnitude had to do with expenditures for promotion. In 1948 savings and loan associations spent twice as much on advertising as they did in 1945. The $12.5 million outlay of 1948 had doubled again by 1952; and by 1957 the advertising expenditure was twice what it had been in 1952; the figure was still climbing as the decade ended. A commercial bank competitor wrote in 1956: "Savings and loans advertise more and, all too often, advertise more effectively. For every $1,000 of deposits the associations spent $1.30 for advertising, while the banks spent only 32 cents."

Truly modern savings and loan advertising meant not only larger budgets but better-quality advertising and greater all around emphasis on promotion of the association. With the advertising budgets mounting yearly the associations did several things. They turned to more specialized talent to achieve maximum productivity. They became regular users of the large mass media—newspapers, radio and television; thus they began to reach an ever larger number of potential customers. By good fortune the savings and loan business was already in a mood to spend increasingly large sums to attract customers at the time when the completely new advertising medium, television, was emerging; they were in on the ground floor, so to speak, with their TV ads.

The definitely more sophisticated approach to advertising taken by the business was simultaneous with the development of greater sophistication in advertising in the business world generally. Where once an association had been far behind in the procession, it now began to march in the front ranks of businesses that were experimenting with new appeals, daring to use types of copy which financial institutions had never before found acceptable.

The promotion of thrift had received a substantial boost during the war from the savings bond campaigns of the United States government. Such devices as the bond-a-month campaign had made a whole new generation conscious of the value of postponed spending. Associations realized that the idea of saving money had to be sold continually to the American public, just as a piece of merchandise or a consumer service had to be marketed. After the government volume of advertising for its savings bonds was cut drastically at the end of the war, savings and loan advertising took up some of the slack in the overall urging of people to save money. Basic in its approach, from 1947 on, was the recognition that the idea of thriftiness had to be planted and nourished in each individual.

Public relations in full bloom

A cofactor with advertising in pushing the business to new heights was the modernized concept of public relations. Going into the postwar period, savings and loan institutions already had a taste of a unique kind of good public relations because of their VA loan participation. Gradually but purposefully they took more care in explaining to the community at large their entire role in the economy. Newspaper publicity was used with increasing skill, because managers were becoming better informed about the news value of their operations. They worked more closely with editors to report news promptly and adequately. A growing number of the larger institutions put the preparation of both publicity and advertising into the hands of specialists, assigning the responsibility either to staff members or engaging the services of outside agencies. As early as the League Postwar Planning Committee's report the attention of management had been directed toward the benefits which would come from offering extra services. A myriad of such things as Christmas clubs, safety deposit rentals and sale of travelers checks were available to them—to increase "traffic" into the associations' offices. It was estimated in 1948 that only 500 to 600 associations provided one or more extra services; but 10 or 12 years later the majority offered at least some of them. Such devices were especially helpful in introducing the public to the association's savings facilities.

Many associations augmented their other-than-financial activities, entering a much more general field of public service. To mention a few, they set up home planning departments, exhibited building materials and provided meeting spaces for community organizations. They thus entered the main stream of public relations emphasis in the late 1950s—the evidence of a social conscience.

The United States League enlarged its public relations staff; periodic communications to the members with ideas for their public relations became a part of the service. Focus of the League's public relations program changed as the 1950s moved along; special efforts now were aimed at making the savings and loan business known for its inherent excellencies rather than on just assuring adequate attention for savings and loan news in all news media. The larger need now was to present the best savings and loan image where the savings and loan position needed to be understood. For example, in 1957 the League (alone among groups connected with the housing industry) vigorously defended the government's "tight money" policy, pointing out that such a policy was invaluable in combating inflation. The organization also directed attention several times to the continuing problem of high building costs.

Rates on savings

All the auxiliary activities to attract savers into the institutions were successful because the rate of return paid to savers remained attractive as compared with that paid by both mutual savings banks and commercial banks. Until the mid-1950s the rate at which associations distributed earnings was a reflection of the prevailing low rates of return on money, but it was maintained above the going rate for competitive savings in both mutual savings banks and commercial banks. The average dividend rate first went over the 2.5% level in 1950, but it stayed below the 3% level until 1956. As the 1950s progressed, banks of all types paid considerably higher rates on their savings than in former years. The only type of investment yield, however, which consistently rivaled savings and loan in these postwar years was that of high-grade corporate bonds.

But savings and loan institutions avoided raising rates on savings as long as possible, because they had to build loss reserves. In some respects the most persistent battle which the business had to fight during the great expansion era was for these reserves. Sometimes it was fought in directors' rooms. Often it kept the light burning late in the manager's office as he went over the cost items in the savings association operation and tried to find where he could cut something out in order to augment allocations to reserves. The faster the business grew the more complex the problem seemed to become.

Reserve policies

On December 31, 1950, the ratio of reserves to total savings accounts was 9.15%. For the remaining years of the 1950s the rate of growth of the business was accelerated. Table 21 shows what happened to reserves.

Reserve ratios, of course, vary widely from association to association. The accumulation depends somewhat on the age of the association; and the battle was most difficult in the 1950s for those not organized until after the depression. The problem varied too with geographical location; some areas by custom permitted associations to make charges which increased incomes, whereas other areas never countenanced these charges.

As early as 1954 the Home Loan Bank Board was working on a new formula for the accumulation of reserves. Finally, on December 15, 1956, a substantial amendment of the Insurance Corporation regulations on reserves went into effect. The Corporation now

Table 21. Reserves* of savings and loan associations as a percentage of savings capital, December 31, 1945-1960

Year ending	Reserve ratios
1945	8.74%
1946	8.79
1947	8.77
1948	8.84
1949	8.87
1950	9.15
1951	9.02
1952	8.64
1953	8.32
1954	8.02
1955	7.95
1956	7.94
1957	8.02
1958	8.01
1959	8.05
1960	8.02

* Reserves, surplus and undivided profits are included in term "reserves"

Source: Federal Home Loan Bank Board, "Savings and Home Financing Source Book, 1961," p. 8

ruled for the first time on the situation of an association which had passed its 20th anniversary of insurance of accounts and which had duly reached the required 5% in the insurance reserve. (That year 1,575 associations had reached the 20th year of insurance.) The new rules of the Corporation called for at least 10% of net income to be added annually to reserves until they equalled 12% of insured accounts. The Corporation also set up new annual yardsticks for reserve accumulations during each of the first 20 years.

Operating expenses

A glance at the income and expense ratios of associations from 1947-1960 demonstrates the one factor which was favorable in the building of reserves during this period of growth. The associations, under new concepts of business management with astute, imaginative men at the head, succeeded in steadily reducing the ratio of operating expense to gross operating income. For reporting members of the Federal Home Loan Bank System in 1947, it was 29.3%. By 1960 it had gone down, year by year, to 22%.

Table 22 shows the year-by-year decline in this ratio.

*Table 22. Ratio of total operating expense to gross operating income
all reporting member savings and loan associations
of the FHLB System, 1947-1960*

Year	Ratio
1947	29.3%
1948	28.9
1949	28.2
1950	27.3
1951	27.3
1952	27.1
1953	26.1
1954	25.6
1955	24.6
1956	24.4
1957	23.8
1958	23.3
1959	22.7
1960	22.0

Source: *Federal Home Loan Bank Board, "Combined Financial Statements,
Members of FHLB System, 1955," p. 47; 1960, p. 71*

Nothing demonstrates more surely the development of management techniques in the savings and loan business than the careful whittling down of the ratio of operating expenses. Actually the manpower at the very helm must get substantial credit for the unprecedented growth of the business.

Management as a profession

The first truly pioneering attention to savings and loan management, as a profession, had come in the management courses of the Institute's Graduate School of Savings and Loan. The fact that many savings and loan presidents had mastered these courses by the late 1940s had begun to show in the operations of the associations. Moreover a career as a savings and loan manager was now for the first time appealing in its own right. This meant that the men who started out in 1947 were more likely to remain in the business. They would thus give the individual institution the priceless asset of management continuity. The continuity was especially significant at a time when most associations, despite their expanding personnel, were still the lengthening shadow of one individual.

Progress had been made in the recovery era toward a more

adequate compensation system and also a more appropriate assignment of authority to the managing officer. But it was not until after the war that the job at the top in an expanding association began to have several facets of genuine appeal to career people.

The situation with regard to the remuneration was righting itself, gradually but surely. Every second year the United States League made a survey of compensation policies, both for the manager and for the men and women down the line; and as each of these biennial reports was published the clear story unfolded of a business that was learning to pay for brains, judgment and experience much more nearly what they were worth. As the late 1950s progressed and "fringe benefits" were an ingredient of practically all business compensation policies, the savings and loan executive began to get his share of these benefits, too.

Washington assistance

Not to be overlooked as a contributing influence to more appropriate management compensation was the change in the salary pattern of the FHLB presidents. The imaginative and effective efforts of the business to strengthen and improve the associations had finally received some support, after the war years, from Washington, D. C. In 1947 Reorganization Plan No. 3, submitted by President Truman, replaced the wartime National Housing Agency with a permanent top housing establishment known as the Housing and Home Finance Agency.

In the establishment of the new government arrangement, the Federal Home Loan Bank Administration headed by a commissioner was abolished. A three-man Home Loan Bank Board (the adjective "federal" was omitted in the Reorganization Plan) was reconstituted. The move was far-reaching in its ultimate effect on the supervisory relationships of the savings and loan business in Washington. Pride in the savings and loan business and the will to increase its prestige was a dominating influence in the new Board. Gone forever was any vestige of the postdepression notion that the instrumentality in Washington had to be apologetic for the shortcomings of the depression-scarred savings and loan business. One way in which the Board moved early to lift the morale of the FHLB System was to permit higher salaries for the bank presidents. The presidents, as the supervisory agents, in their turn became more enthusiastic than before about appropriate salary increases for the heads of savings and loan institutions.

Managerial reorganization and outlook

Coupled with a constantly improving financial status for the savings and loan manager was the enlarged stimulus which the job now presented to the top executive. As the years went along the chores which had been taken for granted as part of the manager's day were handed on to others. Even before World War II, as it has been pointed out, managing executives were beginning to undertake departmentalization. In the immediate postwar years more and more managing executives found it imperative to have intraoffice organization with new clear-cut lines of authority. With the office details less of an hour-to-hour concern, the manager could take time to think, planning for the future of the institution. In the climate in which he was doing his planning in the late 1940s and 1950s this was an altogether stimulating experience.

The title of president became the norm for a savings and loan manager in these years, conferring greater prestige. In adopting this nomenclature the associations were following the custom of banks and insurance companies. But the presidency of a savings and loan institution in 1950 implied many different emphases from those of an executive vice presidency in 1940.

Part of the change was in the president's concept of how his time should be spent. He began to look more and more outward on the world in which his association operated, while still glancing often enough at the details within the confines of the office to see that all went well. The war years provided a basic stimulus for the change in top management's outlook.

Now with the emergency of war and transition ended, managers had a much broader vision of their role in the community. In nearly every city and sizable town savings and loan executives became participants in civic enterprise. Just as the associations moved their offices with increasing frequency into choice downtown locations, the managers were moving into closer contact with the business and civic elite of the community. They were also conspicuous in such strong organizational groups as war veterans and the local committees of the major political parties.

A new and absorbing tool in the hands of management everywhere was economic forecasting. The whole concept of studying a market caused important changes in savings and loan planning. The obvious changes in the social pattern of the community added many nuances to the challenge of building up a financial institution.

Revised federal regulations; Charter N

Before the reconstituted Home Loan Bank Board had been in office a year, it had initiated a most important project for releasing the ultimate energies of federal associations as large and influential financial institutions. This was the complete review of all the regulations affecting federal associations, an accumulation in 1948 of 15 years of rule making under the impact of widely varying economic and social situations. This set of rules was now to be molded into a mid-century framework remarkably well-fitted, in retrospect, to the realization of the opportunities of the postwar world.

The review was in charge of a Board member who had for more than 20 years close contact with savings and loan operations as state supervisor in North Carolina and later as president of the Federal Home Loan Bank of Greensboro. From this review an almost complete rewriting of the federal regulations emerged. Also, a new and relatively brief charter for federal associations, known as Charter N, was provided. The course toward these changes was deliberate and it was characterized by conferences at several different stages between representatives of the savings and loan business and the Board. The final promulgation, along with Charter N, came on August 15, 1949.

The most significant departure from precedent involved in Charter N was the procedure for meeting withdrawal requests. Here the comprehensive listing of the association's legal obligation to its savers, as set forth in the old charters, was abandoned in favor of the simple authority to follow whatever the Home Loan Bank Board prescribed in the way of procedure for paying withdrawals. The plan was similar to that already in use for savings banks in many states. Charter N broke new ground in terminology, using "savings accounts" and "withdrawals" as normal description of operations instead of the more cumbersome "share accounts" and "repurchase" references of depression-influenced years. The change became a continuing target for the more vigorously competitive banks. These latter have persistently implied that a saver in a savings and loan association actually has a "share," so that he is somehow flirting with a type of investment more speculative than a savings account. Occasional litigation over the savings and loan use of the term "account" survived into the late 1950s.

Charter N also provided for optional plans of earnings distribution and thus paved the way for associations to avail themselves of quarterly distribution of earnings and similar later changes in the regulations adopted by the FHLB Board.

On the lending side, Charter N permitted an association automatically to make available any new loan plan authorized by law or regulation. Going beyond the Charter K permission to borrow up to 50% of share capital, the new charter provided unlimited borrowing with prior approval of the FHLB Board.

Then in 1952 the Board issued a new version of Charter K, permitting associations which desired to keep the longer charter many of the privileges of flexibility which had already been conferred in Charter N. With this second change the federal system was well on the way to becoming the up-to-date instrument for thrift and home finance which it represented in the public mind in the later 1950s. The great majority of associations adopted either Charter N or Charter K (Rev.) before the decade was over. A steady conversion process from the old Charter K to either Charter N or Charter K (Rev.) characterized the late years of the decade, largely because the amendments to the federal regulations, which liberalized procedures, were most often reserved to these two later types of charter. Only a handful of associations under the original Charter E remained by 1960.

Before the approval of Charter N by the Home Loan Bank Board in 1949 several states had amended their laws to provide for the simplified savings structure which Charter N exemplified. Also many states followed the trail-blazing done by the new federal charter, especially in the savings structure of the association.

Well-rounded home lending service

The desirability of offering a well-rounded home lending service to the community became increasingly apparent to savings and loan managers in the postwar years. Management had started to grasp the opportunity to meet the demands of the home buyers and builders before all the guns of World War II had ceased smoking. As early as 1945, the first advertisements for loans were being placed. The associations had $2 billion in liquid resources which enabled them to get in on the ground floor with the big job of home financing. The business had taken a long lead in financing veterans who would for years constitute a large part of the market; it had also kept its close identity with moderate-income customers buying moderately priced homes.

Mortgage lending procedures and policies of savings and loan associations acquired subtly, if not spectacularly, a new appearance during the years of great opportunity. Yet the lending operation rested solidly on the foundations of the traditional amortized conventional mortgage. In this period the word "conventional" came to be used to describe mortgages where the risk was not shared by the federal government, either through the FHA or the VA. Up until this time there had been no real need to designate the non-federally assisted mortgage by any particular name.

The savings and loan business followed—with some reservations —the tendency of the times to stretch loan terms to 20 and 25 years and to make higher percentage loans than had been formerly thought wise. The high prosperity of the late '40s and the '50s and the unbroken upswing in the popularity of real estate inevitably changed the thinking of the entire business about the mathematical measures of the risk on mortgage loans. The VA loan experience was on the books to back up their thinking. Considerable apprehension that real estate prices were too high to be sustained had continued up through 1949, but the advent of the Korean War, with its new inflationary implications in the economy, underscored the fact that lending on "today's prices" was the realistic approach. Acceptance of the new price level by the savings and loan business turned the final switch on the green light to expanded lending plans.

Large-scale operations in the financing of operative builders were no longer unusual, as the years moved along. Advance commitments to the builders who would not actually use the funds for several months became a common procedure.

A new emphasis on property improvement loans fitted well into the concept of a well-rounded home lending institution. Interest in this type of lending was stimulated by legislation enacted in 1947. Associations had always made loans to their own borrowers who wished to modernize or repair their homes; they did it simply by refinancing the mortgage to include the whole amount of indebtedness. Then in 1947 for the first time, federal associations obtained the authority to make unsecured property improvement loans on what was known in the business as "their own plan."

The Federal Section Committee of the United States League had developed a plan which incorporated the best experience of some state plans and some of the more remunerative features of the Title I FHA property improvement plan. This was the substance of the new legislation. It meant that federally chartered associations could extend credit for relatively short terms for property improvement without taking a mortgage. The 1947 legislation also permitted federal associations expressly to make Title I FHA loans and unsecured property improvement loans under the GI bill. A few of the state associations had already been doing a volume of business under FHA Title I.

As the 1950s went along, many savings and loan institutions made major use of an open-end clause in the mortgage for extending additional credit to borrowers for such purposes as new equipment, repairs and remodeling. Many made wide use of the package mortgage which, like the open-end clause, had been recommended by the Postwar Planning Committee; it enabled the borrower to include major household equipment items in the original real estate security and thus lower the financing costs for these larger equipment items.

More service from leagues

Obviously the men at the helm of the savings and loan associations in the 1950s did not have the psychology of "letting well enough alone." Thus they naturally moved in new directions with their trade associations. In this era several of the state leagues acquired full-time executives for the first time. The savings and loan manager whose time was freed from many office details by the development of a competent staff could make a more noteworthy contribution to his business beyond his immediate institution. Men such as this, elected to the leadership of their state leagues, recognized the need for more adequate budgets permitting full-time staffing.

State leagues began to add to the services offered their constituents. One area in which several of them moved forward was that of providing group plans for "fringe benefits" for all association employees in the state; arrangements on a statewide basis were especially helpful to institutions whose size did not permit an economical plan for such accepted programs as retirement benefits and group health arrangements. Sponsorship of public relations programs with representatives of educational institutions in the state was also a natural responsibility for many state leagues to assume. More persistent efforts were made to organize local leagues. A few of these emerged with full-time staffs by the end of the decade.

Leaders in the business had revised the United States League Constitution in 1946 to provide for an annual turnover in the Executive Committee membership, with staggered terms for the members expiring after three years. Thus the way had been paved for more and more of the newly emerging leaders to come into the councils of the League.

The League, now 60 years old, had several occasions in its two generations of service to change its emphasis. In the 1950s its destiny was clearly to expand its efforts. It had to serve a business which was growing very rapidly and managers who were telescoping the growth experience of several decades into a few years. It had to do this without de-emphasizing any of the services that had become part of its permanent agenda.

A Committee on Savings and Loan Management became one of the standing committees in 1946. Special studies by the United States League took on added quality as well as variety; they included committee-requested studies by staff members, market surveys by professionals and more elaborate studies by contracts with academic institutions. The staff was notably enlarged to include specialists of many types.

A separate publications department was created. Every few years during this period of great expansion the League launched a new publication to reach a new need in the business. In 1949 the new publication was the *Quarterly Letter* on savings and home ownership, circulated to writers, educators and other opinion-making groups; it offered for the first time a statistical review of data not otherwise given this objective treatment in a general publication. *The Savings and Loan Fact Book* began to appear annually in 1954, for distribution to members of Congress, newspaper writers, schools and colleges, chambers of commerce and other organizations.

The planning of meetings for savings and loan personnel so that they might exchange ideas had been the League's first activity in 1892. The post-World War II expansion era saw many new meetings added to the pattern. The management conference of the early 1940s became in the 1950s the primary source of discussion and exchange of ideas on business details, with the national convention on the other hand affording opportunity for hearing about policies and broader issues of concern to the business. In 1952 the annual late summer workshop devoted each year to a different phase of the savings and loan operation became a permanent fixture. These workshops were attended principally by department heads or junior officers rather than managers.

The United States League had made its first motion picture, a customer relations film for use within the business, in the closing days of World War II; some of the scenes for it were being shot in a suburb of Chicago as the first atomic bomb was being exploded over Hiroshima. This was a limited-purpose, minimum-budget venture. Eight years later, in 1953, the League produced its first sound-color film for the public's understanding of the business, depicting in story form the home loan services of savings and loan associations. A film on the savings function was produced the next year in a similarly interesting, easy-to-understand style. Later a cartoon-type film, especially adaptable to TV showing, was added to the supply. In 1959 it was estimated that around 3.5 million persons had seen these films at schools and community meetings; and around 115 million had viewed all or portions of them on TV.

As the 20th century moved toward its last 40 years—through the startling late 1950s which made the space age a reality—the savings and loan system increased its rate of expansion. Management found itself casting aside the established ways of the year before, or the year before that, to cope with unforeseen challenges to serve their communities. The 30th anniversary of the Great Depression was just around the corner. A whole generation had passed since the "building and loan" movement had begun to turn over that multitude of new leaves which converted it into the savings and loan business. The final chapter will outline some of the responsibilities of management which were different as a result of the new rate of growth and some of the signs on the horizons of the 1960s. The intervening chapter will review the significant federal legislation which affected savings and loan associations in the postwar era.

Chapter 17

Legislation
and the postwar expansion

An event of deep significance to the savings and loan business was scheduled for the White House on June 27, 1950. The chairman of the FHLB Board and ranking Democratic and Republican members of the Senate and House Banking Committees were to be present for the signing by President Harry S. Truman of a new law; it was a major Savings and Loan Act amending many of the federal statutes related to the business. The legislation represented the accomplishment of several objectives pursued by savings and loan leaders for many years.

The swift-moving events of history closed in on this schedule. The Korean War started the weekend before. The fanfare of the ceremonious signing was cancelled, since the President had an extremely busy morning with conferences on the outbreak of hostilities. But he did sign the bill so that it became law that day.

The most vital improvement embodied in the 1950 legislation was the reduction of the Federal Savings and Loan Insurance Corporation premium. Lowering it from 1/8 of 1% to 1/12 of 1% of insured savings, the new law reduced the expense of insurance of accounts by $417 a year for every $1 million of insured accounts. This achievement climaxed the longest and most persistent legislative effort of the savings and loan leaders and their friends in Congress. Over the years the objective had been twofold: to reduce the expense to the associations; to make the premium commensurate with that paid by commercial banks for FDIC insurance.

Since the whole concept of insuring the safety of money in financial institutions was highly experimental in the 1930s, as pointed out in Chapter 6, all anyone could do in 1934 was to guess at an appropriate premium. Within a few years, however, the diligence of the FDIC officials had persuaded Congress to reduce the premium paid by the banks to 1/12 of 1%. The Home Loan Bank Board, in charge of the Federal Savings and Loan Insurance Corporation, did not follow this example. Even after its reconstitution in 1947, it was far from independent in deciding to support or oppose any specific legislation. As a constituent unit of the Housing and Home Finance Agency, it had to accept the dictum of the housing administrator on all matters of public policy.

Previous premium reduction efforts

The first official efforts to put the savings and loan premium on a par with that of the banks came from the Congress. The United States League's Legislative Committee Report back in 1937 included this noteworthy statement: "H.R. 6929, introduced by Mr. Spence of Kentucky, would have reduced the premium to 1/12 of 1%." Representative Spence (who was not yet chairman, although a member, of the Banking Committee) was probably the person most familiar, of all members of the House of Representatives, with savings and loan institutions. For 13 years thereafter he persisted in his efforts to obtain what he deemed "justice for the savings and loan institutions."

Leaders of the business worked with him all these years, but they encountered notable opposition and several hurdles besides outright opposition. Commercial banking interests fought the development of the savings and loan institutions, characterizing them as a "third banking system" competing on "favored terms" with savings banks, savings departments of commercial banks and other financial institutions. Other obstacles included the crowded agenda of Congress in the war years (when any enactments other than those relating to the prosecution of the war were unlikely) and the cumbersome way in which proposals for legislation had to get "clearance" from the executive department.

Wartime procedures introduced the pattern of requiring the consent and support of the affected government agencies before legislation could sail smoothly through Congress. In this case, of course, the Federal Home Loan Bank Board was the affected agency. But legislation affecting the Board had to get "clearance" from the Housing Agency. The Housing Agency had to get the support of the Bureau of the Budget. In its turn the Budget Bureau attached considerable weight to the views of other federal agencies, including the Treasury Department and the Federal Reserve Board. Such an involved routine of executive agency clearance had militated against legislation for reducing the insurance premium, not only because of the time involved but also because somewhere along the line some opposition to the idea was usually encountered. In the Treasury and at the Federal Reserve Board banker attitudes toward savings and loan institutions were frequently encountered.

The premium reduction had been approved by the House of Representatives in 1940, but the legislation was not acted on in the Senate. In 1946 both the House of Representatives and the Senate approved it, but President Truman vetoed it. Thus the 1950 enactment was indeed the end of a long road. It came when its long-time advocate, Representative Spence, had risen to the chairmanship of the House Banking and Currency Committee.

Washington scene, 1950

When, in November 1950, the United States League held its first Washington, D. C., convention in 31 years the outstanding speaker was Mr. Spence. His words to the convention that he would continue to do what he could "to make your fine institutions a success so that they may continue in their good service to the American people" were for savings and loan managers a heartening introduction to the decade. In fact, this gathering at the beginning of the 1950s was a memorable occasion all around. The delegates' wives had the first lady of the land, Mrs. Harry S. Truman, as their luncheon guest at the Congressional Country Club. Mrs. Georgia Neese Clark, the Treasurer of the United States, was the special guest for their annual tea party. The League president in his address urged the business to participate in a 10-year crusade for home ownership; the record of savings and loan lending, described in the last chapter, speaks eloquently indeed of how this challenge was accepted.

The only clouds which gathered on the horizon that convention week came from Korea, for at that time the first overt indication of Red Chinese support for the North Korean government became evident in that dire conflict on the other side of the world. The savings and loan representatives were well aware of the fortunate circumstance that the omnibus savings and loan legislation had cleared the Congress before the start of the conflict on June 24, 1951 —the Korean War.

The early enactment owed something to luck. Typically, legislation of this type could have been expected to emerge only during the closing weeks of the session and then only after a snail's-pace course through the general legislative process. In the year which saw the outbreak of the Korean War in early summer and the consequent concentration of congressional attention on defense matters, it might well have been blocked that year once again and for several years thereafter. It happened, however, that one of the early bitter controversies over civil rights came in that year. A Fair Employment Practices bill was pending. Supporters of it decided to use a rare parliamentary procedure to get their measure considered by the House of Representatives. In order to block this tactic, opponents of the bill had to call up some other measure from some other committee; the parliamentary situation favored one from a committee whose name was near the front of the alphabet —hence the Banking and Currency Committee was picked; and the only major bill which this committee had ready was the savings and loan one, largely processed in the preceding session of that Congress. Thus the savings and loan bill was called up for House action in February and was adopted on a day when 90% of the talk was about civil rights, although the official business was savings and loan legislation. With this unusually early start in the House of Representatives, the legislation was through the Senate and on its way to the White House by the time the North Koreans marched across the 38th parallel into South Korea.

Contents of omnibus bill

The omnibus savings and loan legislation provided several important changes in the Insurance Corporation statute other than premium reduction. The United States Treasury was authorized to lend up to $750 million to the Corporation. This change meant the Corporation could call upon the Treasury in case of need. Also provided for was the retirement of the original government-subscribed capital by application to this purpose of half of the net earnings of FSLIC every year.

The legislation also made important changes in the Federal Home Loan Bank Act. It provided emergency United States Treasury support for the FHLB System up to $1 billion, giving the Treasury authority to buy obligations of the Bank System to this maximum. It included a plan for retirement of the government-owned capital in the Bank System by requiring members to hold capital stock equal to 2% of their mortgage loans outstanding. Already for some years a few of the Federal Home Loan Banks had been accepting voluntary extra stock purchases from member institutions and thus were gradually retiring the government capital. The new plan provided that the balance of the original government advance to the System should be paid off in 12 months.

What was then regarded as the price of these long-sought amendments was a new provision for the FHLB Board to establish a minimum liquidity ratio somewhere between 4% and 8% for all member institutions of the Bank System. The Board had vigorously pressed for this provision.

Higher ceiling on insured accounts

Another major statutory improvement for the business came out of the 1950 session of Congress. Early in the session a move had been started to raise the coverage for the FDIC to $10,000 for each insured bank deposit; it was part of an omnibus bill to make several substantial changes in the FDIC Act. The savings and loan leaders were successful in getting included a provision to lift the ceiling of insured savings and loan accounts to $10,000, effective whenever a similar amendment for FDIC coverage became law.

Also achieved in the new FDIC legislation, enacted in September of 1950, was a highly desirable revision of the language for the payment of insured accounts by an insured savings and loan association in default. Instead of the previous option to the saver of one of three plans, no one of which included getting all his account in cash, the new law provided simply that the saver could have his account either in cash or in an insured account in another association. Most importantly, the sections providing for payouts were made identical for banks and savings and loan associations. From this time forth the competitively inspired whispering campaign of some commercial banks, that the FSLIC was less reliable for savers' protection than the FDIC, could find no support in the statute.

Effects of omnibus legislation

The insurance premium reduction was made retroactive by the 1950 legislation and all insured institutions were able to apply the sum saved to their next payment; thus the associations saved $4.5 million in their expenses that year. Retirement of the government capital in the FSLIC began in 1951 and was completed July 1, 1958. The law directed FSLIC to pay 2% simple interest on the federal funds; a check for $29 million, covering the period from 1934 to 1949, was the Treasury's immediate gain from the 1950 savings and loan legislation.

The major significance of the $750 million Treasury backing for the FSLIC was that this provision placed the agency's relationship to the government in a parallel situation to that of the FDIC and the commercial banks. This authority and the $1 billion Treasury support for FHLB obligations were designed to be operative only in case of the most serious economic crisis. The 10 ensuing years brought no period when there was a remote possibility of their having to be used.

At the end of 1949 the FHLB System had $95.8 million of government-owned capital stock. Through the associations' increase of stock ownership to 2% of loans, the Bank System was able to repay this sum to the Treasury by July 1951.

The invoking of the new control over the liquidity of member institutions of the Federal Home Loan Bank System had little impact on practices. Most of the 2,800 member institutions of the FHLB System were already maintaining liquidity ratios above the 6% rate established by the Federal Home Loan Bank Board. Only a small number had any substantial adjustments to make.

Defense Production Act

The congressional session of 1950 lasted long enough to present the savings and loan business with problems as well as victories. A few weeks after the Korean War broke out the Defense Production Act was proposed. In the excitement of the times it was intended for a swift unopposed course through Congress such as had happened only in the bitterest days of the Great Depression. As introduced, the legislation contained in Title IV the most far-reaching proposal ever made with regard to real estate credit; it was that all credit transactions on real estate should be subject to terms to be set by the executive department, including "credit for the purpose of purchasing or carrying" real property "or constructing buildings or otherwise improving such property."

The United States League decided to oppose the enactment of credit controls on existing housing despite the rush-it-through atmosphere which surrounded the proposal. The leaders in the business realized that the red tape involved in a control over every single real estate credit transaction would retard and complicate immeasurably the acquisition of homes. The proposal had been offered as part of an entire program whose objective was to discourage the construction of new homes and thus relieve pressures on the existing supply of critical materials; the leaders of the savings and loan business reminded the congressional committees that there was no reason why credit on existing real estate should be controlled, since such loans could not conceivably stimulate *new* construction.

Furthermore the proposed legislation included a provision for a new range of liquidity requirements in savings and loan associations up to 20%, instead of the existing 8% ceiling. The Housing Agency was generally regarded as the source of the major proposals to control real estate and savings and loan credit. The League opposed the 20% liquidity proposal, estimating that the imposition of such a high ratio could have taken many associations out of the lending field for months (while permitting other types of lenders to continue normal operations).

The Defense Production Act reached the statute books in September. Its control of conventional real estate credit was limited to new construction. Thus the impact on the total loan volume of the associations was relatively light. The proposed higher ceiling for liquidity ratios for savings and loan associations was completely eliminated from the legislation.

Corporate tax liability

In contrast to 1950, a year in which savings and loan institutions could remember the legislative enactments on the whole with satisfaction, 1951 brought a legislative departure which stirred wide apprehensions among savings and loan managers. The time-honored tax treatment of the savings and loan institutions and mutual savings banks materially changed. Beginning with the taxable year 1952, these institutions were subjected to the federal corporation income tax.

For years the government's constant quest for additional sources of revenue had foreshadowed a strenuous attempt some day to place the savings and loan associations and mutual savings banks in a tax position different from that in effect up to 1951. In that year the government was reaching out for more revenue, because of its heavy wartime expenditures. The staff of the Joint Committee on Internal Revenue Taxation (serving the tax writing committees of both Houses of Congress) and also the staff of the Treasury Department had recommended that the regular corporate income tax be levied on these institutions.

The House Ways and Means Committee disagreed with this recommendation on savings and loans and savings banks, however, and the Revenue Act of 1951, as it passed the House, contained no such provision.

The Senate Finance Committee, however, included such a tax in its version of the bill. The Senate committee had heard testimony from the National Tax Equality Association and from 15 state bankers, all bitterly denouncing savings institutions and calling for imposition of the income tax on total earnings without even an exemption for dividends paid. The United States League's testimony emphasized the clear need for loss reserves in excess of those the business had then accumulated. The Senate Finance Committee reported a tax bill which would have permitted savings and loan institutions to make reserve allocations before taxes on the basis of prior loss experience, with the Secretary of the Treasury determining the allocations permitted.

When the bill got to the floor of the Senate, considerable support for the position of the savings and loan institutions was evident. Several senators claimed that the Finance Committee's bill jeopardized the ability of these institutions to accumulate adequate reserves. The Senate amended the committee bill so that associations and mutual savings banks could make annual allocations to reserves as a deduction from gross income until their reserves were equal to 10% of savings.

When the conferees met, the members from the House of Representatives stood firm, day after day, against the inclusion in the new bill of any change of the existing savings institution situation. The stalemate was finally broken; the bill as it reached the statute book October 20, 1951, permitted the associations to make allocations to bad debt reserves before taxes until such reserves were 12% of their savings accounts.

Internal revenue negotiations

The responsibilities of the United States League officers and staff were multiplied by the new tax status of the institutions. Two major lines of responsibility immediately loomed. One was the delicate matter of negotiating with the Internal Revenue Bureau on the regulations, which could have as great an impact on the operations of a savings and loan institution as the statute itself. The other was to guide the newly taxed institutions in their wisest course in the interim between the enactment of the law and the promulgation of the regulations.

Management Bulletin after *Management Bulletin* went out from League headquarters as the year 1951 passed into history and 1952 began. There were accounting problems, legal problems, numerous new situations to be encountered, at every level; there were new board of directors requirements for all savings and loan associations. Above all, a more complicated system of record keeping was required than had ever been used in the business. From the date of the imposition of the corporate tax upon the savings and loan business the employment of controllers within the institutions became a measure of wisdom. The correspondence of the United States League's staff on tax questions emerged into one of its major occupations. The regulations were put in final form by the Bureau of Internal Revenue in December 1952. And a new chapter in the relations of savings associations with the federal government began.

Dividend reporting changed

In September 1953 the Internal Revenue Bureau amended its regulation for the reporting of dividends paid by savings and loan institutions. Until then associations had to report all earnings distributions of $100 or more in a taxable year. The situation had long been considered prejudicial to savings and loan from the competitive point of view, since other major savings institutions had to file information returns only on amounts of $600 or more paid out. The new language made $600 the minimum required to be reported by savings and loan.

In 1953 when the business was still only $27 billion in size, the new $600 floor under dividend reporting made a substantial reduction of the office burden for savings and loan institutions. It would take a $20,000 account at a 3% rate to earn $600 a year, and $20,000 accounts were not notably numerous in those years. Thus the change in regulations met a wide welcome in the business.

Other legislation of the 1950s

On the whole the 1950s were a fruitful period for the improvement of the federal statutes dealing with savings and loan associations. Changes included: the extension of FBI protection to all insured associations; the transfer of the supervision of nonfederal associations in the District of Columbia from the Comptroller of the Currency to the FHLB Board; permission for federal credit unions to invest funds in all insured savings and loan institutions; a clarification of the definition of "insured member" under the FSLIC statute so that custodial and trustee accounts might have access to larger overall insurance coverage; and an adjustment of the admission fee to the FSLIC giving the Corporation more discretion in providing reasonable costs for admission to insured status.

To meet expanding national needs for savings and loan lending services the Congress increased the investment powers of federal associations more than once during the decade. The law was changed to permit lending up to 20% of assets on the security of improved real estate other than the one-to-four family home types, and without regard to the $20,000 limit on individual loans, whether in or outside the statutory 50-mile radius. As already reported in Chapter 15, the $20,000 loan limit itself was raised

302

to $35,000. Along with these liberalizations, Congress granted federal associations power to purchase FHA-insured or VA-guaranteed home mortgages beyond the 50-mile radius. Late in the decade still further changes in the investment powers of federal associations were made to meet far-reaching new visions of their role, and these will be described in the final chapter dealing specifically with the prospect for the 1960s.

Competitors of savings and loan institutions which wished to curb savings and loan progress by federal legislation had little to show for their efforts in the 1950s. The most conspicuous examples of their failure were the repeated attempts of commercial banking interests to get the branch privileges of federal associations tightly circumscribed by law; and the tremendous efforts throughout this period of major sectors of commercial banking to persuade Congress to rewrite the savings and loan sections of the Internal Revenue Code, which had not been done when the 1960s began.

The savings and loan business did not experience a like degree of success in dissuading the Congress from periodically authorizing greater liberalizations of government-assisted credit programs. Year after year the United States League's representatives stated opposition to the proposals for extremely low down payments and longer maturities; repeatedly they stated the thesis that the interests of the home owner and of a healthy mortgage credit structure are not served by these approaches. Yet the decade saw a step-by-step stretching of the credit terms insurable under FHA.

Likewise, the League's opposition was voiced to the direct use of government funds for the purchase of mortgages, an operation recognized more and more as tantamount to direct lending of Treasury funds. Generally mutual savings banks and insurance companies were found on the same side in this continuing battle; frequently, too, the commercial banks sided with the savings and loan business on this particular issue. Other trade groups, such as the Mortgage Bankers Association, generally took positions against stretching credit terms too far, but they always stood firm for the further development of the Federal Housing Administration system. Shifts of position on the part of various segments of the housing industry inevitably arose over the years because of changes in their own circumstances. But the position of the savings and loan business remained basically that of keeping at a minimum the government's role in the mortgage business.

VA loan interest rate

The entire housing industry, including the financing sector, was generally of one mind throughout the decade in seeking adjustment of the interest rate on veterans guaranteed loans to keep it compatible with the market situation. The United States League, as a pioneer in VA lending, was anxious to continue its own substantial support of the program; and some savings and loan associations continued to make some VA loans, even in the years when the interest rate differential was substantial. But these efforts of the business groups were unsuccessful largely because of an interplay of political forces. Some of the veterans groups continued to make retention of the uneconomic rate part of their platforms, although the American Legion notably led the way in a more orthodox economic position. In the majority of Congress there was throughout the 1950s a strong dislike for higher interest rates (always a position with political popularity), and thus the efforts to reconcile a more realistic VA rate with political issues were generally unsuccessful.

The most widely publicized attempt in the decade of the 1950s to arrive at a revised policy for government participation in housing came with the advent of the first Republican administration in 20 years. Early in 1953 President Eisenhower appointed an advisory committee with membership from all segments of the housing industry and government. He stated its responsibility in these words: "to identify the proper role of the federal government in this field and to outline a more economical and effective means of improving housing conditions of our people." Savings and loan institutions were represented on the committee.

The group reported on December 14, 1953, offering a program designed essentially to ease the transition to smaller government expenditures and lesser government participation in housing. When the Congress started working on the program the "more liberal" provisions found favor while many of the carefully thought out new approaches ran into opposition and eventual rejection. The most conspicuous contribution of the advisory committee to the Housing Act of 1954 was the "urban renewal program," which was an elaboration of the existing slum clearance and redevelopment activity, to include more massive undertakings and more widely varied approaches to rebuilding the interiors of cities.

Housing Act of 1954

As the new Housing Act of 1954 reached the statute books it contained a Title V which substantially amended savings and loan statutes. The new ceiling of $35,000 on loans of federal associations and on mortgages eligible for collateral in the Federal Home Loan Bank System has already been referred to in other connections. Otherwise the most far-reaching of the changes was Section 5(d) of the Home Owners' Loan Act, an extensive new section on procedures in the supervision of federal associations, especially where there were "trouble" situations. The lack of adequate law to safeguard management from arbitrary supervisory exercises of power, as well as the lack of sufficient provision for the FHLB Board to carry out its responsibilities without too drastic effects upon the associations, had been apparent for several years.

Starting with 1946 one celebrated example of controversy between Washington and a federal savings and loan association was a conversation piece in savings and loan discussions of supervisory relations for 15 years. This was the case of the Long Beach Federal Savings and Loan Association, Long Beach, Calif., which was placed in a conservatorship by the FHLB commissioner in 1946 and whose cause was espoused by many members of Congress in the ensuing years. The seizure of the Long Beach Federal had come on the heels of an act of the FHLB commissioner abolishing the Federal Home Loan Bank of Los Angeles and combining it with the Federal Home Loan Bank of Portland, thus creating the Federal Home Loan Bank of San Francisco—itself, a controversial step. Within a year after the Home Loan Bank Board was reconstituted it returned the Long Beach Federal to its former management, but without completely settling many of the financial and other points at issue.

Circumstances which arose in connection with the troubles of this and other associations pointed up deficiencies in the law. Even the 1954 revision of Section 5(d) of the Home Owner's Loan Act did not represent a completely satisfactory statute. This became apparent from the many controversies which developed during the subsequent period, including the second entanglement of the Federal Home Loan Bank Board with the Long Beach Federal. This event occurred in April 1960, when a conservatorship was again appointed after seizure of the association. Congressional hearings on the case went far into the summer of 1960. Amendments to the statute were not only recommended by the Special Subcommittee on the FHLB Board of the House Government Operations Committee but were also widely discussed within the business. The section remains one of the most sensitive parts of the statute and one to which further attention will inevitably have to be given before another decade has passed.

Independent FHLB Board

The achievement in 1955 of independent status for the Federal Home Loan Bank Board was a tribute to the perseverance of savings and loan leaders. Independence for the Board had been the prime savings and loan legislative goal for many years, and a variety of approaches had been explored by the leadership of the business. The possibility of a reorganization plan had been discussed with government officials during the early days of the Eisenhower Administration. The case had been presented to the Bureau of the Budget; the savings and loan leaders had seen to it that the Commission on Organization of the Executive Branch of the Government, appointed by President Eisenhower with former President Herbert Hoover as chairman, heard the case for an independent FHLB Board; the commission did not, however, include such a recommendation in its final report.

Other construction industry groups were invited to make recommendations after the case had been presented to them by savings and loan leaders. Although these efforts led to considerable public discussion of an independent Board, there was little or no promise of success through a reorganization plan. Therefore, in the spring of 1955, savings and loan leaders decided to seek legislation. The chairman of the Banking and Currency Committee of the House, Representative Spence, sponsored a bill to accomplish this goal, and it easily passed the House of Representatives.

In the Senate the independence measure was proposed as an amendment to the omnibus housing bill, and opposition from the Housing and Home Finance Agency was strenuous. The agency officials claimed that precedent would be set for other constituent agencies to seek independence. The term "fragmentation" of the Housing Agency was coined as a shibboleth to ward off the approaching independent status of the Board.

As it happened, the housing bill was the subject of delays and grave controversies between conservatives and liberals, since it contained many provisions which were believed to be expensive and unnecessary by those who wished to diminish the federal stake in housing. As had so often been the case with savings and loan major objectives, the housing bill which carried the Board's independence with it, hung fire until the very last minute; many doubted that President Eisenhower would sign it. The course of the legislation was marked by one of the rare instances of a government official appearing in open controversy with the head of his overall agency. The then chairman of the Home Loan Bank Board, who had come to the Board with long and respected experience as a savings and loan manager, came out strongly for the law granting independence, while the head of the Housing Agency was openly attacking it. The bill was, however, enacted. The Board was set up as an independent agency on August 11, 1955.

A new era of prestige for the savings and loan business and its instrumentalities in Washington was inaugurated by this step. Numerous subsequent developments are traceable to it.

Defeat of Reorganization Plan No. 2

An early test of the permanency of the new concept of an independent FHLB Board came the next year. On May 17, 1956, President Eisenhower sent to Congress Reorganization Plan No. 2. It provided for a complete split-off of the FSLIC from the Board; the Corporation would have been administered by an entirely separate three-man board of trustees. The plan had originated in the middle echelons of the Bureau of the Budget, where the forms of government organization carry a peculiar sanctity; its sponsors relied for support on some language in the recommendations of the Hoover Commission (on Organization of the Executive Branch of the Government).

Savings and loan leaders were unanimous in believing that a costly and confusing conflict of regulations and rulings would ensue from such a separation. A threat of repeated jurisdictional bickering hovered in the background of the proposal. The League decided to oppose Reorganization Plan No. 2. Let it be recalled that defeat for any such plan was then a more difficult achievement than under the later versions of the Reorganization Act. Reorganization Plan No.

2 of 1956 had to be disapproved by a *constitutional* majority of one of the two Houses of Congress in order to be defeated. The Eisenhower Administration had never lost a reorganization plan; thus precedent was also against defeat of this one.

Representative Fascell of Florida, a member of the Government Operations Committee, with jurisdiction over all reorganization plans, introduced a resolution of disapproval in the House. It would need 217 votes, a constitutional majority of the then 435 House members, in order to carry. In the hearings Mr. Fascell brought to light defects which were a result of hasty draftsmanship. Opposition from key members of the Banking and Currency Committees in both the House and the Senate helped swell the number of votes against the plan. On July 6, 1956, by a voice vote Representative Fascell's resolution of disapproval was adopted by the House, with Speaker Sam Rayburn announcing that a "constitutional majority" had voted for the resolution killing the plan. No one challenged his ruling, although few could count 217 members of the House on the floor at the time of the vote.

League Washington office

The defeat of Reorganization Plan No. 2 was an early test of the effectiveness of the enlarged effort of the United States League in Washington. Leaders of the League had decided in the mid-1950s that the time was ripe for more continuous representation of the savings and loan point of view in various contacts with government. A broader-based effort seemed appropriate to keep men and women in government apprised of the performance of savings and loan institutions and the positions of their leaders on issues of the day. The two tangible consequences of this thinking were the establishment of new and impressive offices of the League, on Pennsylvania Avenue in Washington, and the inauguration of an annual early-in-the-congressional-session Legislative Conference.

The effect of the new League offices in Washington may be compared with the rise in efficiency and prestige that comes to an individual association when it acquires a new and larger office of modern design and attractive decor. The new Washington office opened March 1, 1955. The League also provided for the inclusion of a full-time counsel on the Washington staff and for increased personnel to pursue the ever more complex developments with which savings associations would be involved over the years.

The League's decision to expand its Washington activities was doubtless subtly influenced by a gradual change that had come over the entire business community and its attitude toward relations with Washington. The Korean War may have been more decisive than has been generally realized in making the hand of the federal government permanent in American economic affairs. This conflict broke out only a few years after the United States had begun to retreat from government domination brought on by World War II. Rent control indeed was still in effect when the Korean War broke out, and it managed to survive several years longer as a result of getting caught in this net. Because a total dismantling of the emergency establishment had not been accomplished by the time of the new hostilities, the nation lost then possibly its one opportunity to turn the political forces of the mid-century in another direction.

Still another motivation for a Washington office of the United States League with sufficient staff to do its job was the greater frequency with which savings and loan executives came to the capital on business. Association managers had more reason to come to confer with the FHLB Board than in previous years; and many also had business with the FHA or FNMA or other government agencies. The League's Washington office had a welcome mat out to serve as headquarters for these managers and the staff was in a position to make things easier—especially to those on Washington business for the first time.

It must be remembered that the Korean War was still being fought in 1952 when the Republican Party captured the White House and Congress. This party had been regarded for 20 years as more congenial in its policies to the free operations of the business community and less inclined toward government arrangements with business—whether referred to favorably as "partnerships" or condemned as "interference." It is possible that the very circumstances under which the Republicans came to power in 1953 altered some of the basic convictions they were generally assumed to hold. At any rate, out of the years 1953-1960 the familiarly termed "modern Republicanism" came to dominate thinking in Washington.

Far from any real retreat from the ventures of government into business and social welfare, this first Republican administration since 1932 moved slowly by way of commissions and specially appointed advisory groups to determine what course should be taken.

What emerged as authentic doctrine in the Eisenhower Administration was a consistently greater emphasis on financial orthodoxy (despite the recurring crises which made five out of the eight Eisenhower budgets deficit budgets). But along with it came a yielding to pressures in welfare and social legislation which far outdistanced the earlier moves of the Democratic administrations. Out of this new trend, housing emerged as one of the areas in which governmental personnel expanded continually and in which the undertakings of the Housing and Home Finance Agency multiplied with the years. The Democratically controlled Congresses worked for the expansion of housing activities. The combined impact of these trends led to greater vigilance on the part of all concerned with mortgage lending. So it was that the savings and loan business moved toward an expanded Washington program.

Almost equally influential in pointing up the need for more continuous and wider-spread Washington activity of savings and loan spokesmen was the expansion of the business. As the aggregate assets of savings and loan institutions climbed to new high levels year by year the influence of the business in the whole financial community became more significant. By the same token many moves of government and of other financial institutions which had affected only slightly a $5-billion savings and loan business had severe repercussions on a $50- or $75-billion business. Any major change in level of interest rates on the public debt, for example, could materially affect the lending of savings and loan institutions. The long-term Treasury rate is crucial in relation to all other long-term lending; thus savings and loan institutions lending $1 billion a month on terms ranging from 12 to 25 years must be well in touch at all times with the Treasury moves.

Investment in government securities

The business also continued to invest substantially in government issues during these years; it held $4.586 billion of such obligations as of December 31, 1960. In the spring of 1958 the Treasury suggested that the savings and loan business create a committee to act in an advisory capacity on Treasury financing, similar to the advisory group which the bankers had for many years. Thus there emerged as one of the permanent contacts between the Treasury and the savings and loan business an Advisory Committee on Government Securities, which met frequently with Treasury officials and became acquainted, on behalf of the entire savings and loan business, with some of the perplexing problems of debt management of the United States government. Because of their basic belief in a movement of money rates as free as possible from political domination, the savings and loan leaders were prompt to support the Treasury's request to Congress in 1959 and again in 1960 to remove the 4¼% ceiling on long-term government issues. (The problem was later resolved by the Kennedy Administration without legislation.)

The prospect for new and far-reaching legislative changes in the 1960s was already apparent in some of the studies made by the savings and loan business in the last half of the 1950s. Legislation in the discussion stage in Congress as the decade came to a close was also indicative of the new vision which some savings and loan leaders had for their business in fostering further the economic well-being of the nation.

The outward reach of the savings and loan business in this and other directions is more appropriately material for discussion of the significant changes of the last half of the decade. It will be appraised more thoroughly in the final chapter of this volume.

Chapter 18

Entering
the space age

Savings and loan executives stood on the threshold of the 1960s with many forecasts of the "soaring sixties" in their hands. One of the most important of these forecasts was entitled "The Next Decade." This comprehensive analysis, commissioned by the United States League, covered findings from a two-year study by the Indiana University School of Business. What it said in essence was this: Savings and loan institutions may well constitute a $100-billion business by the end of 1965 and a $165-billion business by 1970. Startled by the possibility, leaders of the business nevertheless admitted that this new expansion could come to pass; they recalled that every previous prediction of their generation about the rate of savings and loan growth had been far short of the actuality.

The summary of the preliminary findings in the Indiana University study ended with a remark quite consequential to savings and loan practitioners: "Growth of the magnitude suggested for the savings and loan business and other private institutions will be necessary to avoid further intervention of the federal government in home building and home financing." In 1960 leaders of the business thought about more government in their sphere of service just as their predecessors had in the 1930s: They did not want it. Their duty was to prevent it. Thus they knew they must accept the challenge of the new goals.

Some recalled the observation made by a professional educator in 1959 that the *rate* of change in the entire way of life of the human race had accelerated so greatly that in itself it was a change to be reckoned with. And they could view the last five years of the 1950s in that strange light, noting what had happened to the savings and loan institutions in both proportions and procedures. Such a look helped them to regain their equilibrium when they contemplated more than doubling their assets over the next 10 years.

The business had nearly doubled its assets in the five years 1954-1959, going from $31.7 billion on December 31, 1954, to $59.5 billion on December 31, 1959. The gains of that half decade had averaged $5.7 billion a year. To see that kind of growth in perspective, managers had only to recall that one year's growth at this rate added to the assets of the business more dollars than had constituted the entire savings and loan system in the 1936-1940 period. These enormous strides had been possible because of the prosperity of the times and of changes in the savings and loan business in several salient respects. Some of the changes had touched a relatively few associations, as numbers go, but they were spreading into more and more units of the business; no one imagined that these changes would not spread. Others had already affected practically the entire business by 1960.

Competition for savings

One change affecting all associations was that competition for savings became more vigorous in the late 1950s. Not only between the savings and loan associations and other forms of savings did a strenuous rivalry develop, but also within the savings and loan business. This intrabusiness competition presented a situation which had not existed for the savings and loan institutions since the 1920s. During its way up from doubt and discouragement in the 1930s to the new prestige of mid-century, the business had retained a compelling sense of the competitive threat of other businesses. Therefore, for nearly 25 years it had shown an especially keen appreciation of the fact that all must hang together or they would all hang separately. As the individual associations expanded in a business world which had not expanded quite so much it was probably inevitable that there should be a sharper rivalry among them.

The contest for savings centered more and more on lures of tangible worth to the saver. These included a higher return on the money invested and in many cases gifts, sometimes of a substantial character, to those starting new accounts—they were called "giveaways" in the business parlance of the era.

The return paid to savings and loan accountholders in the later 1950s was higher than in the preceding 10 years because of two factors. One was the competition described above, and the other was the change in the price of money, as the economy surged. To begin with, the artificial damper on interest rates which had been imposed during the war and transition years was removed in the early 1950s; the Federal Reserve System stopped pegging the interest rates on government issues in 1951, as noted in Chapter 15. Money costs, thus allowed to seek their market level, started rising.

What happened to them in a relatively few years is evidenced by new Treasury policies in the United States savings bond program. In April 1957 the Congress lifted the 3% ceiling on savings bonds to 3.26%. Two and a half years later, in September 1959, with interest rates still higher, the Congress sent to the White House a bill permitting the savings bond rate to go to 4¼%. The Treasury, however, acted conservatively and set the new rate at 3¾% on savings bonds held to maturity. This continued as the effective rate throughout 1960.

More remunerative savings plans

The rates at which savings and loan institutions distributed their earnings in the decade of the 1950s are reflected in Table 23.

How much of the rise was due to competition and how much to the basic economic factors varied from locality to locality. Aside from an increase in the basic rate, another area of close competition lay in the greater frequency of distribution of earn-

Table 23. *Dividend rates paid by savings and loan associations,*
1950-1960 (percentage distribution)

Year	Total	2½% and under	3% and 3¼%	3½% and 3¾%	4% and 4¼%	Over 4¼%
1950	100%	67.4%	32.6%			
1951	100	56.2	40.8	3.0%		
1952	100	46.8	45.2	8.0		
1953	100	33.0	51.2	11.9	3.9%	
1954	100	25.3	56.5	11.8	6.4	
1955	100	18.5	61.0	13.5	7.0	
1956	100	11.0	63.8	18.0	7.2	
1957	100		43.3	40.4	16.3	
1958	100		37.6	45.9	16.5	
1959	100		11.7	43.1	41.2	4.0%
1960	100		2.0	22.3	66.0	9.7

Source: United States League

ings. Dollarwise the greater frequency of payments did not mean much. For example, on the basis of the withdrawal experience of the late 1950s, it was estimated that the saver getting earnings semiannually received only 1/10 of 1% less than he would have received from earnings figured as often as daily. But adroit advertising made the small difference seem much more of a boon to the saver than the actual difference. Furthermore there were other advantages which made a difference to savers promised quarterly rather than half-yearly earnings. If they wished to withdraw all or part of their funds between periods of distribution they obviously stood to lose less in the case of a quarterly arrangement, and those savers building retirement income could look forward to receiving checks twice as often. Thus associations in many localities adopted quarterly distributions as a standard procedure.

By 1959 a proposal had come before the Federal Home Loan Bank Board to permit federal associations to distribute income on individual savings up to the month of withdrawal, instead of merely at the stated periods of distribution; this was already the practice in some state-chartered jurisdictions. While the Board had not granted this privilege to federals in general by the end of 1960, the fact that it was seriously advanced as a proposal from parts of the business points to the vigorous efforts to find more and different ways to please savers.

Associations which engaged in expensive giveaways followed the merchandising approaches of the times. People had become accustomed to television programs which gave away thousands of dollars in one evening; hence they did not regard the financial institution which offered costly items to the savers as out of the ordinary. This manifestation of the competitive spirit was eventually put under control by a regulation of the Federal Savings and Loan Insurance Corporation, placing an arbitrary ceiling of $2.50 on the cost of any item that was given as a premium for a new investment. This did not happen, however, before many had acquired such substantial gifts as sets of flat silver, transistor radios, living room lamps and electrical appliances.

In many localities commercial banks also made their bid for the savers' dollars with a new urgency. For years they had shown lethargy in building savings departments and their gradual change of heart was a factor of the postwar era. Limited until December 1961 by Federal Reserve Board regulation to a 3% rate to savers, they used much the same ingenuity as savings and loan associations in offering fractional advantages to savers not expressed in the rate of return as such. Many banks also engaged in the luring of customers by giveaways.

Savings and loan's search for new avenues to the customers' favor probed more deeply by the end of the decade. By mid-1961 the FHLB Board had amended the regulation governing bonuses for systematic savings and permitted for the first time the payment of a bonus on certificate type savings in amounts of $1,000 or more. Peering more deeply into the considerations which might sway a saver, some of the leaders in the business looked seriously at the provisions for federal and most state-chartered institutions to place savers on a rotation basis for payouts in time of emergency. The New York League had led the way in changing its state law so that this emergency stop-gap was no longer permitted. There was also serious discussion at the Federal Home Loan Bank Board of regulation of fees and discounts on mortgage loans as part of an effort to stabilize rates on savings in localities where high income from such charges gave certain associations advantages over their competitors in bidding for savings. Such was some of the ferment in savings and loan circles as the 1960s emerged.

Brokerage of savings accounts

A by-product of the more strenuous rivalry of savings and loan institutions was the use of brokers in the development of savings and loan accounts. As the 1950s went along more associations used brokers to help recruit money. The FHLB Board had proposed regulating the practice as early as 1954. But it was not until January 4, 1960, that a regulation went into effect limiting all insured associations to the following formula for brokered accounts: They could not receive from brokers a dollar volume of savings equal to more than 5% of the total savings in force at the start of the year. The clamor for a regulation of brokers' savings accounts had come from the business, where the majority of the associations did not use the device and believed that the brokers' advertising of higher rates placed them at a disadvantage.

Commercial insurance of accounts

Another phenomenon of the highly competitive era and the aggressive advertising of rates paid on savings was the emergence of the so-called commercial insurance of accounts. Some savings and loan associations which did not have FSLIC insurance contracted with some private insurance companies to insure their savings; they developed insignia closely resembling that of the FSLIC to illustrate their advertisements. The special appeal of most of these institutions was a higher rate than that commonly paid in the area. Several insurance companies of doubtful stability were the first to be used in pursuit of this competitive advantage. Various actions were taken by courts and state insurance departments in attempts to prevent abuses of savers' confidence and to preserve the good name of FSLIC-insured associations.

The problem remained a baffling one by the end of the decade, but it promised to be less pressing because of the enactment in 1961 of a state supervisory law in Maryland where the state legislature for the previous 100 years had refused to enact supervision. The aggressively advertised, privately insured institutions had a heyday in Maryland before the enactment of this legislation but the collapse of their frail structure began within a few months after state supervision went into effect. This closing of the loophole did not come, however, before several thousand persons had put their faith and money in the unreliable associations and stood to lose substantial amounts in closed associations. Several criminal statutes were violated in the course of this unhappy development.

The emergence of this problem portended periodic menaces to the good name of savings and loan institutions by new schemes to use its name and prestige for less desirable ends. The situation was not too different from the 1890s when the United States League had been founded to protect the good name of the savings and loan business from ill-advised and unworthy practices of those who traded upon its earned prestige. Considering the popularity of the savings and loan business and its great size by 1960, the leaders realized that periodic attempts to capitalize unworthily on its good name were one of the things with which they would have to live.

Variety in lending

While the main change in the savings phase of the business in the late 1950s may be regarded as the emergence of a sharper type of competition, the perceptible change on the lending side lay in an entirely different direction. To begin with, the typical multi-million dollar savings association was now dealing in a much wider variety of loans than had ever characterized the business before. Furthermore it was also handling its mortgage loan portfolio in a substantially different manner from even five years before. As the savings and loan executive studied the possibilities of doing the volume of loan business envisioned by the Indiana University study, he could see where the 1950s had ushered in a new day, sometimes with fanfare, and sometimes quietly and gradually.

While the mortgage on a single-family home was as always the staple component of the savings and loan portfolio, some new items could be found in an increasing number of associations. Among them were loans on apartment buildings and on residential sites. The more spectacular of these was, of course, the lending on residential sites.

Lending on residential sites

Again, as in the case of many suddenly expanding practices in the late 1930s, the embryonic idea of lending on raw land had been tried out here and there for some time. State savings and loan laws had been amended as early as the 1940s in some jurisdictions to permit savings and loan institutions actually to own land and develop it. Furthermore many of the state statutes did not carefully circumscribe the type of real estate security a savings and loan association could take for its mortgages and thus did not restrict them to *improved* real estate. So there had been opportunity, as the postwar boom progressed, to experiment with a theory, long held by some leaders in the business, that one way to assure soundly built new homes and sound planning of subdivisions was for the association to become actively engaged in subdivision operations. As early as 1947, the League's Federal Savings and Loan Committee had discussed the possible power to make loans for preparation of residential sites.

Then the Housing Act of 1959 opened the door a crack to the lending by federal associations on unimproved residential sites; and the door was expected to be opened wider if the first performance showed promise. The 1959 statute permitted any association with general reserves, surplus and undivided profits exceeding 5% of its withdrawable accounts to have outstanding at any one time not more than 5% of such accounts in loans "to finance the acquisition and development of land, within the 50-mile radius, for primary residential usage."

Additional push was given to the enactment of such legislation by the growing scarcity of prepared land for home building and the mounting costs of land, as the builders had to move farther and farther out from the center of the city to build their houses. The larger builders had no trouble financing the development of larger plots for building houses in volume; the smaller builders needed special sources of financing, and it appeared, as the new decade began, that savings and loan institutions would have a good chance to be that source.

Over 80% loans

Higher percentage loans on homes without either FHA or VA backing began to show up in savings and loan portfolios by the end of the 1950s. As of December 31, 1960, savings and loan institutions had made 14,729 loans in the over-80% category for a total of $202 million. Two things had occurred to open the way for this divergence from past patterns. One was the liberalization of the regulations for federal savings and loan associations in the late fall of 1958 permitting them to make convential loans up to 90%, so long as their reserve situation made it feasible. The other was the operation of a strictly private enterprise insurance company specializing in insuring the riskiest part of higher percentage mortgage loans, without the red tape and bureaucracy inherent in government insurance schemes—and, very importantly, without the interest rate ceilings which caused FHA and VA to have a feast or famine existence because of changing interest rate levels.

In Great Britain in 1954 a successful program had been started under which an insurance company guaranteed only the top, or riskiest, part of a high percentage home loan; the premium was lower than that for insurance of the entire loan in the FHA fashion and red tape was at a minimum. The idea appealed to leaders in the savings and loan business, and for two years the United States League had a special committee studying how the plan might be adapted for use here. It proposed an insurance system under the administration of the FHLB Board, but paying its own way through stock contributions by the Federal Home Loan Banks. A provision to charter such an insurance corporation was included in the Housing Act of 1958, but the legislation failed of enactment.

Subsequently those savings and loan institutions interested in this type of cushion for their high-percentage loans turned to a privately organized mortgage insurance company already in operation on a small scale. This company was later reorganized with proportionately larger representation of savings and loan executives on its board of directors.

The buying and selling of mortgages had become a common, if not prevalent, practice in the savings and loan business by 1960. The Federal National Mortgage Association, chartered in 1937 and rechartered in 1954, had broken down some of the prejudice against the sale of mortgages in the course of its activities. Dedication of the savings and loan business to heavy support for the veterans home loan program persuaded many institutions as early as the late 1940s to sell some of their VA loans to the FNMA so that they might have money enough to make new loans to veterans. Furthermore the sale of mortgages, while at the same time retaining the privilege of servicing them and getting a fee for doing so, became an important ingredient of an association's receipts as the spread between earnings and expenses of an association dwindled under low interest rates. By December 31, 1960, 155 associations had sold mortgages amounting to $160 million to the Federal National Mortgage Association.

Buying and selling participations

Long before 1960, however, associations were selling participations to each other, to life insurance companies and to mutual savings banks as well. In 1957 the United States League held its first Secondary Mortgage Conference for representatives of associations especially interested in buying and selling a part of their portfolios. A small group gathered at White Sulphur Springs, W. Va., that first year but it made a suggestion which caught fire: Associations should have the right to sell *participations* in mortgage loans. (The sale or purchase of part of a loan had long been common practice in the commercial banking world.)

As a consequence the FHLB Board adopted in March 1957 a regulation providing as follows: An insured association in one area could originate conventional loans and sell a participation in them to an association in a "surplus" area outside the 50-mile limit, provided the seller retained at least a 50% interest; the seller retained the servicing. In 1959 Congress amended the Federal Savings and Loan statute to increase the amount of participation loans that a federal association could buy or sell. Many state laws were amended subsequently to give similar privileges to state-chartered associations.

In November 1960 the FHLB Board and the Federal Home Loan Banks promulgated a regulation permitting insured savings and loan institutions to sell participations in loans to pension funds and other investors. The move had been urged by the United States League, whose leaders saw its use one day as a method of tapping for home mortgage lending the increasingly prolific source of accumulated savings in the pension funds created by industry and labor. (In 1960, $29 billion were invested in noninsured corporate pension funds.) This step was especially significant because it was one way in which savings and loan institutions could reach out to use in their mortgage lending operations savings which had already been accumulated in another type of investment. An attempt at the same type of pioneering was the creation in 1956 by some savings associations of a mutual fund known as the Insured Accounts Fund.

On the whole the sale and/or purchase of participations between associations found much greater acceptability than had been envisioned by its most enthusiastic sponsors. It proved to be an excellent way to move money from one locality to another while still keeping it within the savings and loan system. As of December 31, 1960, 738 insured associations had sold or purchased interests in mortgages under the plan and $617 million of participations were involved. Most of the sales were made by associations in the South and on the West Coast. There was a growing interest in the program as the decade ended, but this device was far from a total solution for the problem of plentiful mortgage money in one sector and dearth in another.

The leaders of the business faced the 1960s with an increasing conviction that the business needed a secondary market for conventional loans, a hitherto nonexistent means for converting mortgage loans in the portfolio into cash. In 1957-1958 a committee of the United States League studied the possibility of a secondary market of this type within the framework of the Federal Home Loan Bank System. Approval for the idea was slowly gaining ground by the end of the decade. The Banking Committee of the House of Representatives had reported a bill in 1960 including a provision for such a secondary market. The Senate Housing Subcommittee in its study of the mortgage credit needs of the 1960s had given the idea favorable comment. A meeting of the American Bankers Association in Washington in the spring of 1961 also endorsed the idea of a secondary market for conventional mortgage loans.

Growing importance of conventional loans

The urgency for establishing such a new device was emphasized by the increasing proportion of the mortgage lending of the nation being done on a conventional loan basis by 1960. In the 15 years immediately after the close of World War II, the conventional loan had showed itself to be the truly stable factor in the flow of home mortgage money. In only four of those 15 years was there a year-to-year drop in dollar volume of such lending. By contrast there were six downward fluctuations in FHA and seven in VA volume. The FNMA, confining its buying and selling operations to FHA-insured and VA-guaranteed mortgage loans, would continue to offer an acceptable market for such loans; but the need for some additional facility less confined in the type of mortgages in which it traded became apparent as the conventional loan gained in relative popularity.

In 1960, $22.7 billion of home loans were made on the conventional basis, accounting for 78% of all home lending. This was the largest part of home financing done on the conventional basis since 1937, the year before the FHA became truly successful. It appeared that any program for channeling more funds into mortgage lending in the years ahead should include some stimulation of funds for conventional lending. In Chart 10 is shown the large proportion of total mortgage recordings accounted for by the conventional type of loan.

Also significantly, objective study was being given by 1960 to the whole idea of central mortgage banking and secondary market facilities through a University of California at Los Angeles project.

Chart 10. Annual volume of nonfarm mortgage recordings under $20,000, all types of lenders, by type of mortgage, 1945-1960

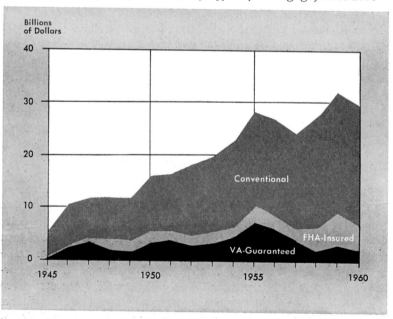

Sources: Federal Home Loan Bank Board, Federal Housing Administration and Veterans Administration, annual reports

The study was financed jointly by the United States League and the life insurance and savings bank businesses. The part taken by the League in this study indicated not only its concern over the sources of mortgage money in the future but also its reconsideration of the one-time view that the sale and purchase of mortgages was antithetical to the savings and loan concept. The world had changed from 1930 to 1960, and no one questioned the need for an objective exploration of the whole idea.

Future of Federal Home Loan Banks

But all the new approaches to opening up the flow of more funds into home mortgages through savings and loan associations were studied against the background of a deepening recognition that the potentialities of the FHLB System had never really been tested. Economic circumstances, the extraordinary success of the FHA from 1938 onward and the predilection of personnel in the FHLB System had all combined to slant policy toward use of the System for short-term credit needs. The result was tantamount to disregard of that part of the original concept which had envisioned it as a supplement to the total volume of long-term mortgage funds available to savings and loan institutions. Furthermore year in and year out, 40% of the member institutions of the System were doing no borrowing.

In 1957 the United States League appointed a special committee to study how the System might be made more useful. The New York League likewise commissioned an objective study assisted by competent economists.

In 1958 the FHLB Board surveyed the membership of the FHLB System to determine the acceptability of a special issue of five-year obligations. As a result, it issued $300 million of such obligations; associations receiving this money agreed to keep it five years. After the Kennedy Administration came into power and urged the lowering of home mortgage interest rates for the quickening of economic recovery, the Board proposed as part of its program for lower interest rates to make an additional volume of special five-year advances available to members.

The Senate Banking Committee's study of mortgage credit needs for the 1960s not only suggested favorable consideration of the secondary market for conventional loans but also asked the FHLB

Board to give the committee some guidance on the possibility of a more significant contribution by the Bank System to mortgage lending. Thus there seems to be developing a thorough exploration of, and possible decisive action on, the role of the FHLB System.

By 1960 the position of home mortgage debt in the economy of the United States had become much more commanding than a generation before. A total home mortgage debt of $134.7 billion was owed by all families of the United States as of December 31, 1960. This constituted 47% of the total indebtedness of all individuals on that date. It compared with a home mortgage debt in 1929 which was only between a third and a fourth of the total private individual indebtedness at the time. True, $70 billion of mortgage indebtedness had been paid off between 1950-1960, but the prospect for the availability of repayments on home mortgage debt as a source of new credits to home owners during the decade of the 1960s was less bright than in the 1950s. The entire mortgage debt of the country was written on a longer term basis, and the payments on principal, therefore, would inevitably be less significant during the decade ahead as a source of new loanable funds.

Furthermore by 1961 broader experiments in the shape of 35- and 40-year maturities for widening groups of home mortgage borrowers were being ushered in by the housing act sponsored in the first year of the Kennedy Administration. There was every reason for savings and loan executives to explore, consider and continually review what needed to be done to help their institutions live up to the goal set in the Indiana University study of "The Next Decade."

Holding companies

A new element was introduced into the organic structure of several hundred savings and loan institutions in the later 1950s. This was holding company participation in savings and loan operations. To understand it, the reader must be cognizant of another development of the 1950s, viz., the revival of interest in the permanent, or capital, or guaranty stock type of savings and loan institution. A generation earlier, in the 1920s, the previous decade of significant savings and loan expansion, the development of stock companies had played a leading part in the growth of the business in California and a notable part in the growth in Ohio. By the end of the 1920s, Texas had joined the ranks of savings and loan states convinced that salvation lay in the direction of the permanent stock association. In Kansas, the state law authorizing permanent stock operations dated back to 1893, and many associations there were proceeding successfully under its provisions.

Then many developments in the depression threw favorable emphasis on the mutual type of institution and away from the stock concept. The Federal Savings and Loan statute, by its exclusive use of the mutual concept, had much influence in this direction. In the 1950s, however, interest developed again in the stock institutions. Some of this interest resulted in the conversion of a few mutual associations into stock associations. Some of it led to the authorization of stock institutions in the laws of states which had not had them before; among these states were New Mexico, Wyoming, Illinois, Washington and Virginia.

The United States League created a standing committee on the Management of Capital Stock Associations in 1956. This group's annual agenda is devoted not only to operational concerns but also to problems peculiar to the permanent stock type of operation in relations with government and other financial institutions.

For instance, the internal organization of a capital stock institution makes it a relatively easy vehicle for merger. The purchase of the capital stock of one institution by another became one of the ways in which some institutions swelled their assets by the merger route in the 1950s. Such mergers, especially where large institutions were involved, drew public attention to this type of savings and loan association. When a mutual converted into a stock association, attention began to be focused on the rights of the savers with regard to the reserves, surplus and undivided profits of the mutual, converting association. Proposals were made for federal legislation to control the conversions of mutual associations which were FSLIC-insured. But these questions did not command as much attention, either inside or outside the business, as did the holding company development.

Holding companies were familiar to the commercial banking scene in the United States long before they stepped onto the savings and loan stage, and they were subjected to federal regulation in May 1956. Between the depression of the 1930s and 1957, there had been no manifestation of holding company operations in

327

the savings and loan business. Some with long memories could re-call that in the mid-1920s mass acquisition of ownership of capital stock associations had begun, but the depression and subsequent association failures had swept the memory out of mind. Then on July 29, 1955, the Great Western Financial Corporation, organized by the New York investment house of Lehman Brothers, acquired the capital stock of the Great Western Savings and Loan Associa-tion of Los Angeles. During the next four years this holding com-pany acquired six more savings and loan associations, 15 escrow companies, a reconveyance company and controlling ownership of a title search company; it also conducts an insurance agency, some-times makes loans to builders and has organized two subsidiaries to participate in joint ventures for land development.

Entrance of Great Western into the situation set the ball rolling for further holding company organizations and acquisitions of con-trolling interest in savings and loan institutions. Table 24 shows the year-by-year development the last half of the decade.

Table 24. *Public holding company control of savings and loan associations, December 31, 1955-1959 (in thousands of dollars)*

Year	Number of public holding companies	Number of controlled associations	Total assets
1955	1	1	$ 128,035
1956	2	3	232,669
1957	3	11	683,185
1958	4	14	937,519
1959	13	54	2,472,417

Source: Federal Home Loan Bank Board

The spread of public and nonpublic holding company activity in savings and loan associations over a relatively wide geographic area is shown in Table 25.

The FHLB Board, in its report to the Banking and Currency Committees of the two Houses of Congress in May 1960 termed the holding company device a "highly profitable promotional ven-ture for the investment banking industry."

In April 1956 a bill had been introduced in the House of Rep-resentatives to limit any holding company to the ownership of one

328

Table 25. *Public and nonpublic holding company activity in savings and loan associations by states, December 31, 1959 (in thousands of dollars)*

State	Number of associations	Total assets
Arizona	1	$ 1,696
California	66	3,764,935
Colorado	6	88,595
Idaho	1	11,796
Kansas	3	16,000
Nevada	1	5,300
Ohio	5	111,738
Texas	9	237,187
Utah	1	22,480
Total	93	$4,259,727

Source: Federal Home Loan Bank Board

savings and loan association. Enactment into law was delayed by the unsuccessful attempt of the Senate to recodify all financial institution laws in 1957-1958, and the hope of Senate leaders to include the savings and loan holding company bill with the larger measure. Thus it came about that the holding companies in the field were able to go ahead without interference in the strides as shown above. Finally in 1959 temporary legislation was passed banning for two years the acquisition by a holding company of more than one FSLIC member savings and loan institution. A year later this law was made permanent.

The savings and loan leaders did not regard this legislation as the end of their thinking about the appropriate place of holding companies in the business. They thought, however, that with this legislation they had a more workable situation from which to arrive at better legislation some time in the future, when time and experience had given them, the supervisors and the lawmakers more perspective.

New office buildings

Some conspicuous changes occurred in the physical characteristics of savings and loan institutions as the 1950s passed into the 1960s. A changing contour could be noticed in most of the new offices—low-lying and stretched out, in contrast to tall structures. During the 1950s at least 55% of all associations built new main or branch office quarters or both, and 23% of them built new main office quarters in the last half of the decade. Many were remodeling quarters built only five or six years before. A 1960 association office was much more likely to devote some space to activities not strictly business than had ever been the custom before. Community rooms were no longer a news item; an employees' lounge and dining room were an accepted part of the new office pattern. The median floor space in new office structures, built in 1955-1959, was 6,000 square feet; upward of 20,000 square feet was the median for associations with assets of $35 million or more. Furthermore a parking lot was considered a necessity, if a new building was going up. A drive-up window where a saver might transact his business without leaving his automobile was no longer a novelty.

Branch development

Branch offices, however, were the most spectacular thing which happened to the housing of savings and loan offices. As of the end of 1949 only 75 associations had branches, roughly one out of 80. The number had multiplied more than 10 times by the end of 1960. At that time almost one out of every eight associations had one or more branches, and one out of every five savings and loan offices was a branch office. On a single day in 1960 the largest savings and loan association in the country opened four new branches. Table 26 shows the geographical distribution of branch operations.

Obviously the history of banking institutions in the United States helped prejudice some jurisdictions against branch offices and was probably responsible for the comparatively late development of the branch pattern in both commercial banks and savings and loan.

Even by 1960 the practice in the United States gave little or no indication of an overall change to the free and easy way of the British Commonwealth, where no supervisory approval is required for the opening of a new branch. Actually, making a case for a new branch office became increasingly difficult as the competitive situation between savings and loan and other financial institutions and among savings and loan associations themselves sharpened. In 1960 the FHLB Board processed 218 branch applications from

*Table 26. Geographical distribution of savings associations
and branch offices, December 31, 1960*

Region	Total number of associations	Number of associations with branch offices	Number of branch offices	Percent of total number of associations with branch offices
New England	323	30	49	9%
Middle Atlantic	1,499	208	318	14
East North Central	1,617	156	337	10
West North Central	514	46	86	9
South Atlantic	1,064	128	217	12
South Central	735	88	159	12
Mountain	167	46	111	28
Pacific	356	124	334	35
Total	6,275	826	1,611	13%

Source: United States League

federal associations, but granted only 137. In California, the state of largest activity in branch applications, state-chartered associations applied for 55 branches during the first half of 1961, and 30 of them were denied.

The savings and loan leagues found their activities also influenced by the branch pattern. The United States League assigned a staff man primarily to the problems of branch operations and had a standing committee on branch operations by the end of the decade. A 50-page League brochure, a study on savings and loan branches emphasizing the factors involved in deciding whether or not they were profitable, appeared in 1961. The California Savings and Loan League had an annual Branch Operations Conference starting with 1955.

Personnel developments

The practical doubling of the assets of the average association between 1955 and 1960 brought greatly increased demands for manpower. So it was that the savings and loan business which had 40,500 persons on its aggregate payroll in 1955 had upward of 65,-000 by 1960. New positions were estimated to be opening up at the rate of 4,500 a year.

This period also saw with increasing frequency the tapering off of duties of many chief executive officers who had borne the burden of business operations in the 1940s and 1950s. They became chairmen of the board, in the most common rearrangement of titles; this meant shifting the responsibilities of the presidency to younger shoulders.

A general expansion of personnel was necessary despite a steady lowering of operating costs from 1955-1960, during which period the business had whittled the average of 1.024 persons per $1 million in assets down to 0.9; this spectacularly low figure compared with two persons per $1 million of assets in the 1940s. In addition the organization structures changed substantially during the two decades. Departmentalization and specialization were present on a much greater scale than ever before.

The tasks which had to be done in savings and loan institutions had multiplied. In 1960 whether one was concerned with the typical association ($12 million in assets and 14 employees) or with the larger institutions (over $100 million in assets and employing hundreds of persons) one was aware that the type of work performed during the hours on duty was often quite unprecedented in terms of earlier savings and loan experience. There was a much greater use of middle management in staff responsibilities. Increasing attention to internal organization and to personnel policies was part of management's approach to maximum efficiency. No wonder the larger savings and loan institutions often found it appropriate by the late 1950s to hire management consultants to look objectively at their in-office arrangements in order to increase their efficiency.

New machines in offices

As the 1960s approached there was yet another way in which the physical being of a savings and loan association was undergoing something of a metamorphosis. Wider use of machine processing offered an almost limitless possibility. In 1958 the United States League commissioned a certified public accounting firm to study data processing in savings and loan associations by the new electronic devices. The result was a three-volume report dealing with the opportunity for using electronic equipment already on the market and with that yet in the planning stage. It helped the associations to know what stage of their growth opened the way for practical adaptation to one or more of the new devices.

When the study was begun some associations had just started to utilize the new aids by farming out their loan accounting operation to firms which specialized in using the wonder machines of the new age. Less than two years later the exhibit hall at the United States League convention was replete with displays of machines which automatically calculated dividends, proved deposits and withdrawals, and prepared trial balances at electronic speeds; also there were several computers which provided low-cost electronic loan accounting within the association, handling the calculation of interest, apportionment to escrow accounts for tax and insurance payments, and the final calculation of payment against principal. There were some few viewing these marvels of the atomic age who recalled what a horror New Year's Eve used to be for the accounting department because the books had to be balanced at the year's end with all the attendant problems of human fallibility. Any hardships in the savings and loan business in the 1960s were obviously not going to be in that category.

As savings and loan executives faced the great demand of the 1960s they could be encouraged about the ability of the business to promote itself. Aside from the spectacular strides that had been made in advertising by individual associations, the late 1950s had seen the fruition of another long-time dream of business leaders. This was savings and loan cooperative advertising on a nation-wide scale. Twice in the 30 years after the Great Depression the United States League had sounded out the possibilities of a large-scale national advertising campaign, and the response had always been insufficient to launch the venture.

Savings and Loan Foundation

Then in December 1954, for the first time in history, advertisements publicizing the insured savings and loan institutions appeared in *Life, Time* and *The Saturday Evening Post;* they were full pages in black and white and went to a circulation of approximately 12 million readers. "Savings and Loan Foundation" was the signature on the ads. How the Savings and Loan Foundation developed is an excellent demonstration of the special ability of the savings and loan business to fashion its own future.

333

The Federal Savings and Loan Advisory Council, the statutory group created in 1935, had appointed a special committee in 1951 to consider proposals for launching a national publicity campaign. Representatives of the United States League and the secretary of the FHLB Board met informally with the committee. The pledges of 311 insured institutions to advance $85,000 to underwrite part of the program were submitted. As a consequence the Savings and Loan Foundation was created, with representatives of 10 Federal Home Loan Banks, some of whom were the presidents, signing the papers of incorporation drawn up under Delaware law.

In 1955 the Foundation had an approved advertising budget of $683,374 and its supporters were some 1,100 associations that paid dues at the rate of $100 per million of assets. By the end of 1960, 2,010 associations were supporting the project, representing 63.8% of the total assets of the business, and the rate of their dues had been cut in half to $50 per million of assets. The operating head of the organization was the man who had been chairman of the FHLB Board when the idea germinated.

A $2-million national advertising budget was voted for 1961. The Foundation had long since moved into color ads six or eight times a year in such magazines as *The Saturday Evening Post, Life* and the *Reader's Digest,* and was supplying its members, large and small—up and down the land—with window cards and other duplicates of the ads proclaiming its familiar slogan, "Where You Save Does Make a Difference." The Foundation in 1961 sponsored one major television network's coverage of President Kennedy's inauguration and had celebrated New Year's Eve by sponsoring the East-West Football Game.

The Foundation's success had been so notable that it prodded the American Bankers Association in 1958 to create a foundation of its own to tell the story of commercial banking to the public.

New associations

Reassuring also was the apparent vigor of the savings and loan idea, as manifested in new institutions. Managers of existing associations might be pardoned for looking upon new institutions as something short of a blessing because of their competitive possibilities, but they would still have to admit in their most objective moments that the new charters augured well for the future. New

The business that builds better communities!

As the nation's largest source of home loans, Insured Savings and Loan Associations play a leading role in residential community development. It is good to know that when you save at an Insured Savings and Loan Association, your money . . . in addition to earning excellent returns for you . . . helps your neighbors buy homes, helps develop your community and stimulates the nation's biggest industry, the construction business.

Insured Savings and Loan Associations

©1961, The Savings and Loan Foundation, Inc., 1111 E Street, N.W., Washington 4, D.C.

A typical Savings and Loan Foundation advertisement

communities and new groups of citizens were starting associations just as they had in the 1880s and 1920s, and the new ones were growing and going well.

Over 600 newly chartered institutions entered the system between 1950 and 1960. Some of them came to fill gaps in sections of the country where, for one reason or another, the development of savings and loan institutions had lagged. Some had been deliberately fostered by leaders of the business in nearby localities so that there might be a more complete network of institutions offering savings and home financing facilities. The widening web of suburbia, while it had made branch offices popular, had also made the opening of brand new institutions of the savings and loan type a natural development. The fact that one out of 10 of the institutions making up the savings and loan system at the start of the 1960s was less than 10 years old certainly meant that the business was not subject to stagnation; nor was it likely to run out of ideas if the manpower of the business as a whole was being freshened periodically by these new infusions.

Changes in United States League

By 1960 the United States League, close to 70 years old, faced the future in a prime position to serve a $72-billion business. Not only did it and its affiliates have a staff of 150 persons with access to three decades of experience with savings and loan institutions, but it also had a workable plan for an adequate income to serve the savings and loan business in the 1960s in ways which were yet unforeseen. The whole national pattern of living in the United States had increased the importance and prestige of trade associations; membership in the League was taken for granted as a business service which associations thought they could not afford to do without. The League represented over 90% of the assets of the business, a situation which was helpful not only in budgeting for projects to serve future needs, but also in representations to the Congress when it was seeking legislative enactment.

As in the savings and loan institutions themselves, the last half of the decade of the 1950s had seen the League making many changes in its arrangements in order to meet the challenges of a new age—a new age represented not only by what was happening in the United States at large, but also by the unprecedented growth of the savings and loan business. A San Francisco office had been added. Four new departments had been created out of projects that were once handled by one man and a secretary; an Investment and Loan Department, Convention Department, Publications Department and Legal Department.

In 1958 for the first time the League added a full-time staff economist. In 1960 it made available for consultation a labor attorney. In 1960 the League took the long step forward of employing a full-time architect to enable the savings and loan business to assume a new leadership role in home building. Two of the League's top specialized staff men had acquired the prestige of university faculty associates in 1960.

The League was keeping closer contact with directors of the associations than ever before. Among its devices to give directors a share in its informational program was the semiannual preparation of slides covering the chief business statistics important to savings and loan; these were available to members for projection on a screen in their own directors rooms.

Mindful at the same time of the changing role of the chief executive within the association, the League started publishing a quarterly, *Management Digest;* its aim was to present pertinent new thoughts by leaders in government, business and the professions, so that top management in savings and loan could encompass them in a reasonably brief reading time.

By the late '50s the League had also tackled the major public relations problem of giving educators an intimate acquaintanceship with the business. It initiated an Annual Conference on Savings and Residential Financing, drawing representation from college and university professors. As the 1960s arrived at least a dozen Institutes of Business Finance for high school teachers were being held at various universities under the joint sponsorship of a state league, the United States League and the particular school at which they were conducted. Every year sees more of these institutes begun and they usually become annual affairs.

Institute expansion

The American Savings and Loan Institute was nearing its 40th birthday by 1960. It, too, like the United States League and the typical association, bore only a slight resemblance to its appearance in 1930. It had a staff of 29 persons. They were writing textbooks, planning additional ones and organizing chapters—just as they had always done. But the staff—more nearly adequate than at any previous time in Institute history—was breaking records in meeting its time schedules on publications, as it completed the ninth Institute-written text for chapter and home study. It added 19 new chapters in 1960 alone. It was instructing 18,500 savings and loan employees that year, many times the number of all persons working for the business before the depression.

The success of its Graduate School at Indiana University had become a byword in the business. The Institute was pioneering in specialized business education by starting middle-management schools at two universities as the decade rounded out. Top management had come to regard the Institute's training as an indispensable tool. Because of it the men who looked at the challenge of the necessary expansion of the business did not have too many qualms about how they could fit new employees into their organizations. A new beachhead for the future had also been prepared through Institute training films which would be used in each association office to facilitate new employees' integration into the work.

Controllers Society

In 1960 the Society of Savings and Loan Controllers, in its 11th year, had an enrollment of 2,300 savings and loan controllers and internal auditors. It had to its credit, in this relatively brief life, over 250 educational papers on accounting and related topics. Its local chapters in 33 cities could see in the possible future no letup in the need for savings and loan associations to do an ever-more minute job of analysis of operations. Such a program was not only needed to safeguard the public trust which was placed in a business with $72 billion in assets, but also was an essential to planning intelligently the future work of the institution. Top management could forget many of its individual problems because the Society of Savings and Loan Controllers existed.

Savings and loan idea exported

Exportation of the savings and loan idea to the underdeveloped countries of the world became an increasing interest of some savings and loan executives in the late 1950s. The United States League had long been affiliated with the International Union of Building Societies and Savings Associations and had participated in international meetings of the business from 1914 on. The missionary spirit was encouraged by the United States government's far-flung aid programs for other countries.

Peru adopted a savings and loan law in 1957 as a direct result of the efforts of some American savings and loan executives, representatives of the home building industry and the FHA. Several associations were in operation under its provisions in the late 1950s.

Chile developed a special variety of savings and loan institutions, geared to cope with inflationary aspects of its economy, along lines recommended by savings and loan executives from the United States who visited the scene and turned their imagination and experience to this problem.

A new statute in Austria permitting a Home Loan Bank System for the small but thriving savings and loan institutions in that country was drafted in 1957 by visiting savings and loan leaders.

Bills proposing the creation of an International Home Loan Bank in which United States savings and loan institutions could invest were introduced in Congress as early as 1960; through this device "seed money" for the development of savings and loan institutions in other countries was sought. It seemed likely that before many years some such law would be enacted, as a result of the increased recognition of savings and loan associations as a key to a better-housed nation.

The new economic era

Possibly just as significant to the ponderings of the savings and loan executive on the threshold of the 1960s as the changes in his own institution was the manifest new character of the economic age that lay ahead. It was an era in which practically every vestige of the economic inheritance from World War II had vanished.

Gone were the scarcities, not only in the shelter of individual families but practically throughout the whole range of commodities and manufactured goods. Changed was the position of the United States of America in world markets so that the mechanism of the market place was beginning to work, making prices, exchange rates and interest rates more dependent on economic factors rather than on manipulations of government. No more was the American economy dependent for its major employment on certain bellwether industries, such as steel and the home building industry. A more general pattern of activity in multiple lines—some up and some down from year to year—was emerging. The essence of the decade seemed to be increased and intensified competition for the buyers' dollar and the savers' dollar. A new type of competition for savings was becoming more pronounced as 37% of the disposable income of individuals was spent on services instead of goods; the ratio had been only 30.6% in the late 1940s.

Large-scale makers of aluminum, plastics and built-in appliances —just to mention a few—had moved into a strategic role in the building of homes. In 1959, 60% of all the home building in the United States was done by builders who built an average of 350 homes a year. Multiple-family residential units, moreover, had risen from 10% of the total new starts in 1955 to over 25% by the spring of 1961.

Associations as community builders

By 1960 the forward-looking leaders in the savings and loan business were already trying to visualize what additional services savings associations should be providing in order to fill more adequately their role as community builders. They concluded that it was important for associations to devote part of their resources to housing for the elderly and for community redevelopment. As a result the League proposed legislation to enable federals to make special types of loans for housing for the aging, for trade-in housing and for participation in joint efforts at urban renewal. These provisions were embodied in the Housing Act of 1961.

An important study, published by the privately sponsored and privately financed Commission on Money and Credit, recommended that the "regulatory authorities be authorized to permit greater flexibility to savings banks and savings and loan associations to acquire a wider range of suitable long-term debt instruments." A savings and loan leader had been a member of the commission—a witness to the prestige which the savings and loan business enjoyed by the turn of the decade.

As the savings and loan executive looked further at the projection made by the Indiana University study he saw an estimated need for the business to do $20 billion of home financing a year instead of $15 billion; but he also saw certain challenges to his appraisers which might turn out to be the most significant problem of all he had to solve in the 1960s. The possible impact of the emerging "quality" house upon the whole level of real estate values was of increasing concern. Two directly opposite theories about the price range of houses which should be built struggled for dominance.

One was the politically popular idea that more and more of the units should be built with the market of the lower income groups in mind; especially popular in political talk was the middle-income family living on $4,000 to $6,000 a year. Such a theory would inevitably center the bulk of the home building activity on the "minimum house."

The other was the theory that a smaller number of low-priced houses should be built and that the 1960s would offer a market for twice as many houses priced over $17,500 as under that figure. Rapid style changes in home building, so that no house which was fashionable in the 1940s would be desirable in the 1960s, and the rapid invention of new conveniences of all kinds fed the popularity of the latter thesis. The savings and loan business, dependent on reliable estimates of long-term residential real estate values, had to grapple with this fundamental dilemma in its whole lending outlook.

The new set of social and economic circumstances had come gradually, of course. But whatever the tempo of their emergence, they spelled for the savings and loan institutions of the '60s, '70s and '80s a situation which probably will be more different from the years of depression, war and postwar described in this volume than were those 30 years different from the preceding century.

Certain portents could already be discerned. Changes in urban living, so emphatically a part of the immediate post-World War II period, seemed likely to come in even more rapid succession as the 1960s emerged. In 1961 the Congress was taking its first serious look in 10 years at the tax status of savings and loan institutions, and its decision on the question could have a profound influence on the direction which savings and loan took in the future. As the Commission on Money and Credit, mentioned earlier, observed, there was a definite prospect that there would be less specialization by any financial institutions in the years ahead and more meeting of general credit needs by all of them. Any of these and still other influences yet undreamed of could speed up the rate of change in the savings and loan business beyond the remarkable pace of even the late 1950s.

But the men and women working in and charting the course of this remarkable system of financial institutions had one basic assurance which surrounded the future with light even if it could not present a crystal ball. This business had found within itself in one generation the strength and the wisdom to surmount the many difficulties and grasp the unparalleled opportunities described in these chapters. There was every reason to think that the business would not be daunted by the new decisions it faced in the years ahead. There was sound foundation for the belief that this business had a better than even chance of becoming a yet more effective instrument for improving the lot of the American citizen, as the 20th century rolled on into its last decades.

Presidents
of the United States League

Ernest A. Hale	Boston, Massachusetts	1930
R. Holtby Myers	Los Angeles, California	1931
William E. Best	Pittsburgh, Pennsylvania	1932
Ward B. Whitlock	Springfield, Illinois	1933
Philip Lieber	Shreveport, Louisiana	1934
I. Friedlander	Houston, Texas	1935
LeGrand W. Pellett	Newburgh, New York	1936
Harold T. Donaldson	Lansing, Michigan	1937
Edward C. Baltz	Washington, D. C.	1938
Clarence T. Rice	Kansas City, Kansas	1939
George W. West	Atlanta, Georgia	1940
Paul Endicott	Pomona, California	1941
Fermor S. Cannon	Indianapolis, Indiana	1942
Ralph H. Cake	Portland, Oregon	1943
John F. Scott	St. Paul, Minnesota	1944
W. Megrue Brock	Dayton, Ohio	1945
Henry P. Irr	Baltimore, Maryland	1946
Walter W. McAllister	San Antonio, Texas	1947
Ralph M. Smith	West Somerville, Massachusetts	1948
M. K. M. Murphy	Rutherford, New Jersey	1949
Henry A. Bubb	Topeka, Kansas	1950
Walter J. L. Ray	Detroit, Michigan	1951
Ben H. Hazen	Portland, Oregon	1952
Charles L. Clements	Miami Beach, Florida	1953
Ralph R. Crosby	Providence, Rhode Island	1954
J. Howard Edgerton	Los Angeles, California	1955
Walter H. Dreier	Evansville, Indiana	1956
Roy M. Marr	Memphis, Tennessee	1957
Joseph Holzka	Staten Island, New York	1958
C. R. Mitchell	Kansas City, Missouri	1959
W. O. DuVall	Atlanta, Georgia	1960
C. Elwood Knapp	Pittsburgh, Pennsylvania	1961
M. L. Dye	Salt Lake City, Utah	1962

Directors, 1930-1946,[*]

and Executive Committeemen,

1947-1962, of the United States League

Alabama

F. B. Yeilding, Jr.	Birmingham	1956-1959

California

E. L. Barnett	Santa Rosa	1947-1950
George B. Campbell	San Jose	1940-1944
Stuart Davis	Oakland	1956-1959
Edwin M. Eaton	Fresno	1934-1936
J. Howard Edgerton	Los Angeles	1950-1953
William Moseley Jones	Los Angeles	1953-1956
Robert R. Sprague	Los Angeles	1959-1962
Harold B. Starkey	San Diego	1944-1947

Colorado

Kenneth King	Denver	1949-1952

Connecticut

Frederick T. Backstrom	New Haven	1948-1951
Arthur J. Brockway	New Haven	1960-1963

District of Columbia

Edward C. Baltz	Washington	1933-1935
Carl J. Bergmann	Washington	1939-1943
C. Clinton James	Washington	1929-1931
Clarence E. Kefauver	Washington	1951-1954

---

[*]For the period 1929 through 1943, members of the eight-man governing body of the League, elected from geographical districts, were known as Directors. They served two-year terms and could succeed themselves. Beginning in 1944 the number of geographical districts was increased to 12 and the term of office of members of the Board of Directors was made three years, with a prohibition against successive terms by the same person. In 1946 the name of this body was changed to Executive Committee.

Directors, 1930-1946, and Executive Committeemen, 1947-1962, of the United States League

Florida

Charles L. Clements	Miami Beach	1947-1950
Ralph W. Sedgwick	Vero Beach	1959-1962

Georgia

J. D. McLamb	Savannah	1950-1953
George W. West	Atlanta	1935-1937

Illinois

E. G. Holzweg	Collinsville	1957-1960
George J. Lorr	Chicago	1948-1951
Frank O. Schneider	Kankakee	1934-1938

Indiana

Walter H. Dreier	Evansville	1951-1954
Arthur G. Shireman	South Bend	1960-1963
Carl J. Weber	Fort Wayne	1929-1931

Iowa

Jonathan M. Fletcher	Des Moines	1955-1958
Halsey R. Hanger	Dubuque	1941-1943

Kansas

F. J. McCue	Eureka	1952-1955

Kentucky

John C. Mindermann	Covington	1944-1947

Louisiana

Allain C. Andry	New Orleans	1945-1948
Herman C. Steger	New Orleans	1951-1954
H. Moss Watkins	Lake Charles	1957-1960

Maryland

Albert R. DeFord	Baltimore	1956-1959

Massachusetts

Harry R. Andrews	Cambridge	1951-1954
Ernest A. Hale	Boston	1931-1933
Raymond P. Harold	Worcester	1935-1937

H. Raymond Johnson	Reading	1929-1930
Henry H. Pierce	Boston	1943-1945
William P. Sawyer	Watertown	1954-1957
Herbert F. Taylor	Boston	1933-1935

Michigan

Harold T. Donaldson	Lansing	1931-1933
James H. Jerome	Saginaw	1954-1957
Walter J. L. Ray	Detroit	1944-1948

Minnesota

Emil C. Lundquist	Willmar	1949-1952
Robert L. Palmer	Pipestone	1958-1961
John F. Scott	St. Paul	1939-1941

Missouri

John C. Hall	St. Louis	1936-1940
George S. Metcalfe	St. Louis	1958-1961
E. Paul Smith	St. Louis	1946-1949

Nebraska

| L. C. Crittenden | Beatrice | 1948-1949 |
| E. L. Hevelone | Beatrice | 1946-1948 |

New Hampshire

| A. Harold MacNeil | Concord | 1957-1960 |
| E. Harrison Merrill | Laconia | 1939-1941 |

New Jersey

Wilton T. Barney	Hackensack	1955-1958
Charles S. Moore	Atlantic City	1934-1936
Everett C. Sherbourne	Elizabeth	1949-1952
Fred G. Stickel, Jr.	Newark	1936-1946
John Warren	Newark	1930-1934

New York

Roy H. Bassett	Canton	1937-1939
George L. Bliss	New York	1959-1962
Louis T. Boecher	New York	1952-1955
Ralph H. Davies	Utica	1946-1949

Directors, 1930-1946, and Executive Committeemen, 1947-1962, of the United States League

Willard K. Denton	New York	1930-1931
E. M. Van Norden	New York	1941-1943

North Carolina

H. H. Strandberg	Rocky Mount	1954-1957
J. F. Stevens	Greensboro	1943-1945
George R. Wootten	Hickory	1931-1933
		1937-1939

Ohio

James V. Davidson	Toledo	1949-1952
L. P. McCullough	Columbus	1929-1938
Russell McKay	Youngstown	1938-1942
E. J. Rupert	Cleveland	1942-1949
		1952-1955
Don L. Tobin	Columbus	1955-1958
Francis L. Vesy	Massillon	1958-1961

Oklahoma

Louis W. Grant	Tulsa	1944-1946
Cleo C. Ingle	Tulsa	1955-1958
George E. McKinnis	Shawnee	1930-1936

Oregon

Guy E. Jaques	Portland	1952-1955
Lee Stidd	Portland	1930-1934

Pennsylvania

Kenneth G. Baily	Waynesburg	1959-1960
William E. Best	Pittsburgh	1935-1943
Norman E. Clark	New Castle	1943-1947
George L. Fuessler	Erie	1960-1962
G. Raymond Greeby	Philadelphia	1947-1950
T. Kirk Heselbarth	Pittsburgh	1953-1956
Albert O. Horner	Pittsburgh	1933-1935
William P. Siegert	Philadelphia	1929-1933
Carl F. Troutman	Pottstown	1950-1953

Rhode Island

Ralph R. Crosby	Providence	1945-1948

South Carolina

Julius Anderson	Anderson	1960-1963
R. G. Childs	Columbia	1948-1951

Tennessee

Roy M. Marr	Memphis	1953-1955
William C. Walkup	Knoxville	1956

Texas

A. C. Bigger	Dallas	1944-1945
Lloyd S. Bowles	Dallas	1960-1963
G. J. Casselberry	El Paso	1940-1944
Louis D. Fox	Fort Worth	1948-1951
Walter W. McAllister, Jr.	San Antonio	1954-1957

Utah

M. L. Dye	Salt Lake City	1955-1958
Thomas T. Taylor	Salt Lake City	1946-1949

Virginia

Hugh L. Dougherty	Norfolk	1957-1960
Dandridge Murrell	Lynchburg	1945-1948

Washington

E. E. Cushing	Seattle	1949-1952
J. T. S. Lyle	Tacoma	1936-1940
Frank S. McWilliams	Spokane	1944-1946

Wisconsin

Charles McKeown	Milwaukee	1952-1955
Charles M. Pors	Marshfield	1943-1946

Wyoming

C. N. Bloomfield	Cheyenne	1958-1961

Chairmen,
Legislative Committee
of the United States League

C. Clinton James	Washington, D. C.	1930-1942
I. Friedlander	Houston, Texas	1943-1944
Paul Endicott	Pomona, California	1945-1948
Ralph M. Smith	West Somerville, Massachusetts	1949
George L. Bliss	New York, New York	1950-1953
Henry A. Bubb	Topeka, Kansas	1954-

Members
of the
Federal Home Loan Bank Board

(Alphabetical list with dates of service)

J. Alston Adams	August 15, 1947-June 30, 1954
Nathan Adams	August 9, 1932-November 10, 1932
William E. Best	August 9, 1932-March 4, 1933
Morton Bodfish	August 9, 1932-March 4, 1933
Fred W. Catlett	April 5, 1934-February 24, 1942
John deLaittre	July 2, 1962-June 30, 1966
William K. Divers	December 20, 1947-December 31, 1954
Ira A. Dixon	September 1, 1954-June 30, 1962
Nathaniel H. Dyke, Jr.	August 11, 1947-December 20, 1947
John H. Fahey	June 13, 1933-December 20, 1947
Franklin W. Fort	August 9, 1932-March 4, 1933
John M. Gries	August 9, 1932-March 4, 1933
William J. Hallahan	August 10, 1955-August 11, 1960
Frank W. Hancock, Jr.	January 5, 1939-February 24, 1942
Russell Hawkins	June 13, 1933-January 16, 1934
Kenneth G. Heisler	August 21, 1951-June 30, 1953
H. E. Hoagland	September 24, 1934-October 21, 1937
William H. Husband	November 1, 1937-February 24, 1942
O. K. LaRoque	April 2, 1948-March 30, 1951
Walter W. McAllister	August 3, 1953-September 14, 1956
Joseph P. McMurray	May 1, 1961-(term to expire June 30, 1965)
C. B. Merriam	April 3, 1933-June 12, 1933
Walter Hughes Newton	June 13, 1933-July 21, 1934
Albert J. Robertson	September 15, 1956-January 20, 1961
W. F. Stevenson	March 6, 1933-July 21, 1938
T. D. Webb	March 9, 1933-February 24, 1942
Joseph J. Williams, Jr.	September 19, 1960-(term to expire June 30, 1963)

Membership

of the

Federal Home Loan Bank Board

(Composition of the Board by years, 1932-1962)*

August 9, 1932-March 4, 1933†

Franklin W. Fort, *Chairman* (R)
Nathan Adams (D)
William E. Best (R)
Morton Bodfish (D)
John M. Gries (R)

March 4, 1933-June 30, 1934

W. F. Stevenson, *Chairman* (D), March 6, 1933-July 21, 1938
T. D. Webb (D), March 9, 1933-February 24, 1942
C. B. Merriam (R), April 3, 1933-June 12, 1933 (Resigned)
John H. Fahey (D), June 13, 1933-December 20, 1947 (Resigned)
Russell Hawkins (R), June 13, 1933-January 16, 1934 (Deceased)
Walter Hughes Newton (R), June 13, 1933-July 21, 1934
Fred W. Catlett (R), April 5, 1934-February 24, 1942

---

*This listing of the composition of the Federal Home Loan Bank Board over the years covered by *A Business Reborn* is included, in addition to the alphabetical listing on page 352, in order to show which five-man or three-man Boards, as the case may be, were in office at any particular point in time. The pattern is less than perfect because of staggered terms, resignations, prolonged vacancies and the five-year period during which there was no Board. Insofar as possible, however, the Board's composition is shown by fiscal years.

The entire period during which each member served is shown opposite his name the first time it appears. If his service was terminated by means other than by expiration of his appointment, this fact is noted. Where a member's service started shortly after the beginning of a fiscal year, he is shown under the grouping for the entire period. Where his service extended into a substantial part, but not the entire fiscal year his name is listed for that period.

The Board has always been bipartisan, by Congressional mandate. The political affiliation of each Board member is shown as (D), Democrat, or (R), Republican, the first time his name appears.

†Original members of the Board; all were "interim" appointments. None was reappointed by President Franklin D. Roosevelt who came to office March 4, 1933. Mr. Adams resigned three months after he took office.

July 1, 1934-June 30, 1936

John H. Fahey, *Chairman*
W. F. Stevenson
T. D. Webb
Fred W. Catlett
H. E. Hoagland (R), September 24, 1934-October 21, 1937
(Resigned)

July 1, 1936-June 30, 1937

John H. Fahey, *Chairman*
W. F. Stevenson
T. D. Webb
Fred W. Catlett
H. E. Hoagland

July 1, 1937-June 30, 1938

John H. Fahey, *Chairman*
W. F. Stevenson
T. D. Webb
Fred W. Catlett
William H. Husband (R), November 1, 1937-February 24, 1942

July 1, 1938-February 24, 1942††

John H. Fahey, *Chairman*
T. D. Webb
Fred W. Catlett
William H. Husband
Frank W. Hancock, Jr. (D), January 5, 1939-February 24, 1942

---

††By Executive Order No. 9070 the five-man Board was vacated February 24, 1942. Its chairman, John H. Fahey, was made commissioner of the Federal Home Loan Bank Administration. Under Reorganization Plan 3 of 1947, which became effective July 27, 1947, a Board of three members was substituted for the single commissioner under the designation "Home Loan Bank Board."

Membership of the Federal Home Loan Bank Board

July 27, 1947-December 20, 1947

John H. Fahey, *Chairman*
Nathaniel H. Dyke, Jr. (D), August 11, 1947-December 20, 1947
(Resigned)
J. Alston Adams (R), August 15, 1947-June 22, 1953 (Resigned)

December 20, 1947-December 31, 1950

William K. Divers, *Chairman* (D), December 20, 1947-
December 31, 1954 (Resigned)
J. Alston Adams
O. K. LaRoque (D), April 2, 1948-March 30, 1951 (Resigned)

January 1, 1951-June 30, 1953

William K. Divers, *Chairman*
J. Alston Adams
Kenneth G. Heisler (D), August 21, 1951-June 30, 1953 (Resigned)

July 1, 1953-June 30, 1954

Walter W. McAllister, *Chairman* (R), August 3, 1953-September 14,
1956 (Resigned)
William K. Divers

July 1, 1954-June 30, 1955

Walter W. McAllister, *Chairman*
William K. Divers
Ira A. Dixon (R), September 1, 1954-June 30, 1962

July 1, 1955-June 30, 1956

Walter W. McAllister, *Chairman*
Ira A. Dixon
William J. Hallahan (D), August 10, 1955-August 11, 1960
(Resigned)

July 1, 1956-June 30, 1960

Albert J. Robertson, *Chairman* (R), September 15, 1956-January 20,
1961 (Resigned)
Ira A. Dixon
William J. Hallahan

July 1, 1960-January 20, 1961

Albert J. Robertson, *Chairman*
Ira A. Dixon
Joseph J. Williams, Jr. (D), September 19, 1960—(term expires
June 30, 1963)

January 21, 1961-July 1, 1962

Joseph P. McMurray, *Chairman* (D), May 1, 1961—(term expires
June 30, 1965)
Ira A. Dixon
Joseph J. Williams, Jr.

July 2, 1962-

Joseph P. McMurray, *Chairman*
John deLaittre
Joseph J. Williams, Jr.

Executive Officers

of the Federal Home Loan Banks

District 1
FEDERAL HOME LOAN BANK OF *BOSTON*
(originally Cambridge)
> Walter H. Neaves, 1932-1947
> Herbert N. Faulkner, 1948-

District 2
FEDERAL HOME LOAN BANK OF *NEW YORK*
(originally Newark)
> George L. Bliss, 1932-1939
> (Vacancy), 1940
> Nugent Fallon, 1941-1953
> M. K. M. Murphy, 1954-

District 3
FEDERAL HOME LOAN BANK OF *PITTSBURGH*
> William F. Bell, 1932-1933
> Ralph H. Richards, 1933-1947
> George R. Parker, 1948-

District 4
FEDERAL HOME LOAN BANK OF *GREENSBORO*
(originally Winston-Salem)
> Julian Price, 1932-1933
> Thomas W. Ellett, 1933-1935
> O. K. LaRoque, 1935-1949
> Joseph W. Holt, 1950-1952
> O. K. LaRoque, 1952-1953
> J. M. Sink, Jr., 1953-1957
> John A. Fogarty, 1957-

District 5
FEDERAL HOME LOAN BANK OF *CINCINNATI*
W. E. Julius, 1932-1935
Walter J. Shultz, 1935-1956
W. E. Julius, 1957-

District 6
FEDERAL HOME LOAN BANK OF *INDIANAPOLIS*
F. B. McKibben, 1932-1934
Fred T. Greene, 1934-1961
G. E. Ohmart, 1961-

District 7
FEDERAL HOME LOAN BANK OF *CHICAGO*
(originally Evanston)
A. R. Gardner, 1932-1953
John E. Stipp, 1953-

District 8
FEDERAL HOME LOAN BANK OF *DES MOINES*
Robert J. Richardson, 1932-1955
Robert H. Bush, 1956-

District 9
FEDERAL HOME LOAN BANK OF *LITTLE ROCK*
Ben H. Wooten, 1932-1943
H. D. Wallace, 1944-1953
J. Curran Conway, 1953-1958
Ennis M. Oakes, 1959-

District 10
FEDERAL HOME LOAN BANK OF *TOPEKA*
C. A. Sterling, 1932-1955
James W. McBride, 1956-

District 11

FEDERAL HOME LOAN BANK OF *PORTLAND*
L. H. Hoffman, 1932-1933
Charles H. Stewart, 1933-1936
Frank H. Johnson, 1937-1946

District 12

FEDERAL HOME LOAN BANK OF *LOS ANGELES*
W. F. Duffy, 1932-1934
M. M. Hurford, 1934-1944
(Vacancy), 1945

District 11

FEDERAL HOME LOAN BANK OF *SAN FRANCISCO*
(a merger of the Portland and Los Angeles Banks)
Gerritt VanderEnde, 1946-1947
Harold C. Holmes, Jr., 1948
(Vacancy), 1949
Frederick W. Ruble, 1950-1953
J. Alston Adams, 1953-

Executive Officers
of the State Leagues*

ALABAMA SAVINGS AND LOAN LEAGUE
William A. Granberry	Montgomery	1957
Frank S. Harris	Montgomery	1958-

CALIFORNIA SAVINGS AND LOAN LEAGUE
Neill Davis	Pasadena	1927-

SAVINGS AND LOAN LEAGUE OF COLORADO, INC.
Edwin G. Alexander	Denver	1954-1959
Byron G. Hooper, Jr.	Denver	1960-

SAVINGS AND LOAN LEAGUE OF CONNECTICUT
John J. Stafford	Hartford	1953-1962
Clayton W. Johnson	Hartford	1962-

DISTRICT OF COLUMBIA SAVINGS AND LOAN LEAGUE
Paul Menk	Washington	1956
Bruce Bryan	Washington	1958-

FLORIDA SAVINGS AND LOAN LEAGUE
Carl F. Distelhorst	Orlando	1955-1962
William D. Hussey	Orlando	1962-

GEORGIA SAVINGS AND LOAN LEAGUE
Ed W. Hiles	Atlanta	1945-

HAWAII SAVINGS AND LOAN LEAGUE
Alan P. Kruse	Honolulu	1961-

ILLINOIS SAVINGS AND LOAN LEAGUE
Ward B. Whitlock	Springfield	1930-1939
Harry Goodsitt	Springfield	1939-

---

*Names of many of the state leagues were changed in the course of the years covered by this volume. The name given in this roster is that which applied to the respective league as of July 1, 1962.

SAVINGS AND LOAN LEAGUE OF *INDIANA*

George F. Ogden	Peru	1926-1938
Ivan E. Cooprider	Indianapolis	1939-1949
Hal Kitchen, Jr.	Indianapolis	1950
Lisle W. Tinsman	Indianapolis	1950-

IOWA SAVINGS AND LOAN LEAGUE

Kenneth F. Neu	Des Moines	1958-

KANSAS SAVINGS AND LOAN LEAGUE

Paul B. Morrison	Topeka	1928-1961
Thomas L. Wilson	Topeka	1961-

LOUISIANA SAVINGS AND LOAN LEAGUE

John J. Crawford	New Orleans	1961-

MARYLAND LEAGUE OF BUILDING, SAVINGS AND LOAN ASSOCIATIONS

C. Philip Pitt	Baltimore	1919-1947
George J. Clautice	Baltimore	1947-1950
James H. Mitchell, Jr.	Baltimore	1950-1955
Robert L. Stocksdale	Baltimore	1955-

MARYLAND SAVINGS AND LOAN LEAGUE

John S. Kerns	Baltimore	1938-1947
Carl F. Gottschalk	Baltimore	1947-

MASSACHUSETTS CO-OPERATIVE BANK LEAGUE

Warner M. Allen	Boston	1931-1957
William H. King	Boston	1958-

MICHIGAN SAVINGS AND LOAN LEAGUE

Karl Hepp	Lansing	1933-1934
Grant H. Longenecker	Lansing	1937-1962
Donald F. Wall	Lansing	1962-

SAVINGS AND LOAN LEAGUE OF *MINNESOTA*

Vernon S. Welch	Minneapolis	1941-

MISSISSIPPI SAVINGS AND LOAN LEAGUE

Albert G. Sanders, Jr.	Jackson	1961-

MISSOURI SAVINGS AND LOAN LEAGUE

H. Merle Smith	Kansas City	1940-1943
T. Victor Jeffries	Lebanon	1943-

NEBRASKA SAVINGS AND LOAN LEAGUE

Dean G. Kratz	Lincoln	1955-

NEW JERSEY SAVINGS AND LOAN LEAGUE

Emil Gallman	Newark	1930-

NEW YORK STATE LEAGUE OF SAVINGS AND LOAN ASSOCIATIONS

George A. Plant	New York	1926-1931
Homer N. Calver	New York	1932-1934
Fred T. Greene	New York	1934-1935
Zebulon V. Woodard	New York	1935-1951

COUNCIL OF INSURED SAVINGS ASSOCIATIONS (New York)

Carl F. Distelhorst	New York	1943-1947
David Ford	New York	1947-1951

SAVINGS ASSOCIATION LEAGUE OF *NEW YORK*

David Ford	New York	1951-

NORTH CAROLINA SAVINGS AND LOAN LEAGUE

Martin F. Gaudian	Greensboro	1937-1940
Harry F. Bauer	Raleigh	1941-1943
C. J. Burns	Raleigh	1944-1946
E. D. Kuykendall, Jr.	Greensboro	1947-1957
William A. Granberry	Greensboro	1958-1961
Herbert W. Wentworth	Greensboro	1961-

OHIO SAVINGS AND LOAN LEAGUE

James A. Devine	Columbus	1920-1939
Don Tobin	Columbus	1940-1959
Joseph E. Linville	Columbus	1960-

OKLAHOMA SAVINGS AND LOAN LEAGUE

John F. Mahr	Oklahoma City	1928-1954
John T. McCarthy	Oklahoma City	1955-1958
John F. Mahr	Oklahoma City	1959-
John L. O'Brien	Oklahoma City	1961-

PENNSYLVANIA SAVINGS AND LOAN LEAGUE

George W. Cliffe	Philadelphia	1927-1940
Raymond F. Talbert	Harrisburg	1940-1941
Paul C. Applegate	Harrisburg	1941-1947
James B. King	Harrisburg	1948-

SOUTH CAROLINA SAVINGS AND LOAN LEAGUE

W. Dean Cannon	Columbia	1957-1959
William N. Bowen	Columbia	1960-

TENNESSEE SAVINGS AND LOAN LEAGUE

Bob Dudley Smith	Nashville	1962-

TEXAS SAVINGS AND LOAN LEAGUE

Jack W. Cashin	Austin	1957-

VIRGINIA SAVINGS, BUILDING AND LOAN LEAGUE

Mark W. Saurs	Richmond	1957-

WASHINGTON SAVINGS AND LOAN LEAGUE

A. R. Gardner	Olympia	1930-1932
Loren Grinstead	Seattle	1941-1945
Kingston S. Lister	Tacoma	1946-

WEST VIRGINIA SAVINGS AND LOAN LEAGUE

Joseph P. Condry	Charleston	1959-

WISCONSIN SAVINGS AND LOAN LEAGUE

Carl Taylor	Milwaukee	1931-1943
John A. Seramur	Milwaukee	1944-

Key Staff Members
of the United States League
and Affiliates

Secretary-Treasurer	H. F. Cellarius	1896-1949
Chief Executive Officer	Morton Bodfish	1930-1953
	Norman Strunk*	1938-

Paul C. Applegate	1939-1941
T. W. Atkins	1935-1939
Charles H. Borsom	1949-
Jack Bruce	1953-
C. J. Burns	1936-1944
Donald M. Burson	1944-1950; 1951-
Charles E. Clifton, Jr.	1958-
Donald Coenen	1955-
Virginia L. Collins	1950-
Lawrence V. Conway	1955-
Don M. Dailey	1938-
Carl F. Distelhorst	1942-1943; 1946-1955
Robert H. Distelhorst, Jr.	1961-
Lee E. Duss, Jr.	1957-
Josephine Hedges Ewalt	1931-
Martin F. Gaudian	1934-1938
Don F. Geyer	1951-
Harry Goodsitt	1932-1936
Fred T. Greene	1933-1935
Franklin Hardinge, Jr.	1935-1951
T. Wade Harrison	1955-1956
Helen E. Heggie	1935-
James A. Hollensteiner	1955-
Walter W. Jasinsky	1946-1953
E. Louise Johnson	1932-1949
Leon T. Kendall	1958-
Marion Kessel	1942-
T. Bert King	1956-

*Chief executive officer since 1952.

364

Robert R. Kocher	1955-1961
John W. Ladd	1934-1943
Max E. Lieurance	1950-
Milton E. Miller	1953-
H. Howard Muller	1954-
William B. O'Connell	1948-
Alice O'Connor	1941-
Harold Paus	1940-
Robert P. Perrin	1939-
Thomas A. Pfeiler	1959-
Eugene Pheiffer	1948-1950
Richard Pokriefke	1954-
Eugenia Potwora	1947-
William C. Prather	1951-
Ralph H. Richards	1931-1933
George A. Rodelius, Jr.	1948-
Horace Russell	1938-1959
Thomas E. Sheridan, Jr.	1949-1955
Stephen G. Slipher	1941-
Frances Smith	1940-1955
H. Merle Smith	1943-
Robert T. Souter	1943-1947
John J. Stafford	1962-
A. D. Theobald	1931-1946
Phyllis Thustan	1934-
Glen S. Troop	1952-
Douglas C. Vaile	1936-1945
Wyn Warman	1954-
Margaret Weir	1931-1946

Presidents
of the American Savings
and Loan Institute

George L. Bliss	New York, New York	1930*
Philip Lieber	Shreveport, Louisiana	1931
Clarence T. Rice	Kansas City, Kansas	1932
C. Harry Minners	New York, New York	1933
William R. Gibbon	Los Angeles, California	1934
Charles F. Axtmann	Youngstown, Ohio	1935
Lawrence H. Marston	Malden, Massachusetts	1936
John A. Sierocinski	Chicago, Illinois	1937
Joseph Holzka	Staten Island, New York	1938
A. J. Bromfield	Denver, Colorado	1939
Herbert N. Faulkner	Boston, Massachusetts	1940
L. H. Allen	Houston, Texas	1941
Edward J. Webb	Kansas City, Missouri	1942
Charles L. Plumb	New York, New York	1943
Jack E. Barry	Oklahoma City, Oklahoma	1944
Francis E. Ingalls	Lynn, Massachusetts	1945
Robert W. Almoney	Dayton, Ohio	1946

*Also served during 1929.

Marc S. Raichle	Aberdeen, Washington	1947
Mrs. Ruth M. Lowe	Milwaukee, Wisconsin	1948
Edward O. Morgan	Los Angeles, California	1949
C. Elwood Knapp	Pittsburgh, Pennsylvania	1950
Oscar B. Keith	Boston, Massachusetts	1951
William E. Poulton	Washington, D. C.	1952
John H. Dempster	Philadelphia, Pennsylvania	1953
Donald A. Squire	Pasadena, California	1954
G. E. Ohmart	Indianapolis, Indiana	1955
Ray B. Owen	Providence, Rhode Island	1956
Robert H. Hazen	Portland, Oregon	1957
Charles F. Kenny, Jr.	Hempstead, New York	1958
W. R. Kamp	St. Louis, Missouri	1959
W. A. Obers	Los Angeles, California	1960
Bill C. Wainwright	Atlanta, Georgia	1961
Ray A. Neumann	Peoria, Illinois	1962

Appendix two

The first 100 years:
a synopsis

The first century

of savings and loan associations

1831-1930

The first savings and loan institution in the United States was organized in 1831 when Andrew Jackson was President and there were only 24 states in the Union. Its birthplace was Frankford, Pa., a borough of some 2,000 inhabitants a few miles northeast of the city of Philadelphia, then the U.S.A.'s largest. Within Frankford's borders stood a tavern where George Washington and some of his staff had held critical conferences during the American Revolution. On the outskirts of Frankford was the mill where one of the daring her-

As background information on the first century of savings and loan development, a synopsis of two earlier publications is presented as Appendix two. One is the 792-page *History of Building and Loan in the United States*, 1931, comprising 49 chapters of the history of the savings and loan business in each of the states, as well as 18 chapters on national aspects of the first century. The other is the 64-page *As It Was in the Beginning*, 1956, commemorating the 125th anniversary of the birth year of the business, and presenting an intensive study and interpretation of the earliest years.

oines of the American Revolution, Lydia Darrach, had passed along to the Continental Army the important intelligence information she had gained from listening through a keyhole during a secret session of British officers in Philadelphia.

A few survivors of those momentous years were still in Frankford and their now dimming eyes could see a startlingly new America coming into being. Industrial activity was just beginning to be a major factor in the economy of some sectors of the young nation; and the predominantly agricultural occupation of the people was giving way to employment in the towns.

This strategic change in the social and economic pattern was crucial to the background of the first savings and loan institution: For the first time a large number of people had to have an urban place to live, and most of them did not have the money to buy or build homes. The 1830 census showed an urban population of 1,127,247—not quite one-tenth of all who lived in the United States. Just 10 years before there had been fewer than 700,000 in all the cities and towns combined. The banks of the time were young, not numerous and they envisioned their destiny as the suppliers of capital to a capital-hungry young nation. Furthermore the nation's commercial banking system was in a period of much experimentation in President Jackson's day and was far from ready to become a source of home owner credit.

Thus between the years of Frankford's incorporation as a borough in 1800 and the launching of the Oxford Provident Building Association, Frankford found the need for more area because industry and population had begun to expand.

The circumstances were ripe for the rise of a financial institution to meet the home seeker's needs. Frankford's major textile industry recently had brought to America two Englishmen with a knowledge of the experiment in self-help among industrial workers which had proved satisfactory in providing money for the needed workers' homes in the Midlands of England; as early as 1781 there had been a building society in Birmingham, England. (In 1959 the International Union of Building Societies and Savings Associations put a permanent marker on the bit of Birmingham earth where the first meeting of this kind took place.)

In 1931 the United States League placed a bronze marker in Womrath Park, Philadelphia, to record the transplanting to American soil of the savings and loan idea. It reads:

The first century of savings and loan associations: 1831-1930

On January 3, 1831, a group of citizens of the Borough of
Frankford, Pennsylvania, assembled at Thomas Sidebotham's Inn,
then situated about two hundred feet due east of this spot, to
organize the first cooperative home financing institution in the
United States of America. On that date Isaac Shallcross, Isaac
Whitelock, Dr. Henry Taylor, Jeremiah Horrocks, Samuel Pilling,
Jesse Y. Castor and others of the Frankford townspeople drew up
the Articles of the Oxford Provident Building Association of Philadelphia County.

On the foundations laid for this institution has arisen the system
of savings, building and loan associations which during its first
century spread into the forty-eight states and fostered the building
of eight million American homes.

To commemorate their contribution to the extension of home
ownership and to the consequent strengthening of the ideals of
individual liberty on the basis of the family dwelling, the United
States Building and Loan League erects this tablet.

August 1931

How the Oxford Provident operated

The essentials of the plan on which the Oxford Provident Building Society began were: 1) the regular payment by each member,
each week, of a small amount of money into a pool; and 2) the
lending of the money in the pool to first one and then another of
the members until each had acquired his home. The first loan of
$500 was made to a man named Comly Rich to enable him to buy
a two-story frame house, with a lean-to and an attic, at 4276 Or-
chard Street, Frankford (now in the city limits of Philadelphia).
The house, which still stands, has been designated Monument No.
168 by the Philadelphia Historical Commission and the Historical
Society of Frankford. By one of the perversities of human nature
this first savings and loan borrower became hopelessly delinquent,
and his loan and his home were eventually taken off his hands
by another member of the first association!

The Oxford Provident was what is known as a terminating society: It was to serve its purpose for the 37 original members and
then cease its operations. The only way in which a new person
could join was to buy the shares of an original member who wanted
to drop out. It actually terminated in 10 years and was succeeded

immediately by Oxford Provident No. 2; this was followed by still another, the Oxford Provident No. 3.

Isaac Shallcross of Frankford was the first outstanding figure in the continuity of the savings and loan movement. He was the secretary of the three Oxford Provident associations, and he was still alive to serve as secretary when other associations were formed in Frankford in the 1840s and 1850s. His chief profession was that of a surveyor; thus the early talents which the savings and loan movement was able to attract were, as in later years, those of high-ranking citizens of the community.

Milestown, Germantown, Philadelphia proper and Kensington were other Pennsylvania places where savings and loan sprang up on the Oxford Provident model before the 1840s were over. The earliest direct descendant of the first association, however, was the Brooklyn (N. Y.) Building and Mutual Loan Association (1836), formed after a group of local citizens went down to Frankford and found out how it was being done there. In 1849 the idea reached Connecticut. The following year the Connecticut legislature put in a state law the designation "savings and loan association," the first known use of this particular nomenclature. The associations which sprang up in these simple and unorganized times had, as can already be seen, a great variety of names.

Economic prosperity, 1840s-1850s

The United States was in a generally prosperous state for more than a decade following the recovery from the disastrous money panic of 1837; from the mid-1840s until the late 1850s savings and loan associations had thus a good economic atmosphere in which to progress. Their development was conspicuous for the absence from their background of any particular theory for solving a social need. As one scholarly European writer about the business put it, "The founders were small people with small aims, using simple and old-fashioned means and the movement was always nonpolitical."

Before the Civil War seven other states besides those already mentioned had seen the first savings and loan association of this type formed within their borders. Chart 11 shows the year in which the first savings and loan association was started in each of the states. As will be noted later, South Carolina had an early start in savings and loan work but along somewhat different lines from

374

that on the northeastern seaboard. The first state laws governing the associations came in this period; they were usually quite
rudimentary statutes which required mainly the incorporation of
the association under the Savings and Loan Act and some form
of intermittent reporting to a public authority.

Savings and loan institutions would have remained small and
retained only the "small aims" mentioned previously had not some
way been evolved to give them permanency. Their first successful
effort in that direction came in the early 1850s in the adoption of
what is known as the "serial plan." The Oxford Provident No. 3,
for instance, became a "serial association" in 1854, following a
general trend of the times. A serial association was actually a
grouping under one roof and under one name and usually under
one secretary of a series of new associations, each starting three
months after the other. When succeeding quarterly series of new
members became part of the pattern of these little financial clubs,
other phases of continuous existence began to emerge, regular
meetings became more frequent, the secretary received an increase in pay (small though it still was) and the solicitor collected fees for the legal transactions (more and more people were
involved in legal transactions when several series were operating
at the same time). These first serial associations were still strictly
for home financing, because people were not yet joining them just

Chart 11. Year of the first savings and loan activity in each state

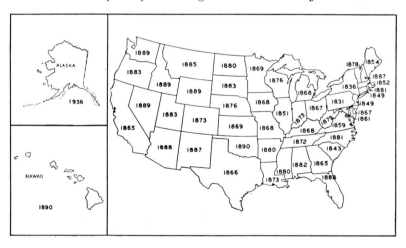

to save money for some miscellaneous purpose: All present and future borrowers were encouraged to make regular installment payments.

The greatest popularity of the serial plan came in the 15 years following the Civil War. Obviously this conflict brought some interruption of the normal development of the nation's social and financial institutions. Certainly the start which savings and loan had made toward permanency before the war had to wait until after Appomattox to evolve into a sizable movement. In the South, of course, it had to wait much longer. Between 1860 and 1880, as the map (Chart 11) shows, 16 more states saw the rise of their first savings and loan institutions. It is noteworthy that despite the ravages of reconstruction, and partly to overcome them, Georgia formed its first savings and loan association in this period, as also did Tennessee and Louisiana. The idea, it will be seen, followed the Conestoga wagons and stage coaches across the vast plains of America, and, as early as 1865, even the postgold rush people of far-off California had established a savings and loan institution.

The serial type of association was far from a flash-in-the-pan or a mere bridge type of operation between the terminating association and the more familiar permanent type of association. Up through the 1920s it was the prevalent form, with some modifications, of savings and loan activity in such major states as Illinois, New Jersey, Pennsylvania, Massachusetts and Wisconsin. This business was relatively simple and easy to operate as long as only a few hundred thousand dollars was the normal unit size of the association. Significantly in most of the states where the serial plan system flourished a larger number of small associations developed rather than a fairly small number of sizable institutions.

Importantly for an understanding of future controversies and decisions in the business over operating policies, the serial plan de-emphasized reserves for the simple reason that all the profits were continually kept in a common fund and not assigned to each individual member. Hence there really was no pressing need for reserves. This was the kind of operation which modern savings and loan executives just couldn't imagine, but it was sufficient for those times. There was actually a verbal battle in the latter part of the 19th century over whether the setting aside of reserves constituted a violation of mutuality!

The New England and New York versions of savings and loan

operation were the subject of a 230-page book published in 1856. But the real impetus to the development of literature on the savings and loan movement came with the heyday of the serial associations, the post-Civil War decade and a half. In 1869 there came off the press in Philadelphia a popular 109-page book known as the *Workingman's Way to Wealth*. It went through six editions and exercised a wide influence on savings and loan development throughout the country, being, as its subtitle indicated, *A Practical Treatise on Building Associations, What They Are and How to Use Them*. The same author wrote another book in 1873 entitled *How to Manage Building Associations, A Director's Guide and Secretary's Assistant*. As a result the author became one of the sources of information on the subject in the United States and was frequently in receipt of letters of inquiry from all over the country and even from foreign countries.

He was also the editor of a *Building Association Journal*. This publication was not the only periodical which might today be called a trade publication. Several were published regularly in Philadelphia in these years. In Cincinnati, too, savings and loan trade publications circulated widely.

In February 1876 *Scribner's Magazine* carried an article entitled "A Hundred Thousand Homes: How They Are Paid For." It stressed Philadelphia experience and the publications which were issued there. The author is unknown, but it was probably the first instance in which a major magazine of general circulation gave attention to the description of an actual savings and loan meeting; of how to organize an association; and of how the financial arrangements work out.

The first 50 years of savings and loan association operation in the United States (1831-1880) represent an epoch in the history of the business. During this period diffusion of the idea into practically every part of the continental United States was accomplished. The idea of installment financing of homes, which is essentially what the savings and loan institution introduced, was tested and found practical. The first idea of having one group of persons band together to accomplish home ownership and then disappear was abandoned in favor of a continuing institution providing for new groups of home-seeking members to be organized every three months. The groundwork for a great system of financial institutions was thus laid, but no one could have foreseen in the United

States of Presidents Ulysses S. Grant and Rutherford B. Hayes, with its stumblings toward a reunited country and its trials and errors on the economic front, that the savings and loan idea was on the verge of a vast growth and development in a new and more attractive direction. It was not even very likely in the decade of the 1870s that many people thought of savings and loan institutions as ever becoming a savings system in which four or five persons were savers for each one person who intended to borrow for a home.

Yet the 1880s did make this major difference in the history of savings and loan operations. In 1879 the financial outlook of the country brightened for the first time since the Civil War. The first four years of the 1880s were especially prosperous. Economic conditions were thus favorable to a great step forward for the savings and loan institutions, and this circumstance was crucial in their rise to a new plateau in size and popularity—as has always been the case then and since. Just as significant, perhaps, was the fact that the urbanization of the United States was continuing at a steady pace. The Census of 1880 showed that more than 14 million persons out of a population of 50 million lived in urban areas. Fifty years before when the savings and loan business received its first impetus from a population beginning to leave the farm, only one out of 10 had been city dwellers; now one out of every three-to-four families lived in cities.

The 1880s were to see, moreover, the stepping up of the tide of immigration to an average of 525,000 persons a year, and most of these people came to live in the cities. Importantly, too, they were thrift minded, on the whole, and above all they desired to own a home. Many came from countries where the typical citizen at that time was not even permitted to own land. The savings and loan idea found some of its most enthusiastic proponents among Middle and Eastern European immigrants. Many formed associations serving principally or entirely their own ethnic groups.

Emergence of the permanent plan

Given this complex combination of external factors to stimulate the development of savings and loan institutions, all that was needed to break into new ground was an internal revolution in the plan of operation. This occurred in the emergence of the so-called "permanent plan." The development of a group of savers apart from those who expected to borrow sometime in the future was generally associated with the rise of the permanent plan. The sequence is not difficult to trace. In the permanent plan the accounts of all members began to be kept separately for the first time. Furthermore accounts could be issued at any time; people did not have to wait until the beginning of the next series, a month or two from now; the retention of shares which had reached their maturity became possible because of the refinements of the bookkeeping system developing out of the decision to keep all member accounts separate. All these changes attracted the money of people who wanted to save for miscellaneous purposes.

The salient features of the permanent plan got a preview in the 1840s in South Carolina, when a Methodist minister, the Rev. S. K. Cox, with a more up-to-date knowledge of the English system than that which lingered in the memories of the Frankford, Pa., industrialists, started a permanent plan association in Charleston, S. C. In the economy of South Carolina, so different from that of the industrial eastern seaboard, the rigid regular payments of the terminating plan did not fit the habits of the average working person. Hence the clergyman found fertile ground for his foray into a different kind of savings and loan operation. He even wrote a book about it, which received considerable circulation. But the story ends there.

It is presumed by most students of the matter that the Rev. Mr. Cox was killed in the war. At any rate the idea of the permanent plan spread no farther at the time, although it became basic to the savings and loan institutions in that state and was known as the "South Carolina plan."

But as early as 1869, Ohio's law had permitted savings and loan institutions to take what were known as deposits. Outside of these two states it was not until the 1880s that the so-called permanent plan with its attractiveness to the saver as apart from the borrower took hold.

A variation of the permanent plan of savings and loan operation, known for the next 60 years as the "Dayton plan," came into use in Ohio in the 1880s and from there spread to other parts of the country. It was the work of a Dayton judge, who had gone to England to observe firsthand the way in which savings and loan institutions (building societies) were operating there—after a century of experience. He came back with the variations from the permanent plan which are associated with the name of his native city.

Dayton plan advantages

In the Dayton plan associations, the operation came nearer to that of a mutual savings bank: Earnings credited to the individual accounts were subject to 100% withdrawal. So-called paid-up stock was issued for the first time, and thus a door was open to the accumulation of a much larger volume of funds. Aside from paving the way for a whole new group of savings members, the Dayton plan made significant changes for the borrower. It was possible now for him to make a larger payment than his regular scheduled monthly installment, if he so desired, and he could reduce the amount of interest on his loan proportionately. This was a more attractive arrangement for the borrower in many cases than was the older savings and loan plan which required him to keep paying in on shares until his savings reached the full amount of his loan and cancelled out his indebtedness.

A clue to the rapid popularity of this simplified savings and loan plan in the 1880s was the public relations sense of the Dayton judge and his associates. They knew the value of newspaper space, and it was not long until the Dayton plan was known among savings and loan people from coast to coast. If any single development is to be given credit for the first great period of savings and loan expansion, it would be the initial push of the publicity-minded persons who fostered the Dayton plan. The decade of the 1880s saw the rise of the first sizable number of institutions still in existence in the 1960s—institutions celebrating 75th and 80th anniversaries these days.

The map (Chart 11) shows that 12 of the states west of the Mississippi recorded organizations of their first savings and loan institutions in the 1880s. Hawaii had its first savings and loan association in 1890, having received its charter from the King of Hawaii before it even became a United States territory. (Obviously some of the other states with savings and loan associations starting in the 1880s were still territories then: Even by 1889 there were only 42 states.) But the real dynamic force was in the older savings and loan states where the idea received new life and vigor.

In 1888 the American Social Science Association made the first study of the extent and size of savings and loan associations. The

380

secretary of its Special Committee on Provident Institutions estimated that there were between 3,000 and 3,500, with assets of approximately $300 million at that time. Significant comment in the secretary's report deserves recording here: "It is doubtful if any system for savings has been devised which has such a tendency to produce frugality among persons of small income, as the building association methods. . . . There are drawbacks and there are dangers in these petty financial ventures which in the aggregate are so vast, but these are not more than attend the usual investments of money. We must therefore expect such associations to increase in number and to absorb more and more the earnings of the people; just as life insurance absorbs more and more of the surplus income of classes a little more prosperous than those who make up the great body of shareholders in the associations we have been enumerating."

From the secretary's remarks it is clear that savings and loan institutions of the 1880s were generally being patronized by persons in what we now call "low-income" categories.

The divergencies in savings and loan plans of operation, which have already been seen as part and parcel of its development, were manifest to anyone surveying the 3,000-odd associations operating in 1888. Some of the far-sighted people connected with the savings and loan institutions either directly or indirectly saw the need for greater uniformity. Most vocal among them, perhaps, was a Cincinnati publisher who did a large volume of business in savings and loan forms, especially with the Ohio savings and loan institutions. He put out a *Manual* for their operation which went through five editions and was revised from time to time. In it came the first talk of the inevitability of the formation of local, state and nationwide leagues for this small but prospering business so that some uniformity, along with many other desirable features, might be achieved.

State savings and loan leagues

Two state leagues had already been formed by 1888; and before another year had passed after the publication of the *Manual* three other states had joined the parade. Pennsylvania savings and loan associations were far ahead, having organized a league in 1877, thanks to the need to defend themselves in litigation being conducted by the state's attorney general who was trying to collect a corporate tax levied by the state upon the savings and loan associations (although they had been specifically exempted by law in 1871). Forty-three associations were the nucleus of this first state league, in which it may be conjectured—in the absence of any authoritative information on the matter—that the term "league" to denote a trade organization of savings and loan associations was first used and thus entered permanently into the vocabulary of the business. Many outside the savings and loan sphere frequently ask the reason for the term "league," which is an uncommon one in the 20th century for business groups. Obviously the unit name of the savings and loan being "association," the pioneers in organization were blocked from using the more common term "association" which bankers, manufacturers and other businesses found ready and practical. They must have delved into the dictionary and found "league" a suitable substitute.

The Illinois League was organized in 1880 with just 11 associations as charter members. These 11, however, represented a fairly wide cross section of the state geographically. In the year in which the *Manual* suggested the imminence of more leagues in the various states, New York, Massachusetts and Michigan formed their original organizations. By 1892, 12 states had formed leagues. In addition to those already mentioned, they were: California, New Jersey, Louisiana, Missouri, Nebraska, Ohio, Iowa, Arkansas, Indiana and Montana. The year 1892 is important in this recounting because this was the time when Judge Seymour Dexter of Elmira, N. Y., issued his call for a gathering to discuss the formation of a United States League, and his call went to each of these state leagues.

The background of the summons by this distinguished jurist of upstate New York to savings and loan leaders must be painted in more colors, however, than the mere existence of a dozen state leagues. The more vivid and striking component of the picture is the great threat of the so-called "national" associations which brought the business to adopt a united front.

Threat of the "nationals"

Somewhere between 1885 and 1887 there came into being in Minnesota an entity known as the National Building, Loan and Protective Union. It issued shares of $100 par value, claiming that buyers paying dues of 85¢ a month would mature them in five years. Out of this monthly dues 10¢ went into an expense fund, 15¢ into an insurance fund and 60¢ was available for the so-called loan fund. The insurance fund was to provide for the payment of par value of the shares to heirs of a deceased member at any time before the five-year maturity. Furthermore there was a membership fee of $2.00 for each share, which went to the agent selling it. This association followed the "tontine" plan of causing a member to forfeit all his payments to date if he did not keep up with the contract. There was no withdrawal value before maturity of the shares.

Within the first six months after the National Building, Loan and Protective Union was organized 100,000 shares were sold, and assets of $250,000 were accumulated. Such was the appearance on the savings and loan horizon of the so-called "national" type of association which was a detour in the history of the business. The nationals were, in effect, a distortion of the system of local institutions which had proved itself for over half a century as a reliable means for home ownership credit, and for well over a decade as a sound method of accumulating savings for whatever purpose the member might wish to use them. More than likely the nationals would never have come into being had it not been for the quickened pace of expansion of the bona fide savings and loan association traceable to the popularity of the Dayton plan and to the public relations awareness of the leaders in Dayton, Ohio.

The development came at a time when speculative activity was booming in the United States. A number of other savings and get-rich schemes, designed primarily to feather the nests of the promoters and agents, had already made their appearance. Agents of such promotions were happy to find new channels for their efforts and the national building and loans provided that channel. Twelve of these associations were formed with Minnesota head offices within the first year after the initial organization. They established branches or local boards throughout the country, the local board generally being composed of persons of prominence in the community, including a banker or attorney whose aid was enlisted for the promise that the local business would be his. It was announced that this national organization had come to the town to place a large sum of loans at once. This helped allay suspicion so that the promise of large returns to savers was not so suspect as it might have been. Of course potential borrowers subscribed to shares in the hope of securing loans.

Subsequently national associations were formed in many parts of the country, and they victimized many prominent men who became associated with the movement without knowledge of their real character. The large front which was put upon this variation of the simple, old savings and loan idea was made glamorous by their advertising in the *National Building and Loan Herald,* a periodical devoted to the operation of this type of finance. A typical ad by one of the national associations claimed it paid a return six times the profit of government bonds and was equally safe; that it was better than a "local building and loan stock," because the profits were larger and the expense smaller; that it was better than a savings bank or an insurance policy.

The essentially unsupervised character of these operations explains why it was easy for the nationals to prey upon the gullibility and desire for gain of a not too suspicious public. There was little supervision as yet of the local building and loan associations. Had there been, it might have been possible to slow down the march of the nationals before they reached their days of trouble. Actually before 1892 the only states which required annual reports to be made by savings and loan associations to a state department were: New York, Michigan, Maine, Minnesota, Wisconsin, South Dakota, North Dakota and Massachusetts. Minnesota passed its act in 1889 largely as a result of the nationals, which already had a foothold. In a sense this was like locking the barn door after the horse was stolen.

Aside from the large drain on these institutions of the expensive salesmen and the loading of the expense budget with remuneration for the promoters, the national associations invested their funds in such a way that, on the whole, little confidence should have been placed in their soundness. Loans were made over a wide geographical area. The promoters claimed that they filled a definite need; that the nationals could supply loans of larger dimensions than the local societies; that they would sell their stock mainly to business and professional men whom the locals could not reach; and that they would supply money to towns and villages which were not large enough to support a local association. Actually, sometimes their loans were made by mail. Of course in a relatively small number of the nationals the local responsible leadership did succeed in carrying on a reputable home lending business, keeping the defects from the bona fide savings and loan plan at a minimum.

Such was the foment in the savings and loan world which made the call for the organization of the United States League a welcome outlet for the feeling that "something must be done." It also explains, incidentally, why the nationwide league had from the beginning the name "United States" League rather than the more obvious name of "National" League; inasmuch as one of its motivations was to put an end to the depredation of the nationals on the good name of the local savings and loan institutions, it could hardly have been expected to call itself the "National" League.

The controversy between the two types of savings and loan operation occupied considerable space in the press of the nation. Taking up the cudgels for the local type of institution was the city editor of the *Daily News* (not related to the present tabloid) of New York, which was then the most widely circulated newspaper in the United States. The editor later became active in the savings and loan business, and president of the United States League. The Elmira judge who had issued the call for the formation of the United States League had also been active in securing legislation to curb the threatening development. In New York state legislation barring "nationals" of other states was adopted in 1888; it required all foreign associations to put up a cash deposit of $100,000 with some designated state office before they could transact business in New York state.

Organization meeting of United States League

On April 14, 1892, the representatives of 13 state leagues—those of Arkansas, California, Illinois, Indiana, Iowa, Massachusetts, Michigan, Minnesota, Missouri, New Jersey, New York, Ohio and Pennsylvania—met in Chicago in accordance with Judge Dexter's call. They were there for two days, elected a president and went home to make plans for a national convention the next year. Their significant work was reported in a bulletin issued May 10, 1892, which described, among other things, the formation of the United States League of Local Building and Loan Associations, to be composed of representatives of the several state leagues of local cooperative savings, building and loan associations. This bulletin further reported that the first annual meeting of the new League would be held in Chicago some time during the summer of 1893. Among the resolutions adopted were the significant statements of opposition to the system of "so-called cooperative financial institutions operating under the name of 'national' building and loan associations," and the further assertion "for the information of working people everywhere" that a "genuine" building association is local in operation and purely cooperative in its character, and these in contradistinction from the so-called "nationals" which operate without limit of territory and are not cooperative either in spirit or in fact.

The final action reported in the bulletin from this founders' meeting was a direction to the president and secretary of the newly formed league to request the chief of the Bureau of Labor Statistics of the United States to gather and publish statistics of building and loan associations.

First savings and loan statistics

As it turned out probably the most significant immediate result of the organization meeting was the development of the first comprehensive statistics on the business. A business depression was hovering in the wings and was to have some part in dismantling the thinly based empire of the national building and loan associations. On the other hand, the census chief's report, which was published in 1894, contained 375 pages of invaluable information about the savings and loan business. Statistical tables featured data from associations all over the country; in fact, there has never been since so detailed an analysis of the savings and loan business as existed then, with even a division as to men and women shareholders in all existing associations. There were chapters on preliminary plans, plans for distribution of profits, withdrawal plans, and finally a chapter containing all the building and loan legislation then current in the several states.

Under the census chief's direction enumerators of the savings and loan census found that there were 5,598 associations with a total membership, borrowers and savers, of 1,349,437, with total assets of $473,137,454. (These figures were for the local associations only and did not include the statistics on the nationals.) Thus for the first time the savings and loan business knew itself to be on the verge of one-half a billion dollars in size and could study the wide variations in systems of operation which had only been guessed at before.

After this initial gathering of data of the business, the main statistical activity was carried on by the United States League. In 1896 a secretary of the League was elected who held this position until 1949. He compiled statistics by states, beginning with the fiscal year ending in 1895, obtaining his figures from the various state supervisors. (It will be recalled that there were no federal associations until 1933.) His compilation became the source of the figures relied upon by the Comptroller of the Currency in publishing statistics of the savings and loan business in the 20th century.

The debacle of the nationals came with the failure of the largest of them all, the Southern Building and Loan Association of Knoxville, Tenn., with approximately $5 million in assets, in 1897. Several other southern associations crashed within a short time and none of the larger nationals remained after a period of two or three years. A quarter of a billion dollars in such investments had collapsed. As is usually the case with a regrettable development in any business, some brands were saved from the burning. Some of the associations which still existed in the latter half of the 20th century represent the continuation of one-time national associations whose affairs fell under the guidance of sure hands and were molded into the more dependable pattern of the local savings and loan institution.

The positive effects on the business as a whole went beyond the scare which brought about the unity of interest by local associations and the formation of the United States League. As has already been seen, the development of state supervision was hastened. And furthermore the possibility of aggressive development of the savings and loan institution was born even though the nationals had regrettable motives in their use of aggressive business development tactics. Some of the nationals produced good accounting systems and aroused interest in the whole area of accounting analysis, which was fairly new to any savings and loan thinking at that time.

The United States League adopted a statement of its objectives when it drew up a constitution and bylaws at the first convention in 1893. Among these was the fostering of proper supervision. The decade of the 1890s saw supervision by a state department enacted in Illinois, Kansas, Missouri, Nebraska, New Jersey, Ohio, Washington, Vermont, New Hampshire, Tennessee, Pennsylvania, Rhode Island, Montana, Wyoming, Indiana and possibly in a number of other states.

These were the years when supervision was advancing from those rudimentary forms that characterized it under the state laws in the 1840s and 1850s. It was no longer considered sufficient for a state merely to require certain things for the chartering of an association. Supervision went through phases where reports to state officials were required and this only; then it moved toward permissive examination by officers representing the state department; and finally toward required periodic examination by state officials. This last phase, taken for granted as a *sine qua non* by supervision in the mid-20th century, was hard to achieve in many jurisdictions.

It should always be remembered that many lacks in the administration of a business or a public service are tied to scarcity of available funds. Savings and loan supervision long suffered from the failure of the various states to provide for sufficient personnel to carry out the provisions of the law. It was not general to assess the expense of examining an association against the association. Acceptance of this pattern came at a relatively late stage of supervision. In the 1920s supervisors were credited with the suggestion to the directors of savings and loan associations that salaries should be paid to the secretaries rather than leave them depending on fees or other sources of remuneration. Their efforts were thus in the direction of a full-time staff, one of the prerequisites of the development of a full-fledged business institution out of a "movement."

It has already been noted that the deep and prolonged business depression which characterized the economy of the United States during most of the 1890s had some part in bringing to a head the difficulties attendant on the erratic and unsound operations of the national savings and loan institutions. The effect of this depression upon the local savings and loan institutions was remarkably mild. This was true despite the fact that there was a deep decline in the prices of real estate and a somewhat marked increase in the number of foreclosures during the period.

In the panic year, 1893, the *New York Post* took editorial notice of the way in which building and loan associations had come through with an increase in influence. It referred to specific examples of the performance of associations in the metropolitan district where several banks had temporarily closed their doors. A dramatic story was reported of the successful effort of a savings and loan board of directors to get its $50,000 deposit out of a closed bank by court action in order that it might pay off its frightened members. They were people "quite unfamiliar with financial affairs and easily taken in by rumors that had no foundation," the *Post* wrote of the members.

Depression and war in the 1890s

There was a general growth of the business during the 1890s—another witness that the several years of less than normal business prosperity did it no serious harm. A decrease in the number of associations did, however, characterize the situation from the years 1897 to 1902, and this doubtless was the result of some shaking out of the marginal units that were unable to keep going in a period of slackened employment and incomes.

The report of the secretary of the United States League for the year 1897-1898 refers to the fact that there had been an increase in the amount invested in these associations notwithstanding some "heavy losses in assets which occurred in several of the larger cities." The report explains that these associations had been able to hold their own under adverse conditions and that this evidenced their strength and permanence and demonstrated also that the "building association" had lost none of its prestige as the most popular financial institution of the common people.

It is obvious that the reference to losses in assets merely meant a decrease in assets and not an actual loss on the books of the association. A $13-million decrease in assets occurred that year in three cities: Chicago, St. Louis and Cincinnati. The League secretary commented that these decreases were due entirely to local causes in the cities in question. Some loss of confidence had followed the disclosures made in connection with the receivership of two large associations in Chicago and the discovery of several shortages; the prevailing business depression was only partly to blame. The decrease in business in St. Louis associations was attributed to the failure of five associations. The League secretary reported these were attributable entirely "to the extravagant, dishonest and incompetent management of the secretary."

"Many associations had recklessly borrowed large sums of money without authority of law, had hypothecated their securities as collateral with banks and trust companies, overvalued the real estate upon which they had made advances and during the hard times were compelled to acquire ownership; many made second mortgage loans." So reads the record of unsoundness in this particular instance. In Cincinnati there was also a lack of confidence resulting from a number of small failures and mismanagement by officers, although the situation there "has improved and is now more reassuring," the report said.

Since this 1897-1898 report covered the period of the start of the Spanish-American War, it is also noteworthy that the secretary said the war "has had little effect upon building associations." During the first scare, he admitted there were some withdrawals by classes of depositors "who are easily frightened," but went on to say that it "has had no appreciable effect upon the volume of business." Table 27 outlines the savings and loan story during the last decade of the 19th century and the first three decades of the 20th.

Beginnings of federal legislative concerns

The story, however, is too significant to be dealt with merely in figures. This period of some 40 years—a full generation of savings and loan activity—saw the beginning of federal legislative concerns of these institutions. The Wilson Tariff Act of 1894 proposed an income tax on corporations' net income (2%), which tax was later held void by the United States Supreme Court. But the act, as it passed, contained a precedent-making provision; "Nothing herein contained shall apply to building and loan associations or companies which make loans only to their shareholders." Subsequently this recognition of the special savings and loan function in the financial community was followed by similar treatment in the Dingley Tariff Act of 1897, the War Revenue Act of 1898, the Payne-Aldrich Tariff Act of 1909 (which levied a special excise tax), the Revenue Acts of 1913 (the first income tax law which was constitutional), of 1914, 1916, 1917, 1918, 1921, 1924, 1926 and 1928. Also the excess profits tax levied in an act of March 3, 1917, included similar savings and loan treatment.

Furthermore this period of 40 years saw court decisions which were highly influential in establishing the relationships between

390

Table 27. Growth in number of associations, total membership, and total assets of savings and loan associations in the United States, 1893-1930

Year	Number of associations	Total membership	Total assets
1893	5,598	1,349,437	$ 473,137,454
1894	5,684	1,447,283	526,382,609
1895	5,770	1,545,129	579,627,765
1896	5,776	1,610,300	598,388,695
1897	5,872	1,642,179	601,130,037
1898	5,576	1,617,837	600,135,739
1899	5,485	1,512,685	581,866,170
1900	5,356	1,495,136	571,366,628
1901	5,302	1,539,593	565,387,966
1902	5,299	1,530,707	577,228,014
1903	5,308	1,566,700	579,556,112
1904	5,265	1,631,046	600,342,386
1905	5,264	1,642,127	629,344,257
1906	5,316	1,699,714	673,129,198
1907	5,424	1,839,119	731,508,446
1908	5,599	1,920,257	784,175,753
1909	5,713	2,016,651	856,332,719
1910	5,869	2,169,893	931,867,175
1911	6,099	2,332,829	1,030,687,031
1912	6,273	2,516,936	1,137,600,648
1913	6,429	2,836,433	1,248,479,139
1914	6,616	3,103,935	1,357,707,900
1915	6,806	3,334,899	1,484,205,875
1916	7,072	3,568,432	1,598,628,136
1917	7,269	3,838,612	1,769,142,175
1918	7,484	4,011,401	1,898,344,346
1919	7,788	4,289,326	2,126,620,390
1920	8,633	4,962,919	2,519,914,971
1921	9,255	5,809,888	2,890,764,621
1922	10,009	6,364,144	3,342,530,953
1923	10,744	7,202,880	3,942,939,880
1924	11,844	8,554,352	4,765,937,197
1925	12,403	9,886,997	5,500,176,154
1926	12,626	10,665,705	6,334,103,807
1927	12,804	11,326,261	7,178,562,451
1928	12,666	11,995,905	8,016,034,327
1929	12,342	12,111,209	8,695,154,220
1930	11,777	12,343,254	8,828,611,925

Source: United States League

state and federal governments and the savings and loan institutions. In 1928 the case of the United States vs. Cambridge Loan and Building Company, widely known in the business as the "Cambridge case," was decided by the Supreme Court of the United States and was one of the most far-reaching in establishing the status of these associations under federal revenue laws.

The first World War also saw the precedent of a federal government corporation making advances to financial institutions including savings and loan institutions. The War Finance Corporation, a $500-million federally financed entity, approved April 5, 1918, was authorized to make advances "to any savings bank, banking institution, or trust company in the United States which receives savings deposits, or to any building and loan association in the United States, on the promissory note or notes of the borrowing institution whenever the corporation shall deem such advances to be necessary or contributory to the prosecution of the war or important in the public interest."

In all these instances the officers and Legislative Committee of the United States League handled the major responsibility of relations with Washington and—one would judge from the records —found their activities often ill-provided for in the scant League budgets of the time. The chairman of the Legislative Committee reported in 1920 that the president and secretary had sent out a circular, as a result of which contributions were received "in aid of the work" from various leagues and associations sufficient to discharge the immediate expenses and liabilities of the committee.

The associations in World War I

The 7,000 associations in existence during World War I came through the disrupting circumstances of this period in the United States without notable mishaps. In 1917 the United States League convention met in Boston, and a committee was appointed to mobilize savings and loan activities for the war effort. A resolution of the convention, which had tendered help to the government in the furtherance of the war, brought the first activity of these institutions in the sale of war bonds to the public, an effort which they expanded many times in the course of World War II, a generation later.

Reporting at the 1918 convention the chairman of the committee estimated that possibly 2,000 of the associations were acting as agents for the Treasury Department in promoting the sale of War Savings Stamps. The report urged, in conclusion, renewed and systematic efforts among the associations in preparation for the flotation of the Fourth Liberty Loan, which would be the largest in amount of all and which in purpose "we hope and pray may be the last great effort necessary for supplying an invincible war machine with the resources of glorious victory."

At this same convention a delegate from Washington, D. C., described the housing shortage in the capital city. He said that with the building of dwelling houses practically suspended and an increase in population estimated between 75,000 and 100,000 the rental situation had become quite intolerable. The first restriction on rents ever to be imposed was authorized by Congress for the capital city at that time.

The Washington situation as to a shortage of housing which was described at the 1918 convention became a national situation when the war was over. The United States League secretary reported to the 1920 convention that the associations had not been able to meet the urgent needs of their communities. "A shortage of homes exists everywhere," he pointed out. "The scarcity of labor and the high price of materials have retarded building activities to some extent, but in most localities there has been a real shortage of mortgage funds."

Home building had virtually stopped during the war years and the depression which came along after the Armistice discouraged immediate resumption of building. This gap in production was superimposed upon the familiar recurring pattern of an America moving still more definitely from the farm to the city. World War I hastened the pace of urbanization. The 1920 census was the first to show more than half the population of the United States living in urban areas. Also the great tides of immigration in the early 20th century were making their physical pressure felt in the need for urban places to live. In the decade from 1905 to 1914, an average of 954,410 immigrants a year were received at Ellis Island. Although the stream was practically halted during the 1914-1918 conflict, it resumed by 1920, and in 1921 the admittance into the United States of 805,228 immigrants represented the last large group permitted entry.

So was the stage set for a home construction activity and a consequent home loan demand of an intensity which was new in the history of this country. The situation explains the fact that the savings and loan institutions were even then discussing the creation of a system of home loan banks which should increase their ability to meet the mortgage loan demand. The establishment of the Federal Reserve System was fresh in the minds of the savings and loan leaders.

Bills were introduced by Senator Calder of New York and Representative Nolan of California to set up a system of Federal Cooperative Banks, as they were first called. Leaders of the United States League worked with the U. S. Department of Labor in perfecting this legislation, and the proposed banks were called "Federal Home Loan Banks" as early as a 1919 draft of the legislation. Although it required another period of different outlook to bring this system into being, this study and the actual congressional, departmental and savings and loan work done on it in the earlier part of the century laid a solid foundation for the future Federal Home Loan Bank System.

Even though the savings and loan institutions did not move during the postwar housing shortage to assure themselves, with the cooperation of Congress, of a reliable reserve credit system, they nevertheless moved into the housing shortage of the 1920s with a natural aptitude born of the fact that they were the only specialized home financing institutions in the nation. Their first real urge to grow into sizable entities came with this great era of housing expansion. This was the time when literally thousands of associations acquired full-time staffs of at least two or three persons and began to operate on a daily, 9-to-5 o'clock basis (these were not years of "bankers' hours" for savings and loan personnel —many still kept open at least one or two nights a week when they went on a daily basis). A hundred or more institutions acquired their own buildings at this time. Altogether they disbursed $15,-377,600,000 in home loans, secured by 4,346,000 properties, both old and new houses. They had a great share in helping the United States achieve a home ownership record of 46% by the end of 1930.

The great expansion era of the 1920s also saw two significant developments in the trade association arrangements of the savings and loan institutions. The decade saw the emergence of 16 state leagues where they had not existed before. Most of them were still on a voluntary basis, without a full-time staff, but they were doing the job that needed to be done at that time. In 1924 the United States League made the important transition from being a mere federation of state leagues to a constitution admitting individual associations as members alongside the state leagues. Thus there was gradually provided a more adequate financing system for the nationwide organization as it moved toward the years when its greatest destiny was awaiting it.

In 1922 the American Savings and Loan Institute was begun and published the first textbook on the savings and loan business written for personnel of the associations below the management rank, *Elements of the Building and Loan Association.* The Institute also had an accounting text and an appraisal book in the hands of students before the 1920s were over and had graduated its first class of three-year diploma holders in New York City in 1928.

The second 50 years of the savings and loan business in the United States, 1880-1930, had proved that the fundamental principles of thrift and amortized home loans had an appeal for Americans under many different skies and on practically every new frontier which American ingenuity was opening up for a dwelling place for this great, free people. It had drawn upon the energies of many humble men and women and paid them relatively little—as is the way of emerging institutions—for their great and lasting contribution to its perpetuity.

It had also known the participation of great names from the history of the various states, governors, supreme court justices, members of Congress-to-be. On the boards of directors of two Ohio associations had sat William McKinley and Warren G. Harding, later to be honored with their nation's highest elective office. The United States League convention had been addressed in 1912 by the Honorable Woodrow Wilson in the first public speech he made after accepting his party's nomination for the presidency, an office in which he was to earn permanent renown.

✻ ✻ ✻

The century of savings and loan beginnings
had been a good century.

Index

Index